Unstuck and On Target!

Unstuck and On Target!

An Executive Function Curriculum to Improve Flexibility for Children with Autism Spectrum Disorders, Research Edition

by

Lynn Cannon, M.Ed.
The Ivymount School
Rockville, Maryland

Lauren Kenworthy, Ph.D.
Children's National Medical Center
Washington, D.C.

Katie C. Alexander, M.S., OTR
The Ivymount School
Rockville, Maryland

Monica Adler Werner, M.A.
The Ivymount School
Rockville, Maryland

and

Laura Anthony, Ph.D.
Children's National Medical Center
Washington, D.C.

·P·A·U·L·H·
BROOKES
PUBLISHING Co.®

Baltimore • London • Sydney

Paul H. Brookes Publishing Co.
Post Office Box 10624
Baltimore, Maryland 21285-0624
USA

www.brookespublishing.com

Typeset by Auburn Associates, Inc., Baltimore, Maryland.
Manufactured in the United States of America by
Versa Press, Inc., East Peoria, Illinois.

Library of Congress Cataloging-in-Publication Data

Unstuck and on target! : an executive function curriculum to improve flexibility for children with autism spectrum disorders / by Lynn Cannon ... [et al.]. — Research ed.
      p.   cm.
Includes bibliographical references and index.
ISBN-13: 978-1-59857-203-2 (pbk.)
ISBN-10: 1-59857-203-2 (pbk.)
1. Autistic children—Education.   2. Autism spectrum disorders.   I. Cannon, Lynn.   II. Title.
LC4717.U67   2011
371.94—dc22   2011015136

British Library Cataloguing in Publication data are available from the British Library.

2015   2014   2013   2012   2011

10   9   8   7   6   5   4   3   2   1

Contents

Contents of the CD-ROM

About the Authors

Lynn Cannon, M.Ed., is a special education coordinator at The Ivymount School. She is responsible for helping to develop and oversee the social learning and academic curriculum for the lower and middle school students at The Ivymount School. Ms. Cannon is the director of Take2 Summer Camp, a program designed to develop interaction skills and social thinking in children ages 8–12. Prior to her work at The Ivymount School, Ms. Cannon was a classroom teacher at the Lab School of Washington, in Washington, D.C. She has been a major contributor to the development of the *Unstuck and On Target!* intervention. Ms. Cannon has led all of the data collection, the implementation of the intervention, and the training of the teachers in the pilot feasibility and development trial.

Lauren Kenworthy, Ph.D., is the director of the Center for Autism Spectrum Disorders at Children's National Medical Center and is an associate professor of psychiatry, pediatrics, and neurology at The George Washington University School of Medicine. She has specialized in the neuropsychological assessment of children with social learning disorders and executive dysfunction for more than 15 years. In addition, Dr. Kenworthy has published more than 20 peer-reviewed papers investigating autism and executive function, as well as developed the most widely used assessment tool in the field, the Behavior Rating Inventory of Executive Function (BRIEF; with Gioia, Isquith, & Guy; Psychological Assessment, 2000).

Katie C. Alexander, M.S., OTR, has dedicated her work since the early 2000s to serving individuals with autism spectrum disorders (ASDs), their families, and the professionals who support them. She is an occupational therapist who has conducted research on cognitive behavioral intervention for adolescents with Asperger syndrome and has provided trainings and presentations both nationally and at the state level. Recently, Ms. Alexander served as the founding program director for the Model Asperger Program (MAP) at The Ivymount School, where she led the development and implementation of a model, evidence-based educational programming, including intervention targeting social competency, positive behavior supports, and executive function. She has since authored two textbook chapters and continues to develop programming for individuals with ASDs and to participate in the research collaboration between The Ivymount School and Children's National Medical Center.

Monica Adler Werner, M.A., is the director of the Model Asperger Program (MAP) at The Ivymount School. In that capacity, she has spearheaded the development of a social learning curriculum that emphasizes problem solving, self-advocacy, and self-regulation. Ms. Werner has been a major contributor to the development of the *Unstuck and On Target!* intervention. In addition, she is a cofounder of Take2 Summer Camp, a program designed to develop social thinking, problem solving, and skills. She also serves as an ad-hoc public reviewer of National Institute of Mental Health (NIMH) autism grants.

Laura Anthony, Ph.D., is a clinical and developmental psychologist at the Center for Autism Spectrum Disorders at Children's National Medical Center and an assistant professor in the Departments of Psychiatry and Behavioral Sciences and Pediatrics at The George

Washington University School of Medicine and Health Sciences. She leads the intervention program at the Center for Autism Spectrum Disorders, an active interdisciplinary evaluation, treatment, research, and training clinic. Dr. Anthony has expertise in developing clinical interventions and more than 20 years of extensive experience in studying and treating behavioral rigidities (executive dysfunction) and stereotyped behaviors in children with developmental disorders. In addition, she and Dr. Kenworthy were awarded an autism spectrum disorders (ASDs) supplement to Children's National Medical Center's Leadership Education in Neurodevelopmental Disorders program to provide interdisciplinary training in evaluation, treatment, and research with children with ASDs.

Foreword

Why do we need a book about getting unstuck? I asked myself that very question when my friend Monica Adler Werner proposed the idea to me last year. As she explained, I realized how important flexibility, and the ability to get oneself unstuck, really is. The more I pondered, the more I saw how flexibility and its attendant traits were key to my own struggles and success in life.

Flexibility is what allows us to accept that there may be more than one way to do things. I had terrible trouble with that as a little boy. I'd see other kids playing with trucks and dinosaurs, and they would be doing it wrong! Sometimes the errors other kids made were so egregious, smoke would curl from my ears and it would hurt to watch.

Green blocks would be haphazardly inserted into collections of red. Dump trucks would be parked upside down on piles of dirt. Helicopters would be mixed with Easter bunnies. The natural order of things—so obvious to me—was either invisible or irrelevant to most other kids.

Whenever I tried to show my playmates the error of their ways, they resisted vigorously. Even worse, they retaliated by making fun of me, calling me names, and excluding me from play groups in the future.

It sure was hard being a kid who knew right from wrong when it came to play. I looked at teachers. They were praised when they showed us kids what we were doing wrong. Then I looked at myself, mocked and ridiculed for doing the very same thing. I never did figure out why, but that's how it was and how it still is today.

When I look back on my childhood, I can date the beginning of my social success to the day I realized that the arrangement of blocks in the sandbox was not worth a fight. The other tykes might still be arranging their blocks wrong, but I learned to ignore them and stay reasonably calm. That was the only way I could tolerate other children playing next to me.

That's the first step in learning flexibility—putting up with other people and the things they do. It's an essential ability, if you want to have friends. However, tolerance is only the first step. Real success requires more.

I took the next step up the social skills ladder when I realized other kids might not be wrong at all. That is, their method of playing might be just as "correct" as my own, even though it was different. Of course, my way remained the best whether they knew it or not, but accepting that other techniques might also be valid opened my eyes. I realized I might learn different ways of doing things from other people.

That was a really important turning point for me in the world of relationships. Suddenly, other people could show me how they did things, and I could watch and learn, without distress. If their methods worked better than mine, I could embrace them and make them my own. If my ideas were better, other people learned from me.

That marked the beginning of give-and-take learning for me. I cannot overstate the importance of that skill. It's how we integrate the knowledge of those who came before us, and it's the foundation of group learning, teamwork, and much social progress. As valuable as that is, it's really hard to do. Accepting that someone else's idea may be better than ours raises the distinct possibility that other people may be as smart as us; maybe even more so. For an Aspergian kid who grew up as the center of the world, that is a bitter pill to swallow.

Unfortunately, I could only accept other ways of doing things in small doses, so my chances to grow through group interaction remained limited. I wasn't very skilled at accepting different points of view, and I didn't know how to practice, so doing so remained stressful. Where might I be, if I had become really flexible and accepting as a kid? I might be a basketball coach, or the president of some big company, instead of a solitary Aspergian book writer.

Kids with Asperger syndrome confront social challenges like I describe every single day. Helping them meet those challenges is vital, because childhood success resolving social issues predicts more general success later in life. A child's ability to emerge from disability depends in large part upon his or her ability to fit in and be accepted by other people.

My recognition of the power of flexibility came much later than it had to, because no one was there to teach me. In fact, when I went to school, school administrators did not even know social skills needed to be taught at all. Some kids, after all, are born with the apparatus for social skills, and they pick them up instinctively. Educators—many of whom were in that "instinctively social" group themselves—assumed everyone was like them.

Kids who did not have working social instincts were, in the thinking of the 1960s, deliberately ignoring the nonverbal signals of those around them. It was only in the 1980s that researchers realized that autism is the cause of this problem. Today we know it's a continuum and that autistic disorder includes both "not speaking" and "not understanding subtle social cues."

That realization led to the definition of what we now call the autism spectrum. We learned that some autism is obvious, when the person's spoken language and functionality are clearly impaired. Other autism, like my own, is hidden, when strong verbal skills mask the inability to read other people's unspoken messages.

Many techniques have been developed to help the autistic population with more obvious impairments. Time and research have shown those interventions to be effective. Unfortunately, we do not yet have a comparable arsenal of well-proven tools to remediate social disability. We are just beginning to develop them. This book represents an important step in that direction.

Some folks would ask why we don't have more clinically validated methods of teaching social skills. The simple answer is that the need to teach these things is just now being recognized. The importance of reading and math has always been self-evident. If you want to prosper in our society, you need to be able to read a menu and count your money. When a kid can't walk or talk, the need to help him or her solve those problems is unmistakable.

Consequently, those are the areas where educators have directed most of their efforts. In choosing where to focus their teaching efforts, they have indeed been "masters of the obvious." Today, we want and expect more. We want to help kids whose disability is real but more subtle and less easily defined.

For example, what about the kids who just don't act right? Kids who don't do what their teachers want; kids who have no friends? Until recently, we did not understand what kind of help children like that might need. We are just now realizing how important skills like flexibility are, and how their lack can keep a person disabled. We've learned that unexpected behavior is often the result of innocent oblivion, as opposed to conscious defiance.

Now that we know unspoken social cues are clear to some people and invisible to others, can we teach the kids who miss those cues how to pick them up? I think we can, but the path to that understanding is not direct.

My friends at Ivymount School and their colleagues at Children's National Medical Center (CNMC) developed the *Unstuck and On Target!* curriculum from their experience teaching social skills to kids with Asperger syndrome. School faculty worked with the CNMC psychologists and researchers to identify the most successful techniques for teaching flexibility, goal setting, and avoiding the trap of circular thinking—three essential abilities for success in today's world.

The techniques in *Unstuck and On Target!* were developed for kids with Asperger syndrome, but they are much more broadly applicable. There are millions of kids with mild social skills impairment but no disability diagnosis and most, if not all, could benefit from the ideas in this work. In addition, therapists who work with adults with Asperger syndrome could adapt the lessons in this book for use with support groups, and they could also be used in one-on-one therapy.

I was very surprised to realize that I could use ideas from *Unstuck and On Target!* in my own life, at age 53! By applying these techniques I am able to avoid the traps of circular negative thought that have plagued me most of my life. I am more receptive to alternate points of view, which makes me more successful on all fronts. As a person with Asperger and a parent of a son with Asperger, I can say from experience that the techniques in this book work and I therefore recommend them based on my own experience.

I hope you are able to put them to good use.

John Elder Robison
Author of *Look Me in the Eye* (2007) and *Be Different* (2011)

Acknowledgments

The authors would like to thank the following people who contributed significantly to this book:

To the families and their children who have taught us what to teach and how to make it enjoyable and meaningful

To Bonnie Beers for her contribution to the development and scope and sequence of curriculum, for her thoughtful consideration of each student's comprehensive needs, and specifically, for her substantial contribution to the development of emotional regulation tools

To Kevan Arevalo, Saundra Bishop, Stephanie Fulford, Joan Galil, Julie Martin, and Brooke Mason for developing countless tools and techniques, carefully tailored to individual students' needs and for finding creative, fun, and salient ways to teach the kids about flexibility

To Laura Batis, Rina Park, Lorin Youngdahl, and Naomi Baum-Skorija for implementing every lesson in social skills groups, for coming up with beautiful and creative ways to engage the kids in the material, and for always giving thoughtful and practical suggestions

To Anne Della-Rosa Pierce, Cat Eike, Pamela Kennedy, Liza Koonin, Brenna Leonard, Nyah Potts, and Grace Welsh for ensuring the students generalize the skills they have learned by keeping the concepts and techniques alive in the classroom throughout each and every school day

To Alexander Plank and Ari Ne'eman, for providing their careful comments on this book

To Jennifer Sokoloff, Kathryn Jankowski, Meagan Wills, Kelly Register-Brown, Katie Kane, James Rutledge, Kelly Powell, Rafael Oliveras Rentas, John Strang, Wendell Wu, Haniya Raza, and Michelle Gucherau for their help with the research behind the development of this manual, formatting the manual, and for making the pilot testing of the manual in school and in clinic social skills groups possible

To Lisa Gilotty, who first developed the idea of a flexibility intervention many years ago; and to Greg Wallace for being there at the beginning

Funding for this project was provided by The Organization for Autism Research and the Isadore and Bertha Gudelsky Family Foundation. Ongoing funding for testing the efficacy of this intervention is provided by an R-34 grant from the National Institute of Mental Health.

*To the children with autism and their families
who have educated and inspired us and who make the world
a richer place through their unique insights and perspectives*

*To Mark Ylvisaker, whose work on
executive function intervention strategies
motivated this curriculum. Prior to his untimely death,
Mark's generous collaboration with us
guided many initial facets of this intervention.*

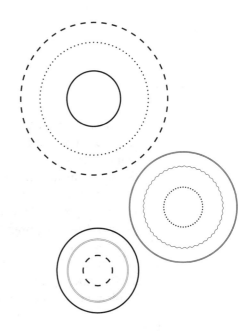

Introduction

HOW WILL THIS MANUAL HELP YOU?

This manual will teach you what flexibility and executive functions are and how to improve them by teaching your students self-regulatory vocabulary, scripts, and routines. It will also show you how to create a flexible classroom, provide just-right cuing, motivate your students to change, and ensure that the skills you teach your students will generalize to other settings.

Understand What Flexibility and Executive Functions Are, Why They Are Important, and How to Teach Them

The manual covers all of the elements of cognitive instruction that are important for students to learn. The first step in learning a new skill is to understand what it is and why it is helpful. In *Unstuck and On Target!*, students, teachers, and parents learn, teach, and consistently practice a new vocabulary and specific flexibility and planning routines and scripts, and they concretely explore the usefulness of flexibility, planning, and goal setting. (See Prerequisites for Successful Implementation of *Unstuck and On Target!* for the what, why, and how of being flexible.)

Create a Flexible, Organized Classroom

Flexibility, like laughter, is contagious. Every educator has an opportunity and a responsibility to establish the culture for his or her classroom. Some classroom cultures are conducive to student success, and others can interfere with student success. This intervention is dedicated to helping the educator create a classroom culture that promotes success for all students, especially for children with autism spectrum disorders (ASD). Children with ASD are most likely to thrive and acquire flexibility in a flexible, organized classroom culture—one in which educators and students alike consistently demonstrate flexibility and in which flexibility is a core value. (See Prerequisites for Successful Implementation of *Unstuck and On Target!* for more on maintaining a flexible classroom.)

Provide Just-Right Cuing

Almost 50 years ago, Teuber (1964) defined the problem of executive dysfunction as "the curious dissociation between knowing and doing." This is especially characteristic of students with ASD, whose adaptive abilities—or what they actually do at home and at school—lag behind their intelligence or what they know (Gilotty, Kenworthy, Black, Wagner, & Sirian, 2002; Kenworthy et al., 2005). Thus, it is not enough to teach the student with ASD what flexibility and goal-directed behavior are and how to be flexible and goal directed. It is also important to have the student practice flexibility and organization skills over and over again in the real world. Flexibility and other executive function skills are taught best through just-right cuing, which means that just enough support is provided for success and support is faded as soon as it is not needed. Extensive, repetitive practice is required to maintain and generalize success. In this way, teaching flexibility and other executive function skills is like coaching a child in athletic skills or teaching a child to play an instrument: The same skills are practiced repeatedly from one year to the next, and the child's ability to perform them in a game or in a concert slowly grows. (See Prerequisites for Successful Implementation of *Unstuck and On Target!* for tips on how to provide just-right cuing.)

Motivate Your Students to Change

Successful interventions are founded on intrinsic motivation and positive reinforcement for success, and not on negative feedback for failures.

Incentives for change and motivational supports are what make learning new habits possible for anyone. Thus, it is essential that all flexibility and executive function interventions are created and supported by adults so that student success is achieved. (See Prerequisites for Successful Implementation of *Unstuck and On Target!* for guidelines on motivating students when change is difficult.)

Help Your Students Generalize What You Teach to Other Settings

To ensure generalization of flexibility and executive function skills, we have designed this curriculum as a multimodal intervention that is embedded in the real-life contexts (home, school, community) in which children with ASD have difficulties because of inflexibility and disorganization. Its primary focus is to give you tools to teach and coach flexibility at school, but all topics are accompanied by Home Extension handouts. These handouts update parents on what you have been teaching and provide home exercises that reinforce this learning. In this way, both teachers and parents will act as coaches for the student, using a combination of teachable moments and direct coaching to reinforce flexibility and good executive functioning in new situations. In addition to engaging parents in the interventions, the information and parent–child activities in the Home Extension handouts help solidify students' learning and give them a sense of ownership of the concepts and strategies they have learned as they teach the concepts and strategies to their parents. *Unstuck and On Target!* also provides Classroom Extensions that encourage the use of specific vocabulary and flexibility and executive function scripts in all classes that a student attends.

HOW EDUCATORS, STUDENTS, AND PARENTS HELPED US WRITE THIS MANUAL

We were first inspired to develop this manual by the work of Mark Ylvisaker and Tim Feeney (Feeney, 2010; Ylvisaker, 2006; Ylvisaker & Feeney, 1998). Working with children with brain injuries, they created key self-regulatory scripts and routines that we have used and modified in the course of developing *Unstuck and On Target!* The Big Deal/Little Deal and Choice/No Choice scripts that we introduce in Topic 7 come directly from their work, as do the concepts underlying the Handling the Unexpected script. The Goal-Plan-Do-Check script described in Topic 6 is also inspired by them, as well as Polatajko and Mandich (2004), who incorporated

Goal-Plan-Do-Check in their occupational therapy intervention, "The Cognitive Orientation to Daily Occupational Therapy Performance." In fact, prior to his untimely death, Mark Ylvisaker was a key early member of the *Unstuck and On Target!* team. His guidance and support for this project included many readings of early drafts and extremely helpful conversations regarding the use of self-regulatory scripts and the importance of building internal motivation in children through the use of heroes, as we describe in Topic 4.

Building on the work of Ylvisaker, Feeney, and others, we developed the manual and materials for *Unstuck and On Target!* through a community-based, participatory approach (Brooke et al., 1986; Israel, Schulz, Parker, & Becker, 1998), which involves engagement with community and policy partners, development of the intervention, a data collection and analysis plan in collaboration with key community stakeholders, assessment of how well the intervention could be used in actual settings, and the pledge that the formative and summative evaluation data will be shared with others who might benefit from the lessons learned (Centers for Disease Control and Prevention, 1999). We also used a bottom-up approach (Sullivan et al., 2005): Instead of developing the intervention in the lab, conducting a trial in a university, and then adapting it to actual settings, we started with the effective techniques that front-line educators were already using to build executive functioning.

Our research team included academic researchers (a clinical and developmental psychologist, and a neuropsychologist), a special educator, two school administrators, an occupational therapist, a parent, and two self-advocates. The development and feedback process then proceeded through a series of stages built on the participatory approach:

1. Classroom observations to identify which currently used strategies work and where students and teachers encounter the most difficulties

2. A needs assessment with experts and stakeholders (e.g., What do professionals, school staff, parents, and students say they need the most? Where are the gaps in skills that need to be addressed?)

3. Compilation of stakeholder-defined key elements of intervention (e.g., What do professionals, school staff, parents, and students say would be most helpful? How should the intervention be structured and delivered?)

4. Focus groups with school staff, parents, and children to evaluate and improve the proposed key elements

5. Translation of the key elements into a comprehensive manual by the research team, which was led by the special educator

6. Review and revision of the comprehensive manual by two young adults with autism

7. A feasibility and acceptability trial: The intervention was tried by two interventionists in three classrooms with 13 children

8. Feedback from the 13 student participants in the feasibility trial (i.e., they developed and delivered formal presentations of feedback to the research team regarding what they learned from the intervention, what they liked best, and what we needed to change)

9. Detailed feedback from interventionists on every lesson in the intervention manual, including revision suggestions

10. Intensive revision of the intervention and manual based on the above process, with new elements being re-reviewed by stakeholders

This participatory process defined the curriculum's structure and the delivery and teaching methods and helped us streamline the lessons. The resulting intervention is feasible and acceptable to participants (93% enrollment rate; no children dropped out or refused, though three left the school for other reasons). The resulting manual describes a curriculum designed for use in a weekly school-based group that teaches what flexibility is, why it is important to be flexible, how to be flexible, how to set and prioritize goals, and how to develop coping skills.

Students who completed the intervention reported positive effects in being better able to compromise, see the benefits of being flexible, and keep their focus on larger, important goals. Teachers who completed the intervention liked how easy the manual and intervention techniques were to use and enjoyed having a new vocabulary system to use every day.

Our approach to developing this intervention was an innovative combination of a participatory process and a theory-driven method based on previously developed executive function interventions and our knowledge of the complex executive function deficits and effective intervention techniques in ASD. Because executive function deficits are primarily expressed, and best assessed, in real-world settings, such as classroom, home, and social settings, it was essential that we develop, test, and modify interventions in a real-world setting and that the interventions be administrable by teachers and other school personnel. Thus, we developed our intervention with a participatory model. This proves the achievability of using an intensive participatory process (including adults, adolescents, and children with ASD) to develop interventions for students with ASD.

DOES *UNSTUCK AND ON TARGET!* WORK?

We also conducted a preliminary test of the intervention as it was being developed, comparing the change from pre- to postintervention. Data were collected from parent and teacher questionnaires and a new group measure assessing executive functioning, especially flexibility, in a socially demanding context (four children working together to complete tasks). In this very small sample of eight children, both parents and teachers reported improved flexibility in 78% of the children after the intervention was completed. The children also showed some change in executive functioning in their ability to shift from one task to another, make a plan, and stay organized (as rated by parents on a questionnaire). On the group-based assessment of executive function skills, the children were significantly more collaborative with each other after the intervention but also made fewer positive comments to each other as rated by a coder who did not know whether the assessments were taken pre- or postintervention. On this same measure, the children trended toward needing to use fewer coping strategies after the intervention and demonstrating an overall improvement in flexibility when working with the other students.

These results suggest that the *Unstuck and On Target!* curriculum implemented in schools is feasible and acceptable to school staff and students with ASD. Furthermore, parents and teachers see promise in such a program, and a blind rater also detected differences in a very small sample of students. The next step in this intervention development process is currently underway to evaluate the effectiveness of this curriculum in inclusive schools, comparing change in larger numbers of students who do and do not receive the intervention.

WHAT YOU NEED TO KNOW ABOUT EXECUTIVE FUNCTION AND FLEXIBILITY

What Is Executive Function and How Is It Impaired in Autism Spectrum Disorder?

Executive function is an umbrella term that captures a set of brain functions that help students regulate their behavior (e.g., stay seated at a desk) and carry out goal-directed behavior (e.g., follow multiple-step directions to complete a task). Specific executive functions include the following (Rogers & Bennetto, 2000):

- Inhibition (or impulse control)
- Flexibility
- Working memory (holding information in mind, e.g., remembering an oral instruction while completing a task)
- Organization (keeping track of materials and seeing the big picture)
- Planning
- Self-monitoring

Clinicians, teachers, and family members agree that students with ASD have difficulties with various aspects of executive function in their daily lives. In fact, any aspect of executive function can be disrupted in students with ASD, but the two most common areas of impairment are organization and flexibility.

Students with ASD tend to be disorganized regarding school materials, homework, and personal articles and space at home; they also have trouble seeing the big picture in what they learn, read, and experience and organizing their thinking. The common expression "can't see the forest for the trees" captures many of the executive organization/integration pitfalls students with ASD experience. The positive side of this weakness, however, is that students with ASD also tend to have excellent cognitive abilities in systematically analyzing and memorizing small chunks of explicit information. Their command of details is often excellent.

Inflexibility is the second major executive challenge in students with ASD. Changes in routine and violations of expectations are particularly challenging, and it is easy for students to get stuck on certain ideas or behaviors. Peter Berg, a middle school student with Asperger syndrome, noted, "Asperger's is like a vise on your brain. And each unexpected event is like another turn on the vise…it just keeps building until you feel like you're going to explode. Sometimes when you explode, it comes out the wrong way."

Taken together, these executive function difficulties significantly and consistently interfere with participation in the social and academic domains of the school day. These observations are supported by scientific research that documents generally poor executive function and specific problems with flexibility and organization/planning in students with ASD (for reviews, see Hill, 2004; Kenworthy, Yerys, Anthony, & Wallace, 2008). Research also clearly links problems with flexibility and organization/planning in ASD to differences in brain structure and brain function (Herbert et al., 2002; Murphy et al., 2002). Brain biology drives executive function differences in ASD.

Unstuck and On Target! targets the problems with flexibility that most students with ASD experience, and it also contains specific supports for organization/planning (e.g., supports for the transportation of Home Extension handouts between school and home, the Target Island and Goal-Plan-Do-Check lessons that promote goal setting and planning). Furthermore, the curriculum builds on common strengths in students with ASD by teaching flexibility and executive skills through explicit, step-by-step routines and scripts. These strategies and concepts will help students not only learn how to be flexible and organized more quickly and easily but also apply them to other new learning in the classroom.

What Is Flexibility?

Flexibility is what enables individuals to generate new ways to solve a problem, adapt to changes in routines, and adjust to the unexpected. Most people have some trouble being flexible some of the time. Adjusting to changes in well-established routines, for example, can be difficult. Beginning a new job or having a first child frequently requires major changes in life routines, which cause stress. Similarly, there are ways that people think about things that are hard to change. It is possible for anyone to get stuck in a rut of doing things in a certain way or thinking in a certain way. Inflexibility, though, can also be adaptive. For example, most of us have a morning routine that we more or less follow when getting ready to leave the house. This prevents us from already being on our way before realizing we forgot to brush our teeth. When difficulties accepting change, making transitions, shifting thoughts, or moving on from an emotional state become so extreme that they interfere with everyday functioning, however, a person will benefit from learning to become more flexible.

Students with ASD have biologically based rigidity and inflexibility, which can manifest as difficulty with the following:

- Making transitions during the school day (e.g., from lunch back to classroom work)
- Tolerating changes in schedules or everyday routines
- Adjusting to changes in staff
- Generating new ways to approach a problem
- Accepting flexible interpretations of rules or events
- Managing an intense emotional feeling
- Responding to the needs or interests of friends
- Negotiating with others
- Accepting differing viewpoints

Students with ASD can be rigid in their approach to tasks, games, and new learning, and it is important to draw their attention to the fact that their peers might want to do something differently than they do. In addition, students with ASDs are highly likely to continue to use one approach to a situation or problem, regardless of the feedback they receive. For example, a student may tell a joke to a group of peers at school and receive no laughter in response. Even with this clear social feedback about the joke, the student tells the joke again to the same group of students later. Research shows that students with ASD are highly likely to display this kind of repetitious behavior, even when there are strong contextual indicators that the action is not the best course.

Driven both by biology and an individual's efforts to cope with the social world, inflexibility plays a major role in determining outcomes for students with ASD. Rigidity frequently leads to serious problems in the academic setting and affects students' options later in adulthood. Currently, only 27% of individuals with average intelligence and ASD in childhood are able to attain functional independence in the community (Farley et al., 2009). Interventions that target and teach flexibility may have a significant, positive impact on participation in school routines, academic performance, and social relationships. In addition, instruction in social communication is essential to help the person with ASD cope with and navigate the social demands presented by a complex and often unpredictable social world. Progress in each of these domains is essential to preparing a student with ASD to meet the expectations of the adult world.

It is also important to understand that inflexibility often serves a protective or even adaptive function for individuals with ASD. Individuals on the autism spectrum can be easily overwhelmed in social, group, and novel situations because social communication, as well as the integration and organization of complex information, is challenging for them. Once overwhelmed, children with ASD tend to experience more anxiety, become more impulsive, and behave inappropriately. The risks they run at such times are profound, given the social isolation, teasing, and bullying they experience at the hands of peers and even adults. An analogy offered by Ari Ne'eman, President of the Autism Self-Advocacy Network, is that of a mine field. In a mine field, anyone would be very cautious and resistant to making any sudden, unplanned moves. "This is similar to what it is like in social situations for those of us with autism," he notes (personal communication). Thus, inflexibility serves a role in limiting the amount of unexpected events to which the person with ASD must respond. It serves an adaptive purpose to reduce anxiety and increase one's overall ability to control responses to others and the environment. For this reason, it is all the more imperative that instructors ensure the presence of the supports listed in Prerequisites for Successful Implementation of *Unstuck and On Target!* These supports will provide the students with a safe, therapeutic setting in which replacing existing patterns of inflexibility with flexible behaviors and responses can be accomplished with success and less anxiety.

> "What purpose does inflexibility serve? For one thing, it is an effective anti-anxiety coping mechanism. It provides order in the context of a world that is confusing and illogical for us."
> —*Ari Ne'eman, President of the Autism Self-Advocacy Network*

The best possible outcome for individuals with ASD occurs when the proper match between their biologically inflexible brain and their environment (e.g., setting, task demands) is achieved. This can happen in three ways:

1. *The student with ASD flexibly adapts to the environment.* A significant part of improving the match between the inflexible brain and the environment is explicitly teaching the student with ASD how to become more flexible and how to readily recognize settings or demands for which he or she should rely on explicitly learned flexibility skills.

2. *The environment is adapted to accommodate the student with ASD.* In some cases the setting or task should be altered to demand less flexibility of the student with ASD. Just as we do not expect a student with dyslexia to read constantly, it is unreasonable and ineffective to expect a student who is constitutionally inflexible to constantly demonstrate unnatural flexibility skills. Because many children with high-functioning ASD are in inclusive environments that are designed for people who are naturally flexible, the match between their brain and the demands of the setting is frequently poor. These children need to develop the self-awareness and self-advocacy skills to determine when it is appropriate to be flexible and when they should ask for flexibility from the environment. Attaining these self-awareness and self-advocacy skills is a long-term process that begins in childhood and extends into adulthood, requiring parents, educators, and treatment teams to continuously calibrate to a student's ongoing development. *Unstuck and On Target!* offers beginning steps to help you start this critical skill acquisition process with your students.

3. *Selected, unacceptable environments are avoided.* There are some situations or tasks that pose unacceptable levels of risk for the student with ASD. They may require such intolerable levels of effort that the student is then incapable of further work. They may overwhelm the student's behavioral regulatory system and create high risk for inappropriate behaviors, or they may create high levels of anxiety. The student with ASD needs to learn how to recognize these situations and avoid them. For example, it is sometimes best for a student to eat lunch in a classroom rather than in a large, crowded cafeteria. Early in a student's educational experience, an adult will need to identify these situations or tasks and create suitable alternatives. With time and development, the student will be better able to recognize these moments and develop appropriate alternatives.

In summary, teaching a student with ASD to function flexibly in a variety of mainstream settings not only helps the student gain flexibility skills but also enables him or her to recognize when it is appropriate to ask for accommodations or avoid a situation or task.

PREREQUISITES FOR SUCCESSFUL IMPLEMENTATION OF *UNSTUCK AND ON TARGET!*

This curriculum teaches students with autism to be more flexible and goal directed, but successful implementation requires a flexible and supportive school context. Next, we describe basic supports that should be in place within the school and classroom and teacher–student interactions.

A Flexible and Supportive School Team and Environment

A supportive school environment includes the following:

School staff and family members must learn to distinguish between willingness and biological differences as causes of behavior in students with ASD. Blaming or punishing a student for a behavior that is not within his or her volitional control will not successfully change the behavior or foster meaningful progress. It will create a toxic atmosphere that contaminates other teaching activities. Table 1 lists some commonly confused sources of behavior in students with ASD. Kunce and Mesibov warned of the dangers of mutual misunderstanding that can occur when adults misinterpret the motivation for specific behaviors in students with autism:

> A failure to understand how a child's typical behaviors reflect this disability can result in misperceptions such as viewing the child as noncompliant, willfully stubborn, or unmotivated, rather than confused, involved in repetitive routines, or focusing on less relevant aspects of the situation. (1998, p. 231)

Ari Ne'eman noted that this perspective-taking exercise is difficult: "This is an exercise that non-autistic professionals struggle with as much and perhaps far more than autistic students struggle with understanding the perspectives of their non-autistic peers" (personal communication). Empathy and understanding are essential, however, as interventions to change behavior can be effective only if the source of the behavior is understood.

Biological and adaptive reasons for inflexibility in students with ASD must be recognized so that accommodations to increase predictability and structure can be made. The fit between the brain of a typical student with ASD and the typical school environment is poor in that school demands a child to learn new skills in large groups of peers through social communication on a daily basis. Although it is the mission of this curriculum to teach the student specific flexibility skills that will improve that fit, it is also important to make accommodations in the school routine that reduce the overall level of stress the student is experiencing. Maintain-

Table 1. Willingness or different brain?

What looks like "won't"	May actually be "can't"
Opposition, stubbornness	Cognitive inflexibility, protective effort to avoid being overwhelmed
Lack of will ("He can do it if he wants to.")	Difficulty in shifting
Self-centeredness	Impaired social cognition, theory of mind, or ability to take another's perspective
Lack of effort ("She doesn't try.")	Poor initiation or impaired planning and generativity
Inability or refusal to put good ideas on paper	Poor fine motor skills, disorganization
Sloppy, erratic work	Poor self-monitoring, overload
Refusal to control outbursts	Overload, disinhibition
Preference for being alone	Impaired social problem-solving
Lack of sensitivity to others ("He doesn't care what others think.")	Impaired understanding and production of nonverbal social cues

ing predictable routines, posting schedules, previewing upcoming changes, offering choices whenever possible, and reducing the number of staff involved with a student are all common accommodations for students with ASD and can benefit all students.

At least one safe person/social coach must be identified at school. A safe person understands the student with ASD and is available to the student on an as-needed basis to review difficult interactions with others, explain confusing situations, and advocate for the student's needs. The safe person/social coach also seeks the student out regularly to monitor, teach, and actively coach social interaction skills. A safe person can be a speech-language therapist, special educator, or counselor who has training and experience in teaching social skills to children with ASD. This person can be any approved adult who the child identifies with and feels comfortable with. It will not be possible for a student with ASD to learn to become more flexible if he or she does not have such support. The social isolation, teasing, and bullying experienced by children with ASD without social support are traumatic events that increase anxiety, decrease flexibility, and impair learning.

Explicit assurance must be made to students with ASD that certain routines will remain unchanged. Self-soothing, repetitive routines (e.g., watching the same video every day after school, following favored eating rituals) that are not otherwise harmful to the student should be respected, as long as they do not interfere with essential social engagement or work completion. If students with ASD can maintain some of these routines, they are better able to handle change in other domains.

A structured behavior management system based on positive behavior supports must be in place. Different settings and different students require different types of specific positive behavior supports. This manual does not dictate which supports should be in place but assumes that the classroom environment is well managed and that students are well supported and set up for successful participation in the classroom setting.

The school team must be able to work together and consistently use the same vocabulary and scripts that are taught in this curriculum and reinforce the same behaviors. The intervention will only be successful if it permeates the student's environment.

A Flexible and Supportive Classroom

Students are better able to develop flexibility in a flexible classroom culture. The following features describe a flexible, organized classroom.

- Educators and students *make smooth and calm transitions between tasks,* activities, and expectations. They respond flexibly when changes and unexpected events occur.

- There is an *absence of power struggles* between educators and students. For example, when a teacher makes a request and a student refuses to obey, the teacher refrains from making a second, more demanding request or imposing a consequence that the student refuses.

- Educators use a *high ratio of praise to corrections* (target 4:1) because they facilitate better performance through positive actions such as scaffolding, elaboration, and modeling *before* trying to stop inadequate performance with consequences and corrections.

- There is *extensive use of active priming,* or a heads-up that something is going to happen. During priming, it is important to reference the concepts and language presented during explicit instruction. Children with ASD experience a high level of stress in response to change in routine or environment, which often develops out of a feeling of losing control. We can all relate to feeling anxious when something important that we had anticipated does not go as planned. For example, imagine that you have planned a formal dinner party, and 30 minutes before the guests arrive you find out that your dog has eaten the roast. By priming for a change or an opportunity to be flexible and referencing the techniques outlined in the explicit instruction, students can experience a sense of control over their environment.

- Educators communicate *clear, explicit, and specific expectations* for the work to be done, expected behavior, and how students should set and achieve goals.

- *The classroom is organized* so that all clutter and visual distractions are eliminated, and there are clear routines for turning in work, getting ready to go home, and making the transition between classes.

A Flexible and Supportive Educator

To maintain a flexible classroom and help students develop flexibility, you must be flexible yourself. Following are some guidelines for being flexible.

Exhibit a calm demeanor, an empathic understanding of the student's perspective, a positive outlook, and high expectations. These personality traits are critical for any educator but especially so for those working with students with ASD.

Problem-solve both internally and externally (with students) to detect when student performance breaks down, and discern and remedy the cause *of the breakdown.* For example, say that a student refuses to write a paragraph on his or her summer vacation. The educator acknowledges the student's difficulty and works to discover why the student has refused the task. Careful consideration may reveal that the student has no idea where to start, does not have a pencil, or has difficulty with fine motor tasks. The educator remedies the situation by introducing a writing rubric, providing a pencil, or allowing the student to work on a computer. In this case, the educator has worked to understand the student's position rather than immediately assume the student's refusal is due to noncompliance.

Know yourself. To be a flexible educator, you must know yourself in the classroom. What upsets you? Are there certain students or behaviors that are triggers for you? Are you ever rigid in the classroom? When are you typically rigid? What do you do when you are rigid? Learning your own early signs for becoming rigid and applying strategies that work for you will increase your flexibility and efficacy.

"Live aloud," or provide explicit instruction. It is not intuitive to the student with ASD that being flexible will increase his or her chances of making a friend or gaining more independence at school and at home. Because students with ASD do not readily draw lessons from experience about how and why to be flexible, these key concepts are taught explicitly and continuously reinforced through the technique of *living aloud,* or making the implicit flexibility demands of situations explicit (Myles, Adreon, & Gitlitz, 2006). By highlighting situations requiring flexibility, highlighting the emotions involved, and explicitly identifying flexible responses, you can provide your students with a working framework for how to be in control of being flexible. For example, you might say, "I was hoping to use the overhead projector to show you this worksheet, but the bulb is burned out. I am going to be flexible and give you each your own worksheet instead."

Treat students with respect and as active partners in their education. You will be most effective as a teacher if you can build a collaborative relationship with your students. This is particularly true for students with autism who strongly appreciate a sense of control. Collaborative relationships do not require teachers to give in to students or give up their expectations. In fact, they often facilitate increased effort and output from students. Collaborative relationships do require a willingness to give choices within the framework of clear expectations (e.g., allowing a student to choose the topic of an essay). They also require both parties to listen to what the other has to say. One student noted that he wished he could be provided with more opportunities to make a choice rather than have decisions made for him. He wished he could be offered these choices "just like regular people." Another student said that he really wanted "teachers to listen to what kids say and not assume things about us, and also take our opinions into account" when appropriate.

Empower your students. As you identify those times of day when a student would benefit from an accommodation (e.g., taking a 5-minute reading break after lunch, using a computer instead of writing by hand) or those environments that are a poor fit for the student (e.g., a loud cafeteria), support the student in discovering for him- or herself what he or she needs. This is an essential first step to teaching effective self-advocacy skills. Here are some examples of what you might say:

- "I noticed that the cafeteria is very loud and you cover your ears when you are in there. That makes it hard for you to talk or eat your food. Can you help me think of a spot that would be less noisy where you could have lunch?"

- "You have told me that you are really tired when you come in the morning. After you went on the swings yesterday you had a lot more energy and you were able to start your work. What strategy should we use when you come in feeling tired in the morning?"

Provide the right level of support through just-right cuing techniques. Use guided practice with faded cuing to gradually build new skills, one step at a time. Guided practice begins with concrete tasks and ample teacher support (i.e., verbal prompting and redirection). Teachers should gradually fade support and guidance as soon as students can demonstrate the skill independently. In the case of this intervention, teachers must be prepared initially to prompt use of flexibility scripts and routines but reduce prompting over time, always providing just the level of support needed for success. The role of the adult is to scaffold behavior only as much as the student needs in order to be successful, not to serve as a crutch or to create a dependency. Use of the Socratic method of asking questions in place of providing answers (e.g. "What do you need to get started?") to find out how much information the student can generate without staff input is helpful in this regard. Students should be guided, not told what to do. Because automatic processes are the most efficient, the goal of guided practice/ faded cuing is for the student to become independent and automatic in using the new vocabulary and scripts. Automaticity takes time, however, and repeated practice is expected. Adopt the model of athletic coaching or music instruction, in which students perform the same drills and routines repeatedly before gaining mastery.

OVERVIEW OF *UNSTUCK AND ON TARGET!* CURRICULUM

Once you have a flexible school team and classroom and are a flexible teacher, you are ready to develop flexibility and goal-directed behavior in your students using the *Unstuck and On Target!* curriculum, which has the following major components:

- *Teaches what flexibility is* through concrete, hands-on experiments with physical and cognitive flexibility. In addition, a specific vocabulary is taught to discuss flexibility with students (e.g., *flexibility, Plan A/Plan B, stuck*), which is then used consistently throughout the implementation of the intervention. See Topic 1: What Is Flexibility? and Topic 2: Flexibility Defined.

- *Explains why it is important to be flexible.* The curriculum provides explicit instruction to students on the concrete utility of being flexible (e.g., it gives them more choices, it helps them become a better friend) in ways that are directly meaningful to students. See Topic 5: Why Be Flexible and Topic 9: Being Flexible Makes You a Good Friend.

- *Teaches students how to be flexible.* The curriculum teaches flexibility skills in a structured format that emphasizes routines and self-regulatory scripts that are continuously practiced and reinforced until they are automatic. See Topic 7: Scripts for How to Be Flexible.

- *Teaches what goals are and how to achieve them.* The curriculum contains lessons to help students focus on what their goals are and distinguish major or target goals (e.g., getting good grades, making a friend) from distracter or "whim" goals. It also introduces a universal self-regulatory script or routine for setting a goal and making and completing a plan to get it done. See Topic 6: Your Goals: Getting What You Want and Topic 8: Journey to Target Island.

- *Teaches students how to want to be flexible and goal directed.* Being flexible and goal directed is hard for students with autism, so some parts of the curriculum are geared to making flexibility and goal-directed behavior reinforcing. Positive reinforcement and humor are embedded throughout the curriculum as they both have magical powers for shaping the behavior of students with autism. We encourage you to freely improvise further positive reinforcements and inject humor wherever you can find it when teaching *Unstuck and On Target!* The curriculum also includes specific lessons that structure students in identifying their own heroes as a way to help organize their understanding of the value of flexibility and goal-directed behavior using the image of a person they admire. This increases intrinsic motivation to be more flexible and goal directed. The curriculum also teaches coping strategies for those times when being flexible is especially hard. See Topic 3: Coping Skills and Topic 4: Personal Heroes.

GOAL OF THIS MANUAL

This manual describes *Unstuck and On Target!:* a plan of action for teaching students with ASD how to be more flexible and goal directed. The goal of this intervention is twofold:

1. To increase the cognitive flexibility and executive function abilities of students with ASD so that they can more easily shift from topic to topic, task to task, and person to person; consider new ideas, alternative beliefs, or another person's point of view; and work independently on multistep tasks in the classroom and beyond

2. To provide the intervention in a way that works in the classroom and ultimately creates more time for the teacher

WHO WILL BENEFIT FROM THIS INTERVENTION?

Students

We designed *Unstuck and On Target!* for 8- to 11-year-old students with ASD who have intact language and cognitive skills (e.g., those with high-functioning ASD) and who have difficulties with flexibility, organization, and planning. Specifically, it is designed to serve school-age children with ASD who have the cognitive and verbal skills to benefit from higher order cognitive and social interventions (i.e., average IQ and at least a second-grade language and reading level) because it is a verbally driven intervention. It is possible to adapt this intervention to meet the needs of older students, and some suggestions are given for these adaptations in each topic.

Staff

This intervention has been specifically designed for use in the classroom by professionals from different disciplines, including teachers, psychologists, social workers, speech-language therapists, occupational therapists, and highly trained teaching assistants. Those implementing this curriculum should have basic skills in working with students with ASD and should read the entire manual before beginning the curriculum.

Parents and Adults in Nonschool Settings

Although this intervention has been designed for the classroom, it has been implemented successfully in other settings (e.g., a small-group therapeutic setting, a social learning camp). In such cases, interventionists report making some adjustments to ensure a fit between the intervention and the setting. As long as the core features of the lessons remain in place, such adjustments are recommended (please see the first page of each topic). In addition, parents have found that *Unstuck and On Target!* is a useful tool to incorporate at home.

GUIDE TO THE LESSON PLANS

This manual includes several topics, each of which requires one to four or more lessons to fully teach the content. Table 2, the Curriculum Map, is designed to help the educator understand the scope and sequence of the curriculum.

Topics

Each topic begins with an overview page that includes a summary of the topic, prerequisite skills, related skills, expected outcomes, special notes to the instructor, and background and rationale. The information on this page covers the material for all of the lessons included in that topic.

Lessons

Most topics require multiple lessons. For ease of use, each lesson plan follows the same organization: a list of the materials required, a description of the activity, generalization activities, and suggestions for modifications. Most lessons also include handouts for the students; full-size color versions of these handouts can be printed from the accompanying CD-ROM. In addition, the CD-ROM also includes Home Extension handouts that can be distributed to parents for home generalization and Classroom Extensions that can be given to each student's classroom teachers.

Every lesson begins with a summary of the previous lesson, highlighting the vocabulary students have learned. It is critical that you completely understand the lessons before beginning them with the students. Read through the entire topic before beginning instruction 1) to gain a full understanding of the skills students will be acquiring and how the lessons fit together and 2) to prepare and gather materials. You know your students best, and an overall understanding of the lessons will allow you to pace lessons as you deem appropriate. Note that some lessons may require you to gather additional materials not typically found in a classroom or school. Those lessons are marked with 🛒 throughout the manual. For other lessons, you may need to spend a bit more time preparing (e.g., cutting), and those lessons are marked with ✂.

Table 2.   Curriculum map

Topic 1: What Is Flexibility?
Lesson 1: Flexibility Investigation
Lesson 2: Flexible Body

Topic 2: Flexible Vocabulary
Lesson 1: Flexibility
Lesson 2: Getting Stuck
Lesson 3: Plan A/Plan B
Lesson 4: Compromise and Consolidation

Topic 3: Coping Strategies
Lesson 1: Recognizing Your Feelings
Lesson 2: What Can You Do to Feel Better?

Topic 4: Personal Heroes
Lesson 1: What Makes a Hero Heroic?
Lesson 2: Who Is Your Hero?
Lesson 3: Hero Movie

Topic 5: Why Be Flexible?
Lesson 1: The Advantages of Flexibility
Lesson 2: Being Flexible Can Make Good Things Happen

Topic 6: Your Goals: Getting What You Want
Lesson 1: Setting and Achieving Goals Using Goal-Plan-Do-Check (GPDC)
Lesson 2: GPDC Application and Practice

Topic 7: Scripts to Help You Be Flexible
Lesson 1: Big Deal/Little Deal
Lesson 2: Choice/No Choice
Lesson 3: Handling the Unexpected

Topic 8: Journey to Target Island
Lesson 1: What Is a Target Goal?
Lesson 2: Your Target Goals
Lesson 3: Conflicting Goals

Topic 9: Being Flexible Makes You a Good Friend
Lesson 1: Flexibility Helps When Your Friend Makes a Mistake
Lesson 2: All Friends Have Similarities and Differences
Lesson 3: Flexibility Helps When You Disagree with Your Friend

Topic 10: Flexible Futures
Lesson 1: *Unstuck and On Target!* Review Game 1: Flexiac
Lesson 2: *Unstuck and On Target!* Review Game 2: Four Corners
Lesson 3: Flexible Futures

Home Extensions

Most topics include Home Extension handouts, which are formatted similarly. The goal of these handouts is to

- Provide additional practice opportunities
- Share language and concepts with families
- Promote generalization across settings by encouraging families to use similar language and practice concepts at home

Read through each Home Extension handout before presenting a lesson. The students will benefit from going over their Home Extension handout before they take it home. A Home Signoff is provided to alert students and parents to due dates for acknowledging receipt of the Home Extensions. Each student's *My Flexibility Notebook* should be sent home, as well (see Topic 1).

Classroom Extensions

Many topics include Classroom Extension handouts. The goal of these handouts is to

- Inform educators who work with your students about key concepts and vocabulary being introduced in the curriculum
- Promote additional practice opportunities
- Encourage all educators who work with the students to reinforce certain flexible behaviors
- Promote generalization across settings by encouraging communication between teachers and social skills instructors
- Promote generalization by encouraging teachers to use similar language and practice concepts in the classroom setting

The pages that follow will lead you and your students on an exciting journey toward more fun, better goal-directed behavior and greater flexibility in the classroom.

REFERENCES

Brooke, R.H., Chassin, M.R., Fink, A., Solomon, D.H., Kosecoff, J., & Park, R.E. (1986). A method for the detailed assessment of the appropriateness of medical technologies. *International Journal Technology Assessment in Health Care, 2,* 53–63.

Centers for Disease Control and Prevention. (1999). Framework for program evaluation in public health. *MMWR, 48* (No. RR-11).

Farley, M.A., McMahon, W.M., Fombonne, E., Jenson, W.R., Miller, J., Gardner, M., et al. (2009). Twenty-year outcome for individuals with autism and average or near-average cognitive abilities. *Autism Research, 2,* 109–118.

Feeney, T.J. (2010). Structured flexibility: The use of context-sensitive self-regulatory scripts to support young persons with acquired brain injury and behavioral difficulties. *Journal of Head Trauma Rehabilitation, 25,* 416–425.

Gilotty, L., Kenworthy, L., Black, D., Wagner, A., & Sirian, L. (2002). Adaptive skills and executive function in Asperger's syndrome and autism. *Child Neuropsychology, 8,* 90–101.

Herbert, M.R., Harris, G.J., Adrien, K.T., Ziegler, D.A., Makris, N., & Kennedy, D.N. (2002). Abnormal asymmetry in language association cortex in autism. *Annals of Neurology, 52,* 588–596.

Hill, E.L. (2004). Executive dysfunction in autism. *Trends in Cognitive Sciences, 8,* 26–32.

Israel, B.A., Schulz, A.J., Parker, E.A., & Becker, A.B. (1998). Review of community-based research: Assessing partnership approaches to improve public health. *Annual Review of Public Health, 19,* 173–202.

Kenworthy, L., Black, D., Wallace, G., Ahluvalia, T., Wagner, A., & Sirian, L. (2005). Disorganization: The forgotten executive dysfunction in autism spectrum disorders. *Developmental Neuropsychology, 28,* 809–827.

Kenworthy, L., Yerys, B.E., Anthony, L., & Wallace, G.L. (2008). Understanding executive control in autism spectrum disorders in the lab and in the real world. *Neuropsychology Review, 18,* 320–338.

Kunce, L., & Mesibov, G.B. (1998). Educational approaches to high-functioning autism and Asperger syndrome. In E. Schopler, G.B. Mesibov, & L. Kunce (Eds.), *Asperger syndrome or high-functioning autism?* (p. 231). New York: Plenum Press.

Murphy, D.G.M., Critchley, H.D., Schmitz, N., McAlonan, G., van Amelsvoort, T., Robertson, D., et al. (2002). Asperger syndrome: A proton magnetic resonance spectroscopy study of brain. *Archives of General Psychiatry, 59,* 885–891.

Miles, B.S., Adreon, D., & Gitlitz, D. (2006). *Simple strategies that work! Helpful hints for all educators of students with Asperger syndrome, high-functioning autism, and related disabilities.* Overland Park, KS: Autism Asperger Publishing.

Polatajko, H., & Mandich, A. (2004). *Enabling occupation in children: The cognitive orientation to daily occupational performance (CO-OP) approach.* Ottawa, ON: CAOT Publications.

Rogers, S.J., & Bennetto, L. (2000). Intersubjectivity in autism: The roles of imitation and executive function. In S.F. Warren & J. Reichle (Series Eds.) & A.P. Wetherby & B. Prizant (Vol. Eds.), *Communication and language intervention series: Vol. 9. Autism spectrum disorders: A transactional developmental perspective* (pp. 79–108). Baltimore: Paul H. Brookes Publishing Co.

Sullivan, G., Duan, N., Mukherjee, S., Kirchner, J., Perry, D., & Henderson, K. (2005). The role of services researchers in facilitating intervention research. *Psychiatric Services, 56,* 537–542.

Teuber, H.L. (1964). The riddle of frontal lobe function in man. In J.M. Warren & K. Akert (Eds.), *The frontal granular cortex and behavior* (pp. 410–477). New York: McGraw-Hill.

Ylvisaker, M. (2006). *Tutorial: Self-regulation/executive function routines after TBI.* Available on The Brain Injury Association of New York State web site: http://www.projectlearnet.org/tutorials/sr_ef_routines.html

Ylvisaker, M., & Feeney, T.J. (1998). *Collaborative brain injury intervention: Positive everyday routines.* San Diego: Singular Publishing.

TOPIC 1

What Is Flexibility?

SPECIAL INSTRUCTIONS: The core goals of these lessons are to help students identify and explore flexibility. Although it is important to provide the vocabulary set forth in this topic, modify the activities as necessary to better meet the needs of your students. A classroom poster should be started during the first topic and lesson, which you will add to during each successive lesson.

Summary: Topic 1 defines *flexible* and *rigid.* In addition, the lessons within this topic provide a conceptual foundation for *flexibility* through concrete, playful activities. Students will begin individual notebooks in which to keep their work.

Prerequisite skills: None

Related skills: Awareness of body

OUTCOME—CRITERIA FOR MASTERY

1. The student defines *flexibility* and *rigidity* in physical, concrete terms.
2. The student identifies whether an object is flexible or rigid.
3. The student demonstrates an understanding of the advantages that flexibility offers a physical object.

TOPIC BACKGROUND AND RATIONALE

Cognitive instruction is the first element of *Unstuck and On Target!* In cognitive instruction, students, teachers, and parents learn and teach new vocabulary, specific flexibility routines and scripts, and why flexibility is useful. The first step in learning a new skill is to understand what it is. *Cognitive flexibility* is a difficult abstract concept; therefore, it is important to make sure that elementary school students understand its meaning and value—its usefulness—in the concrete, physical world first, which is the goal of this lesson.

Lesson 1   Flexibility Investigation

 PURPOSE

The purpose of this lesson is to introduce the concept of *flexibility* and bring salience to its definition. The activities included in this lesson are designed as hands-on, scientific experiments to explore flexibility in its physical form; the activities can be established as stations through which students rotate. At one station, students will experiment with physical force applied to objects that are flexible and rigid; at another, students will explore the physical properties of physical and rigid objects using only the sense of touch; and at the last station, students will create a small art project to demonstrate *flexible* and *rigid*. Students will have a handout for each station that will guide them through the activity. There are four activities in this lesson.

Materials Required for All Activities

 Not Included

- One loose-leaf, full-size three-ring binder for each student
- Uncooked spaghetti noodles
- Rubber bands
- Toothpicks and pipe cleaners or twine
- 8.5" × 11" paper
- Glue
- Two objects that are flexible and two objects that are rigid
- Several blindfolds
- Whiteboard or chart paper
- Dry/wet erase markers or markers
- Four containers and a trash bin
- Magazine pictures or Internet access to download pictures
- Markers, colored pencils, pencils, and/or crayons
- Scissors
- Timer

Included

- Handout: Flexibility
- Handout: Flexible and Strong
- Handout: Flexible Objects
- Handout: Flexible Can Be Faster
- Classroom Extension 1
- Home Extension 1 and Home Signoff

Generalization

School Integration

- Highlight flexibility as a physical attribute as often as possible in the days following this lesson.
- Praise the students when they do the same.
- Start a notebook for each student; label it *My Flexibility Notebook*. Have students add their work from each lesson to the notebook, which should go home with the student on the day of the lesson and come back to school the next day. In addition, once students return their completed Home Extensions, add the handouts to their individual notebooks.
- Complete Classroom Extension 1.

Home Integration

Upon completion of the lesson, send home a copy of Home Extension 1 and Home Signoff.

Modifications

The activities in this lesson are not well suited for older students (middle school and above). It is important to begin with a concrete definition of *flexibility* as it applies to the physical world. Older students can explore more complex applications of flexibility (e.g., skyscrapers).

ACTIVITY 1
What Are Flexibility and Rigidity?

☆ **Presentation**

🕐 **~10 minutes**

Materials

Not Included

- Whiteboard or chart paper
- Dry/wet erase markers or markers
- Magazine pictures or Internet access to download pictures
- Markers, colored pencils, pencils, and/or crayons
- Glue
- Scissors

Included

- Handout: Flexibility

Instructions

In the first part of this lesson, introduce the concept of *flexibility* (Handout: Flexibility) and contrast *flexible* and *rigid* in physical terms. Use the key words on this handout to create a visual at the front of the room.

1. Demonstrate rigid and then flexible posture. You might say, for example, "If you are tired and want to sit down, you have to make your body flexible, right? If you stay rigid, you are *stuck* in one place standing up."
2. Explain that skyscrapers are massive structures but are designed to give a bit in the wind to remain standing.
3. Write key words on the board as you describe flexibility and rigidity.
4. Explore with the students other examples of objects that are flexible.
5. Have the students complete Handout: Flexibility. They should work individually, using visuals that they create themselves or find in magazines or on the Internet (using clipart software) to complete the second column of the handout.
6. Ask students to select at least one word that is a synonym for *flexible* (e.g., *stretchy, bendable*) and another that is a synonym for *rigid* (e.g., *stiff, unyielding*).

Flexible and Strong

📋 **Experiment**

🕑 **~8 minutes**

Materials

Not Included

- Uncooked spaghetti (at least two strands per student)
- Rubber bands (several for use at the station)
- Trash bin for broken spaghetti noodles
- Four containers: one each for rubber bands, uncooked spaghetti, project handouts, and completed project handouts

Included

- Handout: Flexible and Strong

Instructions

1. Establish a station in the room—a single area that is big enough for each student to have his or her own space within the same location.
2. Place a box of rubber bands and a box of uncooked spaghetti in their designated containers at the station.
3. Place the containers and the trash bin at the station in the order of workflow (i.e., project handout, rubber bands, spaghetti noodles, completed project handout bin, and trash bin).
4. The students are going to try to break the rubber bands and the uncooked spaghetti noodles. Before they begin, ask them to make a prediction of what will happen on their handout.
5. Have the students try to break the rubber bands and the uncooked spaghetti noodles.
6. Ask the students to use the handout to report their findings.

ACTIVITY 3
Flexible Objects

□ **Experiment**
🕑 **~8 minutes**

Materials

Not Included

- Two items that are flexible
- Two items that are rigid
- Several blindfolds
- Four containers: one to keep the flexible and rigid items from view, one to hold the blindfolds, and two bins to hold project handouts and completed project handouts

Included

- Handout: Flexible Objects

Instructions

In this activity, students identify objects as rigid or flexible using only their sense of touch.

1. Designate a station in the classroom where students can work independently but within the same general location.
2. Hide four objects—two that are flexible and two that are rigid—in a container at the station.
3. Place the remaining materials in the designated containers.
4. Place the containers at the station in the order of workflow (i.e., project handout, blindfolds, hidden objects, completed project handout bin).
5. First, ask each student how he or she will know whether an object is rigid or flexible. The student should write a prediction about this on the handout.
6. Ask the student to put on a blindfold.
7. Have the student reach into the container of flexible and rigid objects, take out an object, and report whether the object is rigid or flexible, taking the blindfold off between each item to see what it actually was.
8. Have the student complete the handout.

Note: This station will require moderate adult supervision because students will be blindfolded during the task.

ACTIVITY 4
Flexible Can Be Faster

📋 **Experiment**

🕐 **~8 minutes**

Materials

Not Included

- Toothpicks (approximately 10 for each student)
- Pipe cleaners (if pipe cleaners are not available, string, yarn, or twine cut to lengths of 5 inches [approximately three for each student])
- 8.5" × 11" paper
- Glue (enough bottles or sticks for each student at the station)
- Four containers: one each for toothpicks, pipe cleaners or substitute, project handouts, and completed project handouts
- Timer

Included

- Handout: Flexible Can Be Faster
- Home Extension 1 and Home Signoff

Instructions

1. Designate a station in the classroom where students can work independently but within the same general location.
2. Place the materials in the designated containers.
3. Place the containers and glue at the station in the order of workflow (i.e., project handout; toothpicks; pipe cleaners or substitute; 8.5" × 11" paper; glue; completed project handout).
4. Ask the students to create two arches on their paper: one with pipe cleaners and one with toothpicks.
5. Have the students complete Handout: Flexible Can Be Faster to foster their exploration of the efficiency of pipe cleaners for the creation of an arch.
6. Review Home Extension 1 with students.

Flexibility

	Student examples (words or pictures)	Parent examples (words or pictures)
Flexible—bending, changing, switching 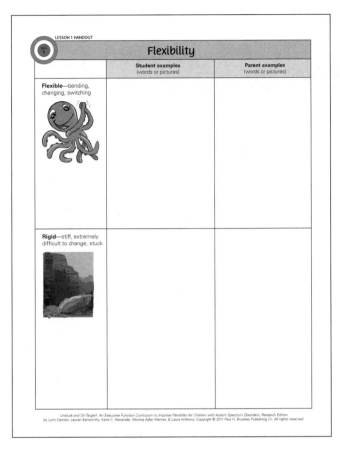		
Rigid—stiff, extremely difficult to change, stuck		

Flexible and Strong

Name: _____ Date: _____

Sometimes, flexibility makes an object stronger. In this experiment, you will discover which is stronger under pressure—flexible objects or rigid objects.

Prediction:

Which do you think will break when you apply pressure? (Underline one.)

Rubber band　　Uncooked spaghetti noodle　　Both

What do you do?

Bend the rubber band. What happened?
___ It broke.
___ It bent.
___ Nothing happened.

Bend the uncooked spaghetti noodle. What happened?
___ It broke.
___ It bent.
___ Nothing happened.

Check your prediction:

Go back and look at your prediction. Circle the item that actually broke.

What happened in your experiment? Which item broke? Why do you think it broke? (If you need help, raise your hand.)

_____
_____
_____

Flexible Objects

Name: _____ Date: _____

Project: Flexible Objects

You can learn to tell when something is flexible, even when you can't see the object.

Prediction:

How will you know whether something you are touching is flexible or rigid?

_____
_____
_____

What do you do?

Gently hold an object while wearing a blindfold. Is it rigid or flexible? Can you tell what it is?

Circle whether the item you touched is rigid or flexible.

| **Object 1:** | rigid | flexible | **Object 2:** | rigid | flexible |
| **Object 3:** | rigid | flexible | **Object 4:** | rigid | flexible |

Check your prediction:

Go back and look at your prediction. Did your ideas for being able to tell whether something was rigid or flexible work?

Circle one:

———1———————2———————3———

Didn't work well　　Worked kind of well　　Worked really well

Flexible Can Be Faster

Name: _____ Date: _____

Project: Flexible Can Be Faster

Sometimes, flexibility can allow things to be done faster. In this experiment, you will find out whether flexibility or rigidity works best. You will create one arch out of toothpicks and one arch out of pipe cleaners.

Prediction:

Which do you think will work better? (Circle one.)

Toothpicks　　Pipe cleaners

What do you do?

Create an arch (the shape of a rainbow), one time with pipe cleaners and another time with toothpicks. Use a timer to track how long it takes to create each arch.

Check your prediction:

1. Which took less time? (Circle one.)
   Toothpicks　　Pipe cleaners

2. How many toothpicks did you need? _____

3. How many pipe cleaners did you need? _____

4. Overall, which worked better? (Circle one.)
   Toothpicks　　Pipe cleaners

Classroom Extension 1

Summary: In group, we have just completed our review of flexibility and rigidity as they are defined in the physical world. Each student has participated in several individual and group activities designed to make the definition of *flexibility* and *rigidity* as meaningful as possible. During group sessions, students are encouraged to use their new vocabulary, *flexibility* and *rigidity*. Teachers will use the language to reflect on student behaviors as well as narrate their own experiences out loud. During their social skills groups, students will continue to be introduced to new "flexible language." As new words are introduced, they will build a visual to help students and teachers remember the concepts and remind them to use the language. To help support generalization of the language and concepts, build your own classroom visual.

Materials:

— Poster board or chart paper

— Glue

— Key word templates (provided)

To Do:

— Cut out key word templates

— Glue them to the poster board

— Name the board something catchy (i.e., flexi-con, or something that ties in with an existing classroom theme)

— Hang the poster board in a prominent place in the classroom

— As often as possible, use the key words in your language by narrating your and your student's experiences out loud and reinforcing students for demonstrating key behaviors.

For example:
*"I know you wanted to use the red marker, great job being **flexible** and using the blue one."*

*"I was hoping to use the color printer to print the handouts. It is out of ink, so I will have to be **flexible** and use the black and white one."*

*"My Internet is not working; I am feeling very frustrated right now. I am going to have to come up with a **Plan B** so I can still get the information I need."*

*"I know you wanted to go outside for recess today. I love that you did not get **stuck** and came up with a **Plan B** to stay inside"*

*"I hope the library has a book on Martin Luther King, Jr. I know they may be all checked out, so I will **keep an open mind** and think about what other books I can check out."*

(page 1 of 3)

CLASSROOM EXTENSION 1 *(continued)*

TOPIC
1

Classroom Extension 1

Notes:

— Students will be introduced to this language throughout the program. Social skills teachers will keep you posted as new language is introduced.

— Feel free to modify key word templates to coordinate with an existing classroom theme.

— You are encouraged to use these words and concepts as part of your classroom reinforcement system (e.g., filling up the classroom marble jar—each time a student is flexible, he or she earns a marble for the group).

EXTENSION ACTIVITY:

The following activity is designed to reinforce flexibility concepts and bring the words *flexibility* and *rigidity* into the classroom.

Materials you will need:

• Computer and printer (if possible)

• Markers, colored pencils, pencils, and/or crayons

• Scissors (1 per student)

• Glue (1 per student)

• Bulletin board or poster board

Instructions:

1. Review each student's flexibility handouts

2. Students will work in groups to develop a poster or bulletin board background.

3. Each student should chose 1–2 images that represent flexibility (it can be a replica of something they have included on Handout: Flexibility or it can be something new).

4. Once that image is found, created, or drawn on a separate sheet of paper, the student should then attach it to the poster or bulletin board.

5. The bulletin board should maintain a prominent position in the classr...

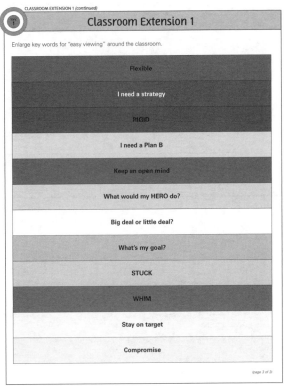

CLASSROOM EXTENSION 1 *(continued)*

Classroom Extension 1

Enlarge key words for "easy viewing" around the classroom.

| Flexible |
| I need a strategy |
| RIGID |
| I need a Plan B |
| Keep an open mind |
| What would my HERO do? |
| Big deal or little deal? |
| What's my goal? |
| STUCK |
| WHIM |
| Stay on target |
| Compromise |

(page 3 of 3)

Home Extension 1

Summary: In class, we have just completed our review of *flexibility* as it is defined in the physical world. Each student has participated in several individual and group activities, all designed to make the definition of *flexibility* as meaningful as possible.

There are several things you can do at home to help your child learn as fully as possible. The more experiences your child has outside the classroom, the better he or she will be able to learn and apply that learning.

1. As often as you can, use the word *flexible* or *flexibility* to point out objects, animals, or people who demonstrate flexibility. For example, you might say, "Look at how flexible the cat is to reach that far under the table for his toy."

2. Please complete the bottom half of this handout with your child and return it to school with your child.

3. You also will find the other handouts that your child has completed in school. Please return them when you have finished your review. This is for your information.

In the upcoming lessons, we will work with students on flexibility of the brain. In this way, we will move progressively from the concrete meaning of flexibility to the abstract meaning.

Flexibility and Rigidity Around the House

1. Find three objects that are rigid (list them here): _____
   _____
   _____

2. Find three objects that are flexible (list them here): _____
   _____
   _____

3. What would happen if your pencil was super flexible? _____
   _____
   _____

4. What would happen if your napkin was super rigid? _____
   _____
   _____

Home Signoff

T

Date sent home: _____

I have read
Home Extension _____

_____
Parent signature

Please return this page to
the social skills teacher by _____.

Lesson 2   Flexible Body

 PURPOSE

Students will continue to develop a concrete definition of flexibility and begin to make flexibility a more personal experience. Two activities are included in this lesson.

Materials Required for All Activities

 Not Included

- Whiteboard or chart paper
- Dry/wet erase markers or markers
- Scratch paper
- Materials for an obstacle course
- A physical space large enough to accommodate the obstacle course (e.g., gym, classroom with desks pushed to the side, playground)
- Timer or stopwatch

Included

There are no included materials for this lesson.

Generalization

School Integration

- Continue to highlight flexibility when opportunities arise.
- Praise flexibility throughout the day (e.g., on the playground and during unstructured time: "Great job being flexible and choosing the swing when the seesaw was not available").

Home Integration

There is no Home Extension for Lesson 2.

Modifications

Rather than completing the activities in this lesson, older students may benefit from exploring the concrete, physical features of flexibility through research activities. For example, students could research the role of flexibility in physical fitness or the advantage that flexibility affords certain animals (e.g., the octopus). The objective of the lesson is the same: to create a solid, salient definition of flexibility. Another option for older students would be to condense these two lessons into one lesson.

ACTIVITY 1
Flexible and Rigid Bodies

 **Group Activity**
🕐 **~10 minutes**

Materials

Not Included

- Whiteboard or chart paper
- Dry/wet erase markers or markers
- Scratch paper

Included

There are no included materials for this lesson.

Instructions

1. Review the previous session.
   a. Ask students whether they can remember the definition of the words *flexible* and *rigid* as well as their findings from their experiments.
   b. Highlight the different ways that flexibility was advantageous in the experiments.
      i. Strength (rubber band)
      ii. Efficiency (arch)
2. Explain the following to the students:
   a. The body can be flexible and/or rigid.
   b. There are times when it works best to have a flexible body.
   c. There are times when a flexible body is very important, such as during class. For instance, students have flexible bodies when they move across the room or raise their hands.
3. Have the students stand up.
   a. Have the students make their bodies rigid and hold their position for 1 minute. You should do this as well. Then, ask them if they are comfortable.
   b. Have the students make their bodies flexible for 1 minute (e.g., wiggle, bend). You should do this as well. Then, ask them if flexible was more comfortable.
4. Have the students attempt to do a simple drawing (e.g., a tree) with rigid arms and then another drawing with flexible arms. Which was easier?

Note: During this activity, highlight salient points on the whiteboard or chart paper.

ACTIVITY 2
Flexibility Overcomes Obstacles

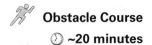 **Obstacle Course**
 ~20 minutes

Materials

Not Included

- Whiteboard or chart paper
- Dry/wet erase markers or markers
- Materials for an obstacle course
- Physical space large enough for obstacle course (e.g., gym, classroom with desks pushed to the side, playground)
- Timer or stopwatch

Included

There are no included materials for this lesson.

Instructions

1. The students will build an obstacle course together.
2. Each student will select three items that he or she will contribute to the obstacle course.
3. Taking turns, each student will place one of his or her three items in succession in order to cooperatively create the obstacle course.
4. Students first will run the course with a rigid body (e.g., arms and legs straight), with the teacher timing completion.
5. Next, the students will complete the course with a flexible body (e.g., arms and legs bent comfortably), with the teacher timing completion.
6. Together, the students will create two bar graphs: one representing ease and the other representing time.
   a. *Ease:* Bars on this graph represent the number of students who vote that one or the other condition—the obstacle course with the rigid body or the one with the flexible body—was easier.
   b. *Time:* One bar on this graph represents the average time for completing the obstacle course with a rigid body; the other represents the time for completion with a flexible body.

Extensions

Generalization

School Integration

- Highlight flexibility as a physical attribute as often as possible in the days following this lesson and praise the students when they do the same.
- Start a *My Flexibility Notebook* for each student with the handouts from the lessons.
- Complete Classroom Extension 1.
- Praise flexibility throughout the day.

Home Integration

- Upon completion of Lesson 1, send home a copy of Home Extension 1 and Home Signoff.
- Send home the student's *My Flexibility Notebook*.

Materials for Home

- Home Extension 1 and Home Signoff

Note: Throughout the *Unstuck and On Target!* program, send home each student's *My Flexibility Notebook*. Parents should return the notebooks the following day. Although not listed on Extensions pages in Topics 2–10, the notebooks should remain a vital part of home integration activities.

Flexible Vocabulary

SPECIAL INSTRUCTIONS: The introduction of each of the five vocabulary words follows a similar set of steps:

Step 1: A playful introduction of the word

Step 2: Exploration of the word in action

Step 3: Performance of an engaging activity in which the students further explore the vocabulary word

Although it is important to implement these three steps in each of the three lessons, modify the activities as necessary to best meet your students' needs.

Summary: In this topic, we build on the foundational understanding of flexibility as a physical property by expanding the concept to include *cognitive* flexibility. Students, teachers, and parents learn and teach a new vocabulary. Specific vocabulary (i.e., *flexibility, stuck, keeping an open mind, Plan A/Plan B,* and *compromise*) is introduced, which is then used consistently throughout the implementation of the intervention. To teach the students most effectively, a common vocabulary is vital. The same phrases must be used over and over and be used consistently between home and school. For example, in any problem-solving situation, students should be asked the following: "Do you have a Plan A?" "What is your Plan B?"

Prerequisite skills: Understanding of the meaning of *flexibility* as a concrete physical property (Topic 1)

Related skills: Core language comprehension, ability to participate in group discussion and role play

OUTCOME—CRITERION FOR MASTERY

The student accurately uses and defines the flexibility vocabulary (i.e., *flexible, stuck, Plan A/ Plan B, keeping an open mind,* and *compromise*).

TOPIC BACKGROUND AND RATIONALE

Having introduced *flexibility* as a concrete physical property in Topic 1, it is important to build on that foundation and expand the concept to *cognitive flexibility*. The primary goal of this lesson, building a common flexibility vocabulary, is vital because it allows teachers, parents, and students to gain access to, with one word or phrase (e.g., "Are you stuck?"), all the teaching and experiences that are provided throughout this intervention. This common vocabulary serves as an essential foundation on which all future work in this curriculum is built.

Lesson 1 Flexibility

 PURPOSE

This lesson forms a bridge from the concept of *physical flexibility* to the more abstract context of *cognitive flexibility*. The lesson begins the work of creating a vocabulary of words and concepts that promote a comprehensive understanding of flexibility. There are two activities in this lesson.

Materials Required for All Activities

Not Included

- Fun putty ingredients (see fun putty recipe on handout)
- Whiteboard or chart paper
- Dry/wet erase markers or markers
- Bulletin board materials (see note at the end of this section)

Included

- Educator Guide: Mystery Word Key (for use throughout Topic 2)
- Handout: Mystery Word 1
- Handout: The Story of Silly Putty
- Handout: Fun Putty Recipe

Generalization

School Integration

- Highlight cognitive flexibility or making a flexible decision or choice versus being rigid as often as possible in subsequent days.
- Pay particular attention to your own actions as the educator and narrate out loud. For example, if you are getting rigid, say, "I want to stay flexible so that I can ____."
- Praise and reinforce students for being flexible.

Home Integration

There is no Home Extension for Lesson 1.

Modifications

General

Students can create their own flexibility dictionaries as a place to store their new vocabulary words and as a reference.

For Older Students

Consider a different work product for older students; Handout: Mystery Word 1 will likely be too easy for them. It also may be helpful to pull video clips rather than use the teacher-enacted scenes in Lesson 2, Activity 3. Make this decision based on your students' interests and abilities. You may highlight different examples from popular adolescent movies, television shows, books, and comics rather than act out scenes. Conversely, older students may be ready to act out the scenes of familiar situations (even if they act out scenes from popular media with which they are familiar).

Note: Students with ASD benefit greatly from salient visual supports. We strongly advise, therefore, that you provide students with a large visual aid that they can view regularly; a classroom bulletin board typically works well for this purpose. Throughout this topic, students will be introduced to several new vocabulary words. A bulletin board or similar visual is a powerful way to remind students of the language they have learned and to foster their use of this critical vocabulary. The bulletin board also serves as a cue for other staff members who may come into your classroom, promoting their use of the vocabulary as well. When all staff members incorporate this language into their conversations with students, students are more likely to generalize their new fund of knowledge.

ACTIVITY 1
Mystery Word—*Flexibility*

👤👥 **Individual or Group Activity**

🕐 **~10 minutes**

Materials

Not Included

- White board or chart paper
- Dry and/or wet erase markers or markers

Included

- Handout: Mystery Word 1

Instructions

Each new vocabulary word will be presented in a unique, enjoyable way. Students will be presented with one mystery word in each lesson. In the first part of this lesson, you will review Topic 1 and guide students through the discovery of cognitive flexibility and the beginning of a new vocabulary related to flexibility.

1. Ask students to reflect on the physical flexibility vocabulary and activities from Topic 1.
2. Distribute Handout: Mystery Word 1 (one per student or one for the group).
3. Once the students have filled in the word *flexibility*, tell them, "We know we can be flexible with our bodies. Raise your hand if you think that you can also be flexible with your mind."
4. Ask students if they have ever been flexible with their minds. They may need some examples to get started. Examples include the following: "The red marker was out of ink, so I used the blue one," or "The book I really wanted wasn't at the library, so I chose a different one." It may be helpful to use examples you have witnessed among your students in recent days.
5. Ask the students to write their examples on the whiteboard.

ACTIVITY 2
As Flexible as Silly Putty

☆ **Presentation and Activity**
🕑 **~20 minutes**

Materials

Not Included

- White glue
- Water
- Food coloring (enough so that the students can choose and share)
- Borax (typically found at the grocery store near the laundry detergent)

Included

- Handout: The Story of Silly Putty
- Handout: Fun Putty Recipe

Instructions

1. Distribute Handout: The Story of Silly Putty.
2. Tell the students the story of the invention of Silly Putty. Use the handout as a guide to your storytelling.
3. Ask the students whether they know what Silly Putty can do. (In itself, Silly Putty is very flexible. It can copy newsprint, bounce, and mold. Astronauts used it on Apollo 8 to keep tools in place.)
4. Explain that people need to be flexible like Peter Hodgson was and in the same way that Silly Putty is. When we are not flexible, we are rigid, the way that James Wright was. Provide the following scenarios for students to consider. Ask students how they would be flexible with their mind in these situations.
   a. "You go to the playground planning to swing, but all the swings are taken. What could you do if you were being flexible? What would you do if you were not being flexible or were being rigid?"
   b. "What if you think that someone really does not like you and then they offer you a cookie from their lunch and ask you to play a game with them?" Incorporate the word *rigid* into the scenario. "What would you do if you were not being flexible or were being rigid?"
5. Summarize the scenarios as follows: "Being flexible is not just about bending; it is also about changing an idea, considering new information, or changing what you are doing." Distinguish between *flexibility* and *giving in*.
6. Distribute Handout: Fun Putty Recipe and the ingredients required to make the fun putty (a generic version of Silly Putty).
7. Make fun putty using the recipe.
8. Post the words *flexible* and *rigid* and their definitions on the bulletin board.

LESSON 1 EDUCATOR GUIDE

Mystery Word Key

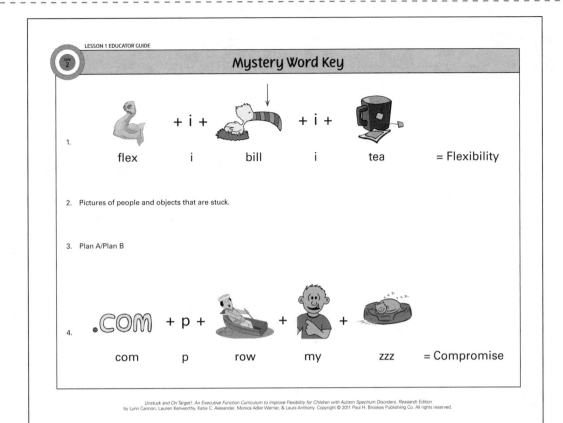

1.

flex   i   bill   i   tea   = Flexibility

2. Pictures of people and objects that are stuck.

3. Plan A/Plan B

4.

com   p   row   my   zzz   = Compromise

LESSON 1 HANDOUT

Mystery Word 1

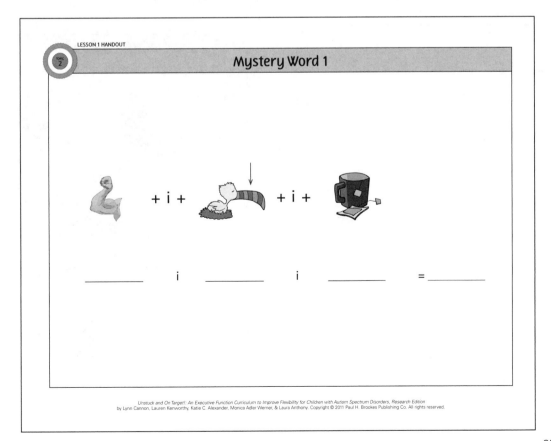

_____   i   _____   i   _____   = _____

LESSON 2 HANDOUT

Fun Putty Recipe

RECIPE

Ingredients:

- 2 cups white glue
- 2 cups water
- Food coloring of choice
- 1 teaspoon borax

Directions:

1. Mix the white glue, 1½ cups of the water, and the food coloring into a bowl until it is no longer sticky. This will be your glue solution.
2. In a separate bowl, dissolve 1 teaspoon borax into ½ cup of water.
3. Add the borax solution to the glue solution.
4. When the two solutions mix, the result will be a very thick clump of slime. Knead the slime with clean hands to get it to mix well. This will take about 10 minutes or so.
5. Enjoy your fun putty!

LESSON 1 HANDOUT

The Story of Silly Putty

James Wright was a thinker who lived during the 1940s. There wasn't enough rubber in the 1940s because of World War II, so he tried to create a substitute for rubber.

Rubber tire

Rubber boots

Because of this, James Wright invented Silly Putty. Unfortunately, Silly Putty did not do what rubber could do; it wouldn't work for tires or boots or other such objects.

James Wright was *not* flexible and gave up on his invention. A few years later, Peter Hodgson, who *was* flexible, thought that although Silly Putty might not be rubber, it still could do lots of neat things.

Peter Hodgson

Silly Putty has now been a popular toy for almost 50 years! Peter is a good example of how being flexible can be fantastic.

Lesson 2 Getting Stuck

 PURPOSE

This lesson extends the concept of *flexibility* and enables students to compare it with the concept of being *stuck*. This lesson uses the students' understanding of *rigid* to link to their conceptualization of *stuck*. There are three activities in this lesson.

Materials Required for All Activities

 Not Included

- Whiteboard or chart paper
- Dry/wet erase markers or markers
- Bulletin board materials
- Silly Putty (or similar substance; one piece per student)
- Craft sticks or tongue depressors (one per student)
- Tape

 Included

- Handout: Mystery Word 2
- Handout: Keeping an Open Mind (each handout has four images; each student will need one image)
- Classroom Extension 2
- Home Extension 2 and Home Signoff

Generalization

School Integration

Distribute Classroom Extension 2 to all teaching staff so that educators can implement these key strategies when working with students.

Home Integration

Upon completion of the lesson, send home a copy of Home Extension 2 and Home Signoff. Home Extension 2 summarizes Lessons 1 and 2 and explains activities that parents can do at home with their children. It also provides families with the beginning of a Flexibility Dictionary.

Modifications

As in Lesson 1, consider activities that would be more meaningful for older students, or condense Lessons 1 and 2 together. See the guidelines offered in Lesson 1.

ACTIVITY 1
Mystery Word—*Stuck*

Individual or Group Activity
~10 minutes

Materials

Not Included

- Whiteboard or chart paper
- Dry/wet erase markers or markers (preferably red and green)

Included

- Handout: Mystery Word 2

Instructions

1. Ask students to reflect on the cognitive flexibility vocabulary and activities from Lesson 1. Ensure that students remember the story of Silly Putty.
2. Distribute Handout: Mystery Word 2 (one for each student or one for the group). Ask the students to think about the pictures of people and objects on the handout and determine what they all have in common (they are all stuck).
3. After students have uncovered the word *stuck,* explain to the students that when they are flexible, they never actually get stuck because they always have a choice. People who are flexible keep an open mind. This may be the first time students have heard the expression *open mind.* Continue to incorporate the expression into your conversation with the students; a detailed description is provided in Activity 2.
4. Reiterate to the students that if they choose to be flexible, they have more choices; however, when they are stuck, they have only the one choice—being stuck.
5. Create a flowchart as you review the examples below. See the example below. Use green and red markers to illustrate the difference between *flexible* and *stuck,* respectively.
   a. James Wright, who invented Silly Putty, got stuck on the fact that his invention could not be used for the purpose he intended. In contrast, Peter Hodgson was flexible and saw everything that Silly Putty *could* be. Hodgson made many children happy and earned a great deal of money because of his flexibility.
   b. If two friends are playing and they get stuck because they want to play different games, they will end up not playing anything; however, if they are both flexible, they can think of many different games to play.
   c. Add additional examples from familiar situations until you feel that students understand the concept.

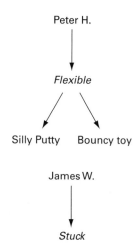

ACTIVITY 2
Keeping an Open Mind

👤 **Individual Activity**
🕐 **~5–10 minutes**

Materials

Not Included

- Whiteboard or chart paper
- Dry/wet erase markers or markers
- Tape

Included

- Handout: Keeping an Open Mind

Instructions

1. In this activity, students will use the *open mind* image from the handout to categorize the examples they discussed and generated in Activity 1 of this lesson.

2. Distribute one image from Handout: Keeping an Open Mind to each student. Remember, you will want to have the sheets cut ahead of time.

   a. Tell students, "When you are flexible, you are keeping an *open mind*. The expression *keeping an open mind* means that you come up with more than one choice or option."

   b. Go back to each example from Activity 1, and ask students to describe how the examples of flexibility, written in green, reflect an open mind.

   c. Ask students to write (or, have someone available for dictation) their answers above the image of the brain in each picture.

   d. Tape the sheet next to the flowchart on the board. See the example provided below.

3. Summarize the lesson thus far for students, reiterating that keeping an open mind helps them to be more flexible and also shows others that they are being flexible. Furthermore, state that when students keep an open mind, they avoid being rigid and getting stuck. Go back and highlight the ways in which people in the examples throughout this topic profit from flexibility.

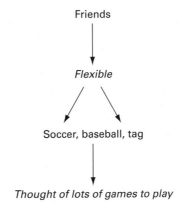

Friends

Flexible

Soccer, baseball, tag

Thought of lots of games to play

ACTIVITY 3
Flexible/Stuck Role Play

Group Activity

~5–10 minutes

Materials

Not Included

- Whiteboard or chart paper
- Dry/wet erase markers or markers
- Craft sticks or tongue depressors (one for each student)
- Silly Putty (or similar substance; one piece for each student)

Included

- Home Extension 2 and Home Signoff

Instructions

1. Distribute one craft stick or tongue depressor and one piece of Silly Putty to each student.
2. Act out the following scenarios; recruit assistants to help if desired. As they watch, students should decide whether the person in each scenario is being rigid or flexible. Following each scenario, ask the students to raise their craft sticks or tongue depressors in the air if the person is being rigid or their Silly Putty if the person is being flexible.
   a. Look for a particular color of marker that you do not have. When you are unable to find the color you are looking for, abandon writing on the board altogether.
   b. Once again, look for a color of marker that you do not have. When you are unable to find that particular color, decide instead to use a color that you have. On the board, write *I love my students* or something that your students will love to read. Once the students have voted on whether the scenario demonstrated flexibility or rigidity, emphasize that the color of marker did not matter but the message did; it was far better to express the message using a nonpreferred color of marker than to abandon writing the message altogether.
   c. Act out two additional scenes with contrasting outcomes (e.g., unable to find a preferred article of clothing, unable to find a preferred toy), again highlighting the advantages of flexibility.
   d. If you have time, ask students to give you examples to act out. You also may ask students to tell you the advantages of flexibility in the different scenes.
3. Conclude the activity by reiterating the value of flexibility and the burden of being stuck. Briefly summarize the vocabulary and activities that have been covered thus far in Topic 2.
4. Post the word *stuck* and its definition as well as the phrase *keep an open mind* and associated images on the bulletin board.
5. Review Home Extension 2 with students.

Mystery Word 2

= _____

Keeping an Open Mind

Classroom Extension 2

Teacher: _____ Student initials: _____ Date: _____

Summary: Students have built on their understanding of *flexibility* as a physical property by expanding the concept to include *cognitive* flexibility. Specific vocabulary (*flexibility* and *stuck*) has been introduced and must now be consistently used as a common vocabulary by teachers, parents, and students to be effective.

What is cognitive flexibility? The ability to generate more than one solution or answer; recognize when a strategy or response is not working and generate a new approach; entertain complex or conflicting information (e.g., Johnny is a good friend even though he won't let me use his Gameboy right now); and negotiate and compromise.

What difference will this make in the classroom? Increasing the cognitive flexibility of students reduces the amount of time the teacher must spend negotiating during class time and the number of disruptive episodes created by a student who does not know how to shift gears. The *flexibility* and *stuck* vocabulary gives teachers a one-word cue to help students monitor and change their behavior.

Key words and phrases

- Flexibility
- Flexible
- Stuck

What should I do to help my student(s)?

1. As often as possible, highlight the advantages of cognitive flexibility or making a flexible decision or choice over being stuck.

2. Pay particular attention to your own actions as the educator, and narrate out loud. For example, if you are getting stuck, say, "I want to stay flexible so that I can ___."

3. Praise and reinforce students for being flexible and identifying when they are stuck.

4. If a student is stuck, bring it to his or her attention privately.

Home Extension 2

Summary: In class, we have just completed our review of *flexibility* as it is defined more abstractly as a cognitive skill. Specifically, your child has learned the definitions of *flexible* and *stuck*. In addition, your child has learned about the phrase *keeping an open mind*. Attached, please find the first two word cards that will form the beginning of a Flexibility Dictionary for your child.

There are several activities you can do at home that will help your child comprehend the idea of *cognitive flexibility* as fully as possible. The more experiences a student has outside of the classroom, the better he or she will be able to learn and apply that learning.

1. Talk with your child about where the best location is for his or her Flexibility Dictionary. It should be kept somewhere where it also can work as a visual cue for you to reference at key times.

2. Continue to use the word *flexibility*, and highlight when your child (or you or someone else) is displaying cognitive flexibility. For example, you might say the following: "I know you had expected pizza, and I love how flexible you're being with the change in plans."

3. At mealtime, try an activity during which you (as well as any other available adults) play out *flexibility* and *getting stuck*. The game for your child is to point out when flexibility and getting stuck occur. For example, you might say, "I really wanted to sit there," gesturing to someplace that is taken or where there is no chair. Pause to see if your child notices. There are many possibilities during mealtime or other times. Have fun with this!

4. Please return the handouts (child's *My Flexibility Notebook*) when you have finished your review. This is for your information and will help you promote your child's understanding of the concepts. Please keep the Flexibility Dictionary at home for easy reference.

In the coming lessons, we will continue to build a vocabulary related to cognitive flexibility.

Home Signoff

Date sent home: _____

I have read
Home Extension _____

_____
Parent signature

Please return this page to
the social skills teacher by _____.

TOPIC 2

My Flexibility Dictionary

Flexible

- Just as we can be flexible with our bodies, we also can be flexible with our minds.

- This means that we can
  o Change our ideas
  o Do something different than what we thought we would do
  o Think something different
  o Consider new information
  o Keep an open mind
  o Identify other flexible mind accomplishments

Stuck

- Just like we can be rigid with our bodies, we also can be rigid with our minds and get stuck.

- When we are rigid and stuck, we
  o Do not change our ideas or think differently
  o Do not do something different than what we thought we would do
  o Do not consider new information

- When we are stuck, we only have one choice: to remain stuck.

- When we are flexible, we do not get stuck.

- When we are flexible, we have many choices.

(page 2 of 2)

Lesson 3 Plan A/Plan B

 PURPOSE

In this lesson, students continue to build a vocabulary foundation for the concept of flexibility. There are two activities in this lesson.

Materials Required for All Activities

 Not Included

- Whiteboard or chart paper
- Dry/wet erase markers or markers
- Videocamera to record the skits (optional)
- Bulletin board materials

Included

- Handout: Mystery Word 3
- Handout: Flexibility Skit Framework: Plan A/Plan B (one for each student)
- Home Extension 3 and Home Signoff

Generalization

School Integration

Continue the previous extension strategies, but expand the vocabulary to include *compromise* as well as *Plan A/Plan B*.

Home Integration

- Upon completion of the lesson, send home a copy of Home Extension 3 and Home Signoff.
- Home Extension 3 contains entries for My Flexibility Dictionary and a blank Handout: Flexibility Skit Framework: Plan A/Plan B. Students will generate an example with their parents showing the concept of *Plan A/Plan B* as it relates to their life at home.

Modifications

Have older students break into pairs and generate their own scenarios using page 2 of Handout: Flexibility Skit Framework: Plan A/Plan B. If they would like, they can select situations from popular media with which they are familiar.

ACTIVITY 1
Mystery Phrase—*Plan A/Plan B*

👤 👥 **Individual or Group Activity**
🕐 **~10 minutes**

Materials

Not Included

- Whiteboard or chart paper
- Dry/wet erase markers or markers

Included

- Handout: Mystery Word 3 (one handout for each student in the group)

Instructions

1. Ask students to reflect on the vocabulary they have learned thus far.
2. Distribute Handout: Mystery Word 3 (one handout for each student or one for the group).
3. After students have uncovered the phrase *Plan A/Plan B,* write the words *Plan A* and *Plan B* on the whiteboard.
4. Explain that people often have a plan for how they want something to go. For example, a student may plan to be the first person at the swings at recess. This is the student's Plan A because it is his or her first plan.
5. Sometimes Plan A does not work out. For example, what if all of the swings at recess are already taken?
   a. Without a Plan B, the student may get mad because he or she did not get what he or she wanted, and the student might be bored because he or she is not doing anything fun.
   b. With a Plan B, the student would have another good plan for backup. For example, the student might play on the jungle gym until one of the swings is available and then swing.
6. Reinforce the idea that when students think of a Plan B at the same time that they think of Plan A, they can make a choice more quickly and avoid getting stuck.

ACTIVITY 2
Role Play

Group Activity

~20 minutes

Materials

Not Included

- Videocamera to record the skits (optional)

Included

- Handout: Flexibility Skit Framework: Plan A/Plan B (one handout for each student)
- Home Extension 3 and Home Signoff

Instructions

Students will work in pairs to create skits using Handout: Flexibility Skit Framework: Plan A/ Plan B. Teachers and students can create other possible situations, using the framework to shape their ideas. Record video of the skits if desired.

1. Divide students into pairs.
2. Distribute one Handout: Flexibility Skit Framework: Plan A/Plan B to each student pair. (Students need a working understanding of the term *consequence*—what would happen as a result of choosing an option.)
3. Students will act with each other (and teachers, if possible) to perform the scenarios described on the handout.
4. Discuss the options and corresponding consequences on the handout to highlight the positive consequences of being flexible. This should be highlighted at every opportunity.
5. If extra time is available, have students write their own examples on the second page of the handout. They may then perform them as skits.
6. Post the phrases *Plan A* and *Plan B* and their definitions on the bulletin board.
7. Review Home Extension 3 with students.

LESSON 3 HANDOUT *(continued)*

TOPIC 2

Flexibility Skit Framework: Plan A/Plan B *(continued)*

Directions: Think of an example of a time when two students could choose to be flexible by creating a Plan B or could choose to get stuck by staying with a Plan A. Write your example below.

Plan A/Plan B

Who: _____ and _____

When:

What:

Describe the student using Plan A.

What would be the consequences?

Options	Consequences

Describe the student using Plan B.

What would be the consequences?

Options	Consequences

LESSON 3 HANDOUT

TOPIC 2

Flexibility Skit Framework: Plan A/Plan B

Directions: In these skits, students and teachers act out different scenarios. Act out what the different options and consequences (see the table below) would look like. Following each skit, discuss the consequences and the options.

Who: _____ and _____

When: During independent work time

What: Student working on own is trying to solve a math problem and is stuck

Options	Consequences
The student keeps trying the same approach to the problem even though it doesn't work.	• The student does not get his or her work finished in time for free time. • The student gets frustrated and angry with the assignment.
The student stops trying the Plan A approach that isn't working and comes up with a Plan B approach to the problem.	• The student completes the problem quickly and gets to enjoy free time. • The student feels happy.

Home Extension 3

Summary: In today's lesson, we continued to expand the students' flexibility-related vocabulary. Specifically, students learned about *Plan A/Plan B*. Please review the attached Flexibility Dictionary for more information.

There are several things you can do at home to help your child learn as fully as possible. The more experiences a student has outside the classroom, the better he or she will be able to learn and apply that learning.

1. Continue to use the word *flexibility*, and highlight when your child (or you or someone else) displays cognitive flexibility. Begin to use the phrase *Plan A/Plan B*.

2. Attached, you will find a copy of the *Plan A/Plan B* scenario the students worked through in class. Use the blank template to think through a Plan A/Plan B situation at home (e.g., There was no vanilla ice cream; what was my Plan B? I was having trouble with my homework assignment; what was my Plan B? We were supposed to have chicken for dinner; what was our Plan B?).

3. Continue to embed playful times during your day when you act out the different vocabulary words.

4. Talk with your child about the best location for his or her Flexibility Dictionary. It should be kept somewhere where it also can work as a visual cue for you to reference at key times.

The next lesson is our final vocabulary-building lesson.

Home Signoff

Date sent home _____

**I have read
Home Extension**

_____
Parent signature

Please return this page to
the social skills teacher by _____

Mystery Word 3

Decode these words using the key below.

___ ___ ___ ___ ___
16 12 1 14 1

&

___ ___ ___ ___ ___
16 12 1 14 2

KEY

A = 1	G = 7
B = 2	H = 8
C = 3	I = 9
D = 4	J = 10
E = 5	K = 11
F = 6	L = 12

M = 13
N = 14
O = 15
P = 16
Q = 17
R = 18
S = 19

Use your decoded words to fill in the following sentence.

If my _____ _____ doesn't work

then I use my _____.

I am being FLEXIBLE!!

My Flexibility Dictionary

Plan A/Plan B

"With a Plan B, I have a good backup plan if Plan A doesn't happen."	• We all have a way that we would like things to go. Our top plan is called *Plan A*. • Plan A does not always work out. • Without a *Plan B,* an alternative plan, you may get upset and then get bored because there is nothing to do. • With a Plan B, you have another good plan for backup. • Remember to make a Plan B when you make your Plan A.

(page 2 of 4)

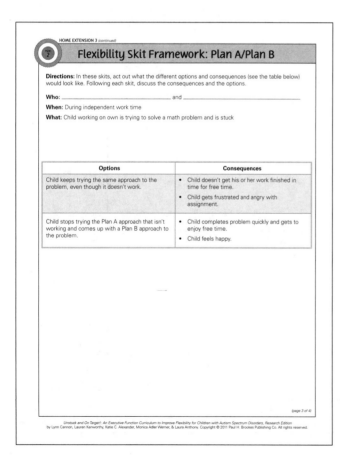

Flexibility Skit Framework: Plan A/Plan B

Directions: In these skits, act out what the different options and consequences (see the table below) would look like. Following each skit, discuss the consequences and the options.

Who: _____ and _____

When: During independent work time

What: Child working on own is trying to solve a math problem and is stuck

Options	Consequences
Child keeps trying the same approach to the problem, even though it doesn't work.	• Child doesn't get his or her work finished in time for free time. • Child gets frustrated and angry with assignment.
Child stops trying the Plan A approach that isn't working and comes up with a Plan B approach to the problem.	• Child completes problem quickly and gets to enjoy free time. • Child feels happy.

(page 3 of 4)

Flexibility Skit Framework *(continued)*

Directions: Think of an example in which two children could choose to be flexible by creating a Plan B or could choose to get stuck by staying only with a Plan A. Write your example below.

Plan A/Plan B

Who: _____ and _____

When: _____

What: _____

Describe the child using Plan A.

What would be the consequences?

Options	Consequences

Describe the child using Plan B.

What would be the consequences?

Options	Consequences

(page 4 of 4)

Lesson 4 Compromise and Consolidation

 PURPOSE

In this lesson, students continue to build a vocabulary foundation for *flexibility*, adding the term *compromise*. There are four activities in this lesson.

Materials Required for All Activities

 Not Included

- Whiteboard or chart paper
- Dry/wet erase markers or markers
- Microphone and props for news broadcast (optional)
- Videocamera to record news broadcast
- Bulletin board materials

Included

- Handout: Mystery Word 4
- Handout: "The Curse of the First" Song Sheet
- Handout: Special News Report Skit Outlines (two versions)
- Handout: Mystery Words Crossword Puzzle
- Classroom Extension 3
- Home Extension 4 and Home Signoff

Generalization

School Integration

Distribute Classroom Extension 3 to all teaching staff so that educators can implement these key strategies when working with students.

Home Integration

- Upon completion of the lesson, send home a copy of Home Extension 4 and Home Signoff. Home Extension 4 contains entries for My Flexibility Dictionary.
- Send home a copy of the completed Handout: Mystery Words Crossword Puzzle.

Modifications

When providing examples of compromise, use examples that relate directly to your students.

ACTIVITY 1
Mystery Word—*Compromise*

 Individual or Group Activity
🕐 **~10 minutes**

Materials

Not Included

- Whiteboard or chart paper
- Dry/wet erase markers or markers

Included

- Handout: Mystery Word 4 (one for each student or group)

Instructions

1. Begin by reviewing the previous vocabulary words. Review what it means to be flexible and to keep an open mind. Revisit the word *stuck;* highlight that when a person is stuck, there are no choices but to be stuck. Ask students what they can do when they are stuck or when their Plan A does not work (make a Plan B). Tell students that today they will be learning another way to avoid getting stuck.
2. Distribute Handout: Mystery Word 4 (one for each student or one for the group).
3. Once the students have uncovered the word *compromise,* write the word on the whiteboard.
   a. Give the students an example of compromise: "If you want to play Connect 4 for recess and your friend wants to go outside, you can compromise by going outside for half of the time and playing Connect 4 for the other half of the time."
   b. Provide additional examples, and ask students to come up with ways the people in the example could make a compromise. Discuss that compromise is different from giving in, which means that you do not get anything that you want. Give examples of giving in, and discuss what a compromise solution might have been.

ACTIVITY 2
The Curse of the First

 Individual or Group Activity
🕐 **~10 minutes**

Materials

Not Included

All materials for this lesson are included.

Included

- Handout: "The Curse of the First" Song Sheet (one for each student or one for the group)

Instructions

1. Ask students whether they have ever played a game with a friend. Explore the things that they have to do to get ready to play the game (e.g., set up, choose a player to go first). Discuss what happens if both people want to go first and are stuck (e.g., no one gets to play the game, friends are upset with each other). What is a solution to this problem? (Make a compromise.) Discuss the benefits of this solution.
2. Sing the song "The Curse of the First" with the students. There is no set tune for this song.

ACTIVITY 3
Newscast

 Group Activity
🕐 **~15 minutes**

Materials

Not Included

- Microphone, props for news broadcast (optional)
- Videocamera to record news broadcast (optional)

Included

- Handout: Special News Report Skit Outlines (two versions)

Instructions

1. Tell the students that they are going to become news reporters for the [name of your school] nightly news. Their job is to report on an exceptional moment when two people compromised so that they would not stay stuck.
2. Distribute Handout: Special News Report Skit Outlines (both versions). Have the students fill out the details of their compromise scenario.
3. Have students act out the news reports, and record them on video if desired.

ACTIVITY 4
Mystery Words Crossword Puzzle

👤 **Individual Activity**
🕐 **~10 minutes**

Materials

Not Included

All materials for this lesson are included.

Included

- Handout: Mystery Words Crossword Puzzle
- Home Extension 4 and Home Signoff

Instructions

1. Wrap-up: Review the vocabulary words on the bulletin board. Ask students to identify examples and/or give definitions for the words listed.
2. Distribute Handout: Mystery Words Crossword Puzzle to each student, and have students complete it.
3. Review Home Extension 4 with students.

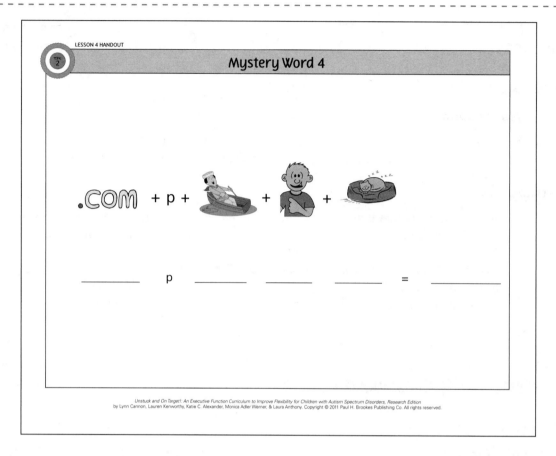

LESSON 4 HANDOUT

"The Curse of the First" Song Sheet

Have you heard of the terrible, horrible curse?
It's the worst kind of curse,
It's the "Curse of the First."

It's when I must always be first
Or else I will burst.
There's only one way to reverse this curse,
It's to say, "Why don't you go first?"

Say, "Why don't you go first?"
And folks will love to play.
Maybe they'll play all day.
See, I'll get the next turn.
It was so simple to learn
To say, "Why don't you go first?"

—Naomi Baum-Skorija, M.S., CCC-SLP

Written by Naomi Baum; reprinted by permission.

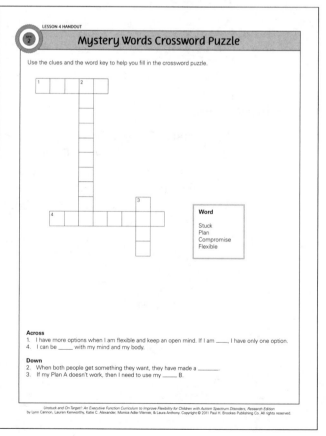

LESSON 4 HANDOUT

Mystery Words Crossword Puzzle

Use the clues and the word key to help you fill in the crossword puzzle.

Word
Stuck
Plan
Compromise
Flexible

Across
1. I have more options when I am flexible and keep an open mind. If I am _____, I have only one option.
4. I can be _____ with my mind and my body.

Down
2. When both people get something they want, they have made a _____.
3. If my Plan A doesn't work, then I need to use my _____ B.

LESSON 4 HANDOUT *(continued)*

TOPIC 2

Special News Report *(version 2)*

Who: Two siblings, Pat and Ben

What: This brother and sister were on vacation together. They were so excited to go to the beach. Pat wanted to play in the waves. Ben wanted to make a sand castle.

What would happen if they became *stuck?* _____

_____

_____

How could they *compromise?* _____

_____

_____

Before you present your newscast, think of

- Your reporter name
- The name of your news channel

LESSON 4 HANDOUT

TOPIC 2

Special News Report *(version 1)*

Who: Two students, Jamie and Chris

What: The students have been friends for 2 years. They like to hang out on the playground together. Jamie wants to play tag. Chris wants to play soccer.

What would happen if they became *stuck?* _____

_____

_____

How could they *compromise?* _____

_____

_____

Before you present your newscast, think of

- Your reporter name
- The name of your news channel

Classroom Extension 3

Teacher: _____ Student initials: _____ Date: _____

Summary: Students have now learned more vocabulary to help them be flexible when they disagree with someone *(keeping an open mind)*; need to switch plans *(Plan A/Plan B)*; or have to meet someone in the middle *(compromise)*. Because a common vocabulary is vital, the same phrases must be used over and over and used consistently between home and school. For example, in any problem-solving situation, children should be asked, "Do you have a Plan A?" and "What is your Plan B?"

What is *keeping an open mind?* *Keeping an open mind* means avoiding black-and-white thinking and accepting inconsistencies and mistakes without coming to global conclusions regarding their implications.

What is *Plan A/Plan B?* We often have a plan for how we want something to go. For example, a teacher may want to complete a lesson on a given day. This is her first plan, or *Plan A.* Sometimes Plan A does not work out; for example, a fire drill may interrupt the class and prevent the teacher from completing her lesson. If *Plan A* does not work, the teacher needs to have a *Plan B.* Having a Plan B allows one to keep an open mind, maintain choices, and avoid getting stuck.

What is *compromise?* In contrast to *giving in,* which means that the student does not get anything that he or she wants, *compromise* means that two people each give up part of what they want or are flexible about the order in which they get what they want.

What difference will this vocabulary make in the classroom? Increasing students' cognitive flexibility and giving them a vocabulary for accepting and accommodating others reduces the amount of time the teacher must spend negotiating during class time, the amount of time spent repairing ruptured student relationships, and the number of disruptive episodes created by a student who does not have a vocabulary for *compromise.* The *Plan A/Plan B* vocabulary gives students a tool for independent problem solving, which reduces the amount of time a teacher must provide individualized attention for students to complete their work.

Key words and phrases

- Keeping an open mind
- Plan A/Plan B
- Compromise

What should I do to help my student(s)?

1. Continue previous generalization activities but expand the vocabulary to include *keeping an open mind, compromise,* and *Plan A/Plan B.*

2. If a student's approach to solving a math problem, making a friend, or any other situation is not producing good results, ask the student if he or she has a Plan B.

3. Pay particular attention to your own actions as the educator, and narrate aloud. For example, tell students that you have had to compromise to get a desired goal.

4. Praise and reinforce students for keeping an open mind, compromising, or coming up with a Plan B.

5. Begin a group-based rewards system (e.g., a small jar that you fill with a symbolic object such as rubber bands). Students receive a rubber band each time they demonstrate that they are being flexible, keeping an open mind, creating a Plan B, or making a compromise. Once students have achieved the target goal for collection, they receive a group reward (e.g., popcorn party or something else that is meaningful to the students).

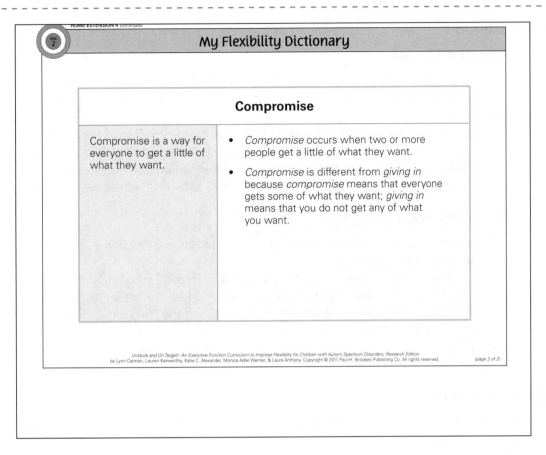

HOME EXTENSION 4 *(continued)*

TOPIC
2

My Flexibility Dictionary

Compromise

Compromise is a way for everyone to get a little of what they want.	• *Compromise* occurs when two or more people get a little of what they want. • *Compromise* is different from *giving in* because *compromise* means that everyone gets some of what they want; *giving in* means that you do not get any of what you want.

(page 2 of 2)

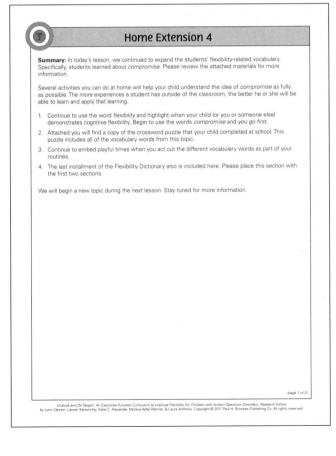

TOPIC
2

Home Extension 4

Summary: In today's lesson, we continued to expand the students' flexibility-related vocabulary. Specifically, students learned about *compromise*. Please review the attached materials for more information.

Several activities you can do at home will help your child understand the idea of *compromise* as fully as possible. The more experiences a student has outside of the classroom, the better he or she will be able to learn and apply that learning.

1. Continue to use the word *flexibility* and highlight when your child (or you or someone else) demonstrates cognitive flexibility. Begin to use the words *compromise* and *you go first*.

2. Attached you will find a copy of the crossword puzzle that your child completed at school. This puzzle includes all of the vocabulary words from this topic.

3. Continue to embed playful times when you act out the different vocabulary words as part of your routines.

4. The last installment of the Flexibility Dictionary also is included here. Please place this section with the first two sections.

We will begin a new topic during the next lesson. Stay tuned for more information.

(page 1 of 2)

TOPIC
2

Home Signoff

Date sent home: _____

I have read
Home Extension _____

_____
Parent signature

Please return this page to
the social skills teacher by _____

Extensions

Generalization

School Integration

- Upon completion of Lesson 1, highlight cognitive flexibility or making a flexible decision or choice versus being rigid as often as possible in subsequent days. Praise students for being flexible.
- Upon completion of Lesson 2, distribute Classroom Extension 2 to all teaching staff.
- Upon completion of Lesson 3, continue the previous extension strategies, but expand the vocabulary to include *compromise* as well as *Plan A/Plan B*.
- Upon completion of Lesson 4, distribute Classroom Extension 3 to all teaching staff.

Home Integration

- Upon completion of Lesson 2, send home a copy of Home Extension 2, including the attached Flexibility Dictionary.
- Upon completion of Lesson 3, send home a copy of Home Extension 3, including the attached copy of Handout: Flexibility Skit Framework: Plan A/Plan B (send both of the provided scenarios as well as the blank framework) and the Flexibility Dictionary.
- Upon completion of Lesson 4, send home a copy of Home Extension 4, including the Flexibility Dictionary, and a copy of the completed Handout: Mystery Words Crossword Puzzle.

Materials for Home

- Home Extension 2 and Home Signoff
- Home Extension 3 and Home Signoff
- Home Extension 4 and Home Signoff
- Copy of the completed Handout: Mystery Words Crossword Puzzle

TOPIC
3

Coping Strategies

SPECIAL INSTRUCTIONS: The core goals of these lessons are to help students identify and explore internal states in response to flexibility requirements and to learn coping strategies for managing negative feeling states. To help your students master these two goals, modify the activities as necessary to better meet students' needs. It is also important to note that the students should make the choice to use coping skills. These skills cannot be forced on students for the educator's convenience. Think about this from their perspective: Does it usually help you when someone tells you to calm down? The purpose of these lessons is to help students recognize their triggers, their emotions, and when a situation might become overwhelming and to provide them with the coping skills to be flexible and to meet their larger goals.

Summary: The first goal of Topic 3 is to teach students how to use a visual rating tool to identify their feelings, with a particular emphasis on identifying when they are feeling frustrated, angry, or anxious as a result of demands to be flexible. The second goal of the topic is to teach common coping techniques for managing these feelings, such as getting more information, asking an adult for help, requesting a break, requesting to meet (with a safe address), and using deep breathing.

Prerequisite skills: Understanding of what flexibility is, basic ability to self-rate feelings

Related skills: Awareness of body, use of rating scale

OUTCOME—CRITERIA FOR MASTERY

1. Using a visual chart, the student rates his or her internal level of frustration when asked to be flexible.
2. The student identifies and accesses several coping strategies and uses them when stressed by flexibility demands.

TOPIC BACKGROUND AND RATIONALE

Being flexible is difficult for children with ASD and creates stress. Furthermore, these children often struggle with identifying their feelings. As a result, they can fail to recognize their own stress until it is very high and they feel overwhelmed. It is important that instruction in flexibility be accompanied by active support for increasing coping skills that will help students know what they feel and will give them strategies for handling negative feelings.

Lesson 1 Recognizing Your Feelings

PURPOSE

If students can identify the emotion they are feeling and with what intensity they are feeling it, they can make better choices about what to do next. To this end, Lesson 1 includes three activities to support each student's skill acquisition.

Materials Required for All Activities

Not Included

- Whiteboard or chart paper
- Dry/wet erase markers or markers

Included

- Handout: Feelings and Actions
- Handout: Recognizing Your Uncomfortable Feelings
- Handout: Recognizing Your Good Feelings
- Handout: Flexibility Thermometer
- Home Extension 5 and Home Signoff

Generalization

School Integration

- Keep a Feelings Thermometer in the classroom or in each student's *My Flexibility Notebook*, and have students practice identifying and rating their feelings repeatedly during the week.
- Rate your own feelings in front of students at least once a day, using instructive self-talk. For example,
    a. "I felt unbelievably good, like a 5, when I saw Billy share his favorite toy with Sam. I could tell by Sam's smile that he felt like a 4 or 5 because he smiled and thanked his friend three times!"
    b. "I feel very good, like a 4, when I get to read this Roald Dahl book. He is my favorite author."

Home Integration

Upon completion of the lesson, send home a copy of Home Extension 5 and Home Signoff. Home Extension 5 includes a blank Handout: Flexibility Thermometer. Ask each student to rate his or her feelings with a parent. Ask the parent to rate his or her own feelings, too.

Modifications

Try modifying your language to better match your students' language use. For example, if a student says that he feels like "the whole world is going to explode!" ask him (gently, and with humor), "How can we make it so only half of the world explodes, or only Antarctica. Oh, but what about the seals and the penguins that live in Antarctica, how can we make the explosion even smaller?"

ACTIVITY 1

Introduction and Emotions Brainstorm

Group Activity

~10 minutes

Materials

Not Included

- Whiteboard or chart paper
- Dry/wet erase markers or markers

Included

- Handout: Feelings and Actions

Instructions

Say the following to the students: "It is kind of hard to control how you feel, but you can change how you act when you have certain feelings and what you allow yourself to do because of those feelings. We will talk next time about different strategies you might use to change your feelings; however, in order for you to know when to use the strategies, you have to be able to identify the need for them first." Pull out Handout: Feelings and Actions. Show the students how feelings are different from actions and explain, "Today we are going to talk about our feelings and actions."

1. Brainstorm with students a list of feeling words, both positive and negative (e.g., *happy, sad, nervous, mad, frustrated, elated, silly, angry, ecstatic*), and write them in two columns on a whiteboard or sheet of chart paper. The students likely will be better at identifying negative emotions, so try to even things out between positive and negative as much as you can.

2. Depending on student level and ability to identify emotion words, you may want to use pictures or act out brief scenes to elicit emotion words.

3. Have the students choose at least one positive (e.g., excited) and one negative (e.g., frustrated) emotion. Help the students define the emotion and describe how it feels in the body.

ACTIVITY 2
My Feelings

  Group and Individual Activity

🕐 **~10 Minutes**

Materials

Not Included

All materials for this lesson are included.

Included

- Handout: Recognizing Your Uncomfortable Feelings
- Handout: Recognizing Your Good Feelings

Instructions

1. Show students the two Feelings Thermometer handouts (Recognizing Your Uncomfortable Feelings and Recognizing Your Good Feelings).
2. Have the students help you complete a thermometer for your feelings. Good choices for your demonstration are *excited* for positive and *frustrated* for negative. Fill in the thermometer with examples (see example in Figure 3.1).
3. For each feeling chosen in Activity 1, have the students give examples of times when they imagine they would feel each degree of emotion.
   a. Some examples for *interested* might be *watching a favorite movie, reading a good book, watching a long baseball game on television, waiting for my turn, sitting in traffic, listening during math class, looking at YouTube videos,* and *doing homework.*
   b. Some examples for *frustrated* might be *computer crashing while I'm playing a game, losing a game, having trouble opening a snack, losing the prize I wanted to someone else, being interrupted by someone, not being able to find my favorite book, having difficulty tying my shoes, the movie I want to see being sold out, the dog next door barking continuously, dropping my books,* and *having difficulty zipping my backpack.*

5 = When they told me I got this job!

4 = When I am leaving for a family vacation

3 = When I was learning how to ski, and I made it downhill smoothly and without falling

2 = When I am meeting my best friend for lunch

1 = When I am making my lunch at home

Figure 3.1. Excited thermometer.

ACTIVITY 3
Self-Monitoring Flexibility

👥 **Group Activity**

🕐 **~10 minutes**

Materials

Not Included

All materials for this lesson are included.

Included

- Handout: Flexibility Thermometer
- Home Extension 5 and Home Signoff

Instructions

In this lesson, you will show students how to self-monitor flexibility. Self-monitoring flexibility is similar to rating emotion except that the student is rating flexibility. See the example in Figure 3.2. Students, teachers, and parents will rate how flexible the student was five times each day using page 2 of Handout: Flexibility Thermometer. Look in particular for the student's use of such flexibility skills as compromising, using a Plan B, asking for help, trying another way, or letting something go.

1. Role-play with scenarios and have the students use the Flexibility Thermometer to rate how flexible the participants are. Use the following examples, or make up others that relate to your students' experiences.
   a. You are in math class, and your teacher asks you to show your work, which you do not want to do. You can feel yourself becoming very frustrated. You refuse to do any more math.
   b. You are in science class, and your body feels like it has a lot of extra energy. You cannot sit still in your seat. You ask to have a short break because you know how important it is to listen in science.
   c. You are in the classroom, and your friend is reading the book you wanted to read during free time. You are feeling very upset and take the book away from your friend.
   d. You are in science class, and your friend gets to answer a question you wanted to answer. You feel disappointed that you cannot share your answer, but you do not get upset because you know you will get a chance on another question.
2. Ask the students if they can predict situations during which they find it particularly hard to be flexible.
3. Review Home Extension 5 with students.

5 = I am keeping a totally open mind.

4 = I am willing to consider other options.

3 = I cannot be flexible now, but I am trying strategies to help me be more flexible.

2 = I know there is another way to see this, but I am having a hard time.

1 = I have to do it my way. I am stuck.

Figure 3.2. Flexibility thermometer.

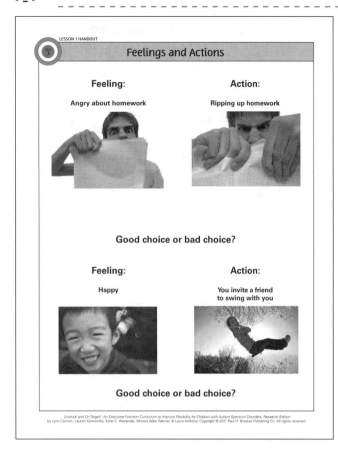

LESSON 1 HANDOUT

Feelings and Actions

Feeling:

Angry about homework

Action:

Ripping up homework

Good choice or bad choice?

Feeling:

Happy

Action:

You invite a friend to swing with you

Good choice or bad choice?

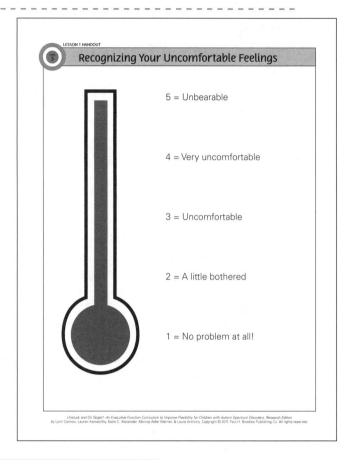

LESSON 1 HANDOUT

Recognizing Your Uncomfortable Feelings

5 = Unbearable

4 = Very uncomfortable

3 = Uncomfortable

2 = A little bothered

1 = No problem at all!

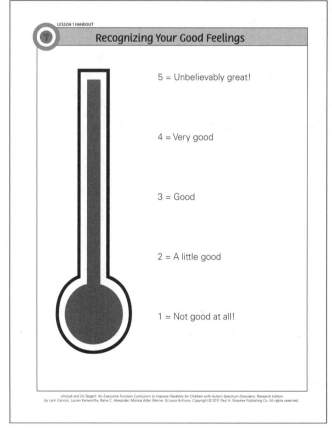

LESSON 1 HANDOUT

Recognizing Your Good Feelings

5 = Unbelievably great!

4 = Very good

3 = Good

2 = A little good

1 = Not good at all!

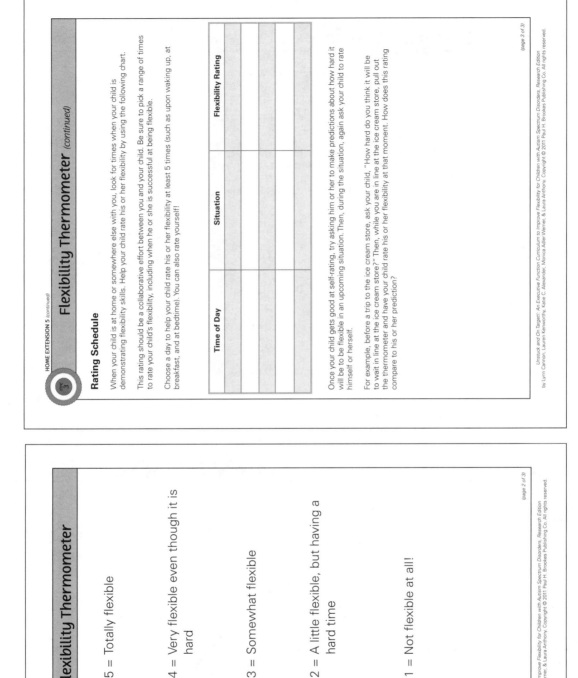

Flexibility Thermometer (continued)

Rating Schedule

When your child is at home or somewhere else with you, look for times when your child is demonstrating flexibility skills. Help your child rate his or her flexibility by using the following chart.

This rating should be a collaborative effort between you and your child. Be sure to pick a range of times to rate your child's flexibility, including when he or she is successful at being flexible.

Choose a day to help your child rate his or her flexibility at least 5 times (such as upon waking up, at breakfast, and at bedtime). You can also rate yourself!

Time of Day	Situation	Flexibility Rating

Once your child gets good at self-rating, try asking him or her to make predictions about how hard it will be to be flexible in an upcoming situation. Then, during the situation, again ask your child to rate himself or herself.

For example, before a trip to the ice cream store, ask your child, "How hard do you think it will be to wait in line at the ice cream store?" Then, while you are in line at the ice cream store, pull out the thermometer and have your child rate his or her flexibility at that moment. How does this rating compare to his or her prediction?

Unstuck and On Target!: An Executive Function Curriculum to Improve Flexibility for Children with Autism Spectrum Disorders, Research Edition
by Lynn Cannon, Lauren Kenworthy, Katie C. Alexander, Monica Adler Werner, & Laura Anthony. Copyright © 2011 Paul H. Brookes Publishing Co. All rights reserved.

Home Extension Flexibility Thermometer

5 = Totally flexible

4 = Very flexible even though it is hard

3 = Somewhat flexible

2 = A little flexible, but having a hard time

1 = Not flexible at all!

Unstuck and On Target!: An Executive Function Curriculum to Improve Flexibility for Children with Autism Spectrum Disorders, Research Edition
by Lynn Cannon, Lauren Kenworthy, Katie C. Alexander, Monica Adler Werner, & Laura Anthony. Copyright © 2011 Paul H. Brookes Publishing Co. All rights reserved.

Home Extension 5

Summary: The students have just begun a new topic in which they are learning about their feelings. They are focusing on how to recognize different emotional states and the degrees of those states. We are working on self-ratings of flexibility.

There are several things you can do at home to help your child learn as fully as possible. The more experiences a child has outside the classroom, the better he or she is able to learn and apply that learning.

1. Please post your child's Flexibility Thermometer at home, where it will be easily accessible. Your child has practiced using this rating in school to identify times when it is easy to be flexible, and times when it is hard to be flexible.

2. Use the attached Rating Schedule to help your child monitor his or her flexibility.

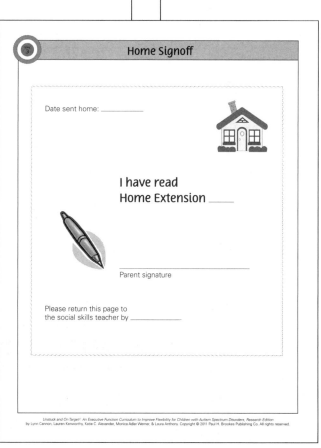

Home Signoff

Date sent home: _____

I have read
Home Extension _____

_____
Parent signature

Please return this page to
the social skills teacher by _____

Lesson 2 What Can You Do to Feel Better?

 PURPOSE

This lesson helps students learn coping strategies to use when being flexible is really difficult. There are four activities in this lesson.

Materials Required for All Activities

 Not Included

- Five blank index cards for each student and for the teacher
- Markers
- Access to clipart, a computer, or magazines with lots of pictures
- Hole punch
- String or D-ring to hold cards together
- Cups
- Water
- Gum
- Access to space for running
- Access to swings

Included

- Handout: Recognizing Your Uncomfortable Feelings (from Lesson 1)
- Handout: Disappointment and Coping
- Handout: How to Feel Just Right
- Handout: Just-Right Strategies Investigation
- Handout: Deep Breathing
- Handout: My Mission to Get Back to Just Right
- Handout: Strategy Card Examples
- Home Extension 6 and Home Signoff
- Handout: Just-Right Strategies Rating Sheet
- Home Extension 7 and Home Signoff

Generalization

School Integration

- Use the coping strategies repeatedly in class when appropriate. Model aloud your own coping strategies: "I am feeling very frustrated right now, so I am going to ask for help [take a deep breath, take a break]."
- Create a feelings bulletin board in the classroom with a Feelings Thermometer, feelings words, and coping strategies.

Home Integration

- Have the students share their strategy cards with their parents. Have the students teach their parents how to do the deep breathing exercise using the script.
- Upon completion of Activity 3, send home a copy of Home Extension 6 and Home Signoff, along with a copy of the student's strategy cards.
- Upon completion of Activity 4, send home a copy of Home Extension 7 and Home Signoff.

Modifications

To simplify this lesson, you can give the students one simple thing to try for a coping strategy instead of doing the investigation—such as count to 10, take 3 deep breaths, or think of the last episode of your favorite TV show—and make a simpler reminder for them instead of the strategy cards.

ACTIVITY 1
Disappointment and Coping

👥 **Group Activity**

🕐 **~10 minutes**

Materials

Not Included

All materials for this lesson are included.

Included

- Handout: Recognizing Your Uncomfortable Feelings (from Lesson 1)
- Handout: Disappointment and Coping

Instructions

1. Discuss the word *disappointment* (when what you want does not match what happens).
2. Ask students to identify feelings they have and/or words they think of when they are disappointed (e.g., *sad, frustrated, mad, angry*). Ask them to think about how their body feels when they are disappointed (e.g., *face gets hot, stomach hurts, teeth clench, fists clench*).
3. Relate different scenarios, and have each student rate the intensity of his or her feelings for each of those scenarios on the Feelings Thermometer. Scenarios might include the following: *I really wanted the new Wii game, but the store was sold out* or *I wanted to play with Susie at recess, but she chose to play with Ann.* You may also use examples from your classroom.
4. Display Handout: Disappointment and Coping. Help students brainstorm ideas for what they can do when they cannot get what they want and they feel disappointed or frustrated (i.e., use coping skills). Ideas might include getting more information, asking an adult for help, requesting downtime, requesting to meet (with safe address), using thought-stopping skills, breathing deeply, thinking about something that makes them really happy, and politely advocating for a change. Write these ideas on Handout: Disappointment and Coping and post the handout on the wall while you complete Activity 2.

ACTIVITY 2
Coping Skills Investigation

📋 **Experiment**

🕐 **~10 minutes**

Materials

Not Included

Items for the investigation:

- Cups
- Water
- Gum
- Access to space for running
- Access to swings

Included

- Handout: How to Feel Just Right
- Handout: Just-Right Strategies Investigation
- Handout: Deep Breathing
- Handout: My Mission to Get Back to Just Right

Instructions

1. Read Handout: How to Feel Just Right. Discuss with students what it feels like to "be red hot." Have they ever felt red hot? Share a time when you have felt red hot. Remind them that everyone feels red hot. Their job is to figure out what strategies help them get back to "just right."
2. From the list of brainstormed ideas from Activity 1 or Handout: Just-Right Strategies Investigation, have students choose some of the coping skills and try them. Students will rate how helpful the strategy was for them.
3. Demonstrate deep breathing using Handout: Deep Breathing. Have the students rate this technique on the Handout: Just-Right Strategies Investigation.
4. Read through Handout: My Mission to Get Back to Just Right. Have students brainstorm what strategies they would use to get back to "just right."

ACTIVITY 3
Strategy Cards

👤 **Individual Activity**

🕐 **~10 minutes**

Materials

Not Included

- Five blank index cards for each student and for the teacher
- Markers
- Access to clipart, a computer, or magazines with lots of pictures
- Hole punch
- String or D-ring to hold cards together

Included

- Handout: Strategy Card Examples
- Handout: Just-Right Strategies Investigation (from Activity 2)
- Home Extension 6 and Home Signoff

Instructions

1. Each student will identify five just-right strategies that he or she thinks will work best in high-emotion situations based on his or her responses to Handout: Just-Right Strategies Investigation. Students will make a strategy card for each strategy they choose, showing the strategy in words and images. Make cards for yourself in advance, and show them to the students. Following are some examples (see also Handout: Strategy Card Examples).
   a. Picture of something that represents deep breathing
   b. Picture of the student hugging a loved one
   c. Picture of the words *Ask for help*
   d. Picture of something that represents taking a break
   e. Picture of the student's favorite place or activity
2. For each strategy, students should write a word or phrase and draw, cut out, or download a picture to put on the strategy card. Have them punch a hole in each index card and bind the cards with a loop or ring. Students may use other visual strategies to capture their Just-Right Strategies if they prefer; they do not have to use the strategy cards.
3. Review Home Extension 6 with students.

ACTIVITY 4
Coping Choices

🏃 **Skits**

🕐 **~20 minutes**

Materials

Not Included

All materials for this lesson are included.

Included

- Handout: Just-Right Strategies Rating Sheet
- Home Extension 7 and Home Signoff

Instructions

1. Read aloud or act out the scenarios at the end of this activity, using plenty of humor.
2. Ask students to give examples of good and bad coping strategies in response to each scenario, or you may choose to read or act out the sample strategies that follow each scenario. Ask the students to indicate whether each coping strategy is a good choice or a bad choice. If the strategy is a bad choice, ask students to suggest alternatives.
3. Have students practice the scenarios using the just-right strategies they have selected for their strategy cards. Ask students watching to indicate whether the participants showed good use of the coping strategies.
4. Review Home Extension 7 with students.

Scenarios and Sample Strategies

Scenario: You are in math class and cannot figure out how to do a problem. You can feel yourself becoming very frustrated.
- *Coping strategy 1:* You ask to take a break, then return to the math class. Now you can figure it out.
- *Coping strategy 2:* You scream and throw your book on the floor and get sent to the principal.

Scenario: You are in science class, and your body feels like it has a lot of extra energy. You cannot sit still in your seat.
- *Coping strategy 1:* You take a long, deep breath and feel calmer, and you are able to pay attention.
- *Coping strategy 2:* You get more and more wound up and get up and run around the room.

Scenario: You are in the classroom, and your friend is reading the book you wanted to read during free time. You are feeling very upset.
- *Coping strategy 1:* You try to grab the book from your friend and get in trouble.
- *Coping strategy 2:* You look at your list of just-right strategies and decide to read a comic book instead.

Scenario: You are in science class and your friend gets to answer a question you wanted to answer.
- *Coping strategy 1:* You interrupt and do not earn your points.
- *Coping strategy 2:* You wait for the next question and try again.

You may want to include a visual supports, such as a flowchart. You can use a flowchart to make predictions about "what would happen if…" or to replay a problematic scenario and then rewrite the scene the way the student wishes it had gone. Built into these flowcharts is a logical progression that visually demonstrates to the student that the problem scenario did not result in the outcome the child wanted and when the student should have used a coping strategy. See Figure 3.3 for a sample flowchart.

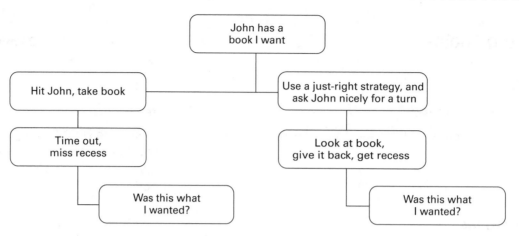

Figure 3.3. Sample flowchart.

Disappointment and Coping

Feeling:

Disappointment

Action:

Coping skills

Can you think of anything that would help you feel less disappointed?

- Playground
  - o Run a lap
  - o Swing
  - o Bounce a ball
- Take a break
  - o Bean bag
  - o Headphones
  - o Weighted blanket or vest
  - o Body sock
  - o Soft pillow
- Edible
  - o Drink of water
  - o Juice
  - o Something chewy
  - o Gum
- Music
  - o Listening with headphones
  - o Humming
- Reading
- Drawing
- Journaling
- Deep breathing
- Cognitive strategies
  - o Positive thoughts
  - o It's okay, I made a mistake
  - o Count to 30
  - o Think of my favorite place or activity

How to Feel Just Right

Sometimes I feel red hot.

I can feel red hot because I am feeling angry.

I can feel red hot because I am feeling upset.

I can feel red hot because I am very excited.

When I feel red hot, it is hard for me to do my work or pay attention.

When I feel red hot, I need to use my strategies to cool myself down to "just right."

**I am going to be a detective.
I am going to be a "just-right detective."**

Just-Right Strategies Investigation

Try these out and see how you feel:

Just-right strategy	How much does this strategy help me get to "just right"?					I like this strategy	I don't like this strategy
	1 None	2 A little	3 Some	4 A lot	5 I feel just right		
Take five deep breaths.							
Close your eyes and think of a "happy place" (e.g., the beach).							
Close your eyes and think of your favorite activity.							
Run outside.							
Think to yourself over and over, "I am okay; I feel calm."							
Have a drink of water.							
Ask to take a break.							
Try the deep breathing script.							
Read.							
Count to 30.							
Draw.							
Sing or hum.							
Swing on the swings.							
Make your own strategy:_____							
Make your own strategy:_____							

Handout 1

Deep Breathing

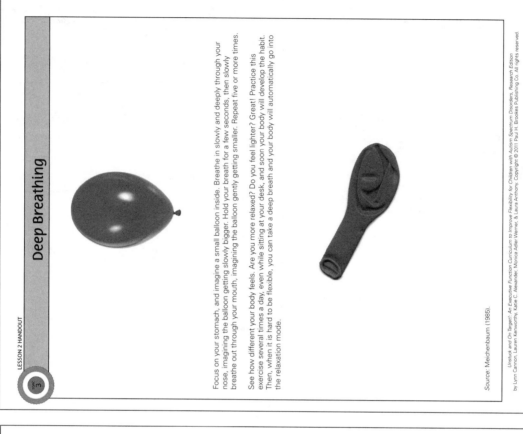

Focus on your stomach, and imagine a small balloon inside. Breathe in slowly and deeply through your nose, imagining the balloon getting slowly bigger. Hold your breath for a few seconds, then slowly breathe out through your mouth, imagining the balloon gently getting smaller. Repeat five or more times.

See how different your body feels. Are you more relaxed? Do you feel lighter? Great! Practice this exercise several times a day, even while sitting at your desk, and soon your body will develop the habit. Then, when it is hard to be flexible, you can take a deep breath and your body will automatically go into the relaxation mode.

Source: Meichenbaum (1985).

Handout 2

My Mission to Get Back to Just Right

My mission: to figure out what strategies I like to use to get back to just right.

I get to select the strategies that I like. These will be my just-right strategies.

I can use these strategies any time I am feeling too hot and I want it to feel just right.

All I have to do is ask my teacher. My teacher will be very proud of me for using my strategies. I will feel very proud of myself for getting back to just right.

I will earn bonus points for using my strategies when I need them.

Mission 1

During lunch, I realize I do not have enough money to buy the snack I want. This makes me feel very angry. I am red hot.

Mission 2

In the library, I realize the book I want to read is being used by someone else. I feel very upset. I am getting hot.

Mission 3

I yelled when I was using my computer. My teacher had to take my computer away from me. I feel very angry. I am red hot.

Mission 4

My friends and I were making jokes. They made me laugh a lot. I can't stop laughing. I am starting to feel hot.

LESSON 2 HANDOUT

Strategy Card Examples

Ask for a hug

Take a break

Ask someone for help

Take three deep breaths

Think of my favorite things/activities

Think of my favorite place

LESSON 2 HANDOUT

Just-Right Strategies Rating Sheet

Good Just-Right Strategies (asking for help, advocating for a change, trying another way, taking a break, talking to a friend, etc.)	Poor Just-Right Strategies (tantrums, aggression, giving up, etc.)

Home Extension 6

Summary: In this lesson, we explored the feeling of being disappointed and how to cope with that disappointment. Each student has had an opportunity to explore coping strategies, called *just-right strategies,* to see what works best for him or her.

There are several things you can do at home to help your child learn as fully as possible. The more experiences each student has outside the classroom, the better he or she is able to learn and apply that learning.

1. Review your child's strategy cards with him or her.
2. Ask your child to teach you how to use deep breathing exercises.
3. Review the attached social story, My Mission to Get Back to Just Right, with your child.

Deep Breathing

Focus on your stomach, and imagine a small balloon inside. Breathe in slowly and deeply through your nose, imagining the balloon getting slowly bigger. Hold your breath [...] slowly breathe out through your mouth, imagining the balloon gently get[...] or more times.

See how different your body feels. Are you more relaxed? Do you feel lig[...] this exercise several times a day, even while sitting at your desk, and so[...] the habit. Then, when it is hard to be flexible, you can take a deep breath[...] automatically go into the relaxation mode.

Source: Meichenbaum (1985).

Home Signoff

Date sent home: _____

**I have read
Home Extension** _____

_____
Parent signature

Please return this page to
the social skills teacher by _____

Home Extension 7

Summary: During this lesson, we continued to help students apply their new knowledge of feelings and how to change them. We have also reviewed good and poor coping strategies.

There are several things you can do at home to help your child learn as fully as possible. The more experiences each student has outside the classroom, the better he or she is able to learn and apply that learning.

Directions
Choose a television show or movie to watch together. As you watch, keep track together of the good and bad coping techniques that you see characters using. Shows with frequent situations that elicit coping strategies and are funny are the most helpful for this activity, such as *SpongeBob SquarePants*, *Jimmy Neutron*, *Pink Panther*, *Drake and Josh*, *iCarly*, and *The Brady Bunch*.

Good Just-Right Strategies (asking for help, advocating for a change, trying another way, taking a break, talking to a friend, etc.)	**Poor Just-Right Strategies** (tantrums, aggression, giving up, crying, etc.)

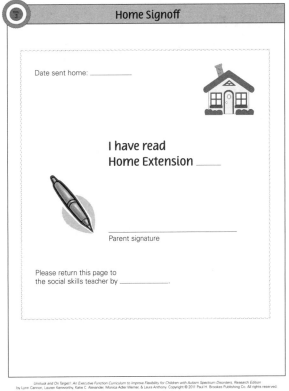

Home Signoff

Date sent home: _____

I have read
Home Extension _____

_____
Parent signature

Please return this page to
the social skills teacher by _____

Extensions

Generalization

School Integration

- Upon completion of Lesson 1, keep a Feelings Thermometer in the classroom or in each student's *My Flexibility Notebook*, and have students practice identifying and rating their feelings repeatedly during the week. Rate your own feelings in front of students at least once a day.
- Upon completion of Lesson 2, use the coping strategies in class when appropriate. Model aloud your own coping strategies, and create a feelings bulletin board in the classroom with a Feelings Thermometer, feelings words, and coping strategies.

Home Integration

- Upon completion of Lesson 1, send home a copy of Home Extension 5 and Home Signoff, including the attached Flexibility Thermometer.
- Upon completion of Lesson 2, Activity 3, send home a copy of Home Extension 6 and Home Signoff. Home Extension 6 has an attached deep breathing script and My Mission to Get Back to Just Right. Also send a copy of the student's strategy cards.
- Upon completion of Lesson 2, Activity 4, send home a copy of Home Extension 7 and Home Signoff.

Materials for Home

- Home Extension 5 and Home Signoff
- Home Extension 6 and Home Signoff
- Copy of student's strategy cards
- Home Extension 7 and Home Signoff

Reference

Miechenbaum, D. (1985). *Stress innoculation training.* Elmsford, NY: Pergamon Press.

TOPIC

4

Personal Heroes

SPECIAL INSTRUCTIONS: The core goals of these lessons are to help students identify a personal hero and explore the hero's characteristics. Although it is important to implement the three primary components of this lesson, you can modify the activities as necessary to better meet the needs of your students.

Summary: Through a series of three lessons, Personal Heroes enables students to identify a hero and explore that hero's meaning to themselves. The hero concept is then extended to help students explore their own identity and consider ways they would like to be more like their hero. This topic involves explicit instruction as well as two activities designed to solidify the learning experience for each student.

Prerequisite skills: Understanding of the meaning of *flexibility, stuck, Plan A/Plan B,* and *compromise* (Topics 1 and 2)

Related skills: Intrinsic motivation, self-concept, goal setting

---

OUTCOME—CRITERIA FOR MASTERY

1. The student identifies a hero and that hero's meaning and relevance to him or her.
2. The student references the hero as an internal resource for making productive, positive flexibility choices. *At first the student will require prompting in order to access the hero in this way; fading those prompts across time will foster student independence.*

TOPIC BACKGROUND AND RATIONALE

Students are motivated to learn new skills that are congruent with their sense of identity and the attributes of people they admire. The rationale and practice of identity mapping and identity-oriented goal setting as a tool for improving outcomes in cognitive/behavioral intervention, particularly in students with executive dysfunction, such as those with ASD, is provided in *Metaphoric Identity Mapping: Facilitating Goal Setting and Engagement in Rehabilitation After Traumatic Brain Injury* (Ylvisaker, McPherson, Kayes, & Pellett, 2008). Individual work with students to help them concretize their ideal self is the first step in developing a positive identity. Related to this is identifying heroes that students want to emulate. The identity map and selection of a hero to emulate provides students who are cognitively disorganized with a structured cognitive support that sums up several important skills into one emotionally meaningful label.

Lesson 1 What Makes a Hero Heroic?

 **PURPOSE**

This lesson introduces students to the concept of a hero as a concrete role model. Following this lesson, students should be familiar with how people use heroes to guide choices and be able to give examples of heroes showing flexibility. Four activities make up this lesson.

Materials Required for All Activities

Not Included

- Whiteboard or chart paper
- Dry/wet erase markers or markers
- Computer with Internet access and speakers

Included

- Handout: Movie Poster Example: Benjamin Franklin
- Handout: The Insect Hero (optional)
- Handout: Mr. Bones to the Rescue (optional)
- Handout: Hero Qualities

Generalization

School Integration

- As opportunities for flexibility arise throughout the day, talk about the ways one of the heroes you have discussed might respond to such opportunities.
- Provide verbal praise when students offer examples or contribute to the discussion.

Home Integration

There is no Home Extension for Lesson 1.

Modifications

General

- Shorten Handout: Hero Qualities as needed based on available time and/or student ability.
- If the Internet links provided for hero stories do not work, search the web for appropriate alternatives. You may also present different heroes based on your students' interests.

For Older Students

- Consider using the term *role model* or *mentor* as a substitute for *hero.*
- Normalize the identification of a role model/mentor/hero by noting that many adults identify and look to mentors.
- Describe how adults use mentors or thinking about mentors as a type of compass to make better decisions.
- After the students complete Handout: Hero Qualities, ask them to choose three questions and tell the group why they answered them as they did. Alternatively, they may give an example of how a hero behaved in the way described.

Additional Resources

For examples of hero stories, see http://www.myhero.com/myhero/go/directory/index.asp and videos at http://www.biography.com/video/index.jsp.

ACTIVITY 1
Hero Introduction

⭐ **Presentation and Group Brainstorm**
🕐 **~5–10 minutes**

Materials

Not Included

- Whiteboard or chart paper
- Dry/wet erase markers or markers

Included

- Handout: Movie Poster Example: Benjamin Franklin

Instructions

1. Briefly review the vocabulary from Topic 2. Ask students to recall the definitions of *flexibility, stuck, keeping an open mind, Plan A/Plan B,* and *compromise.*

2. Introduce the concept of a hero. Have students brainstorm what comes to mind when they hear the word *hero.* Record their answers on a posterboard or flipchart and post it in the room so it can be used again for the next activity.

3. Introduce the hero movie project.
    a. Explain that students will select their own hero for this project. It can be a person from history, another famous person, someone they know, a cartoon character, or someone else students admire. Students will make a movie poster to advertise their hero movie, which will be completed in Lesson 3. The movie poster will tell moviegoers what makes the featured person a hero.
    b. Show students the movie poster example of Benjamin Franklin (or you may make your own), explaining that Ben Franklin is your hero. Highlight the words that describe the hero's characteristics and tell the students how he inspires you. Tell the students that they will be making their own posters and short movies about the heroes that they choose.

4. Explain that you are going to give some examples of heroes by telling a short story about each one. You can present two or three heroes depending on time. Ask students to listen carefully and decide what makes that person (or animal) a hero.

ACTIVITY 2
Hero Videos

🎞 **Video**
🕐 **~10 minutes**

Materials

Not Included

- Whiteboard or chart paper
- Dry/wet erase markers or markers
- Computer with Internet access and speakers

Included

- Handout: Movie Poster Example: Benjamin Franklin
- Handout: The Insect Hero (optional)
- Handout: Mr. Bones to the Rescue (optional)

Instructions

1. Using key words (e.g., *Neil Armstrong video moon landing*), do an Internet search ahead of time for video clips of heroes, or explore these sites: http://www.myhero.com/myhero/go/directory/index.asp and http://www.biography.com/video/index.jsp.
   a. Preview the video clips and save them to your favorites before showing them to students. Prior to having students watch each video, give them a brief summary of what makes that person a hero.
   b. If you do not have Internet access, read the summaries provided in this activity.
2. You may read the following hero summaries to your students, or you may create your own summaries based on the video clips you have selected.
   a. *Neil Armstrong:* Neil Armstrong was an adventurous man. He is most well known for being the first American to walk on the moon, but before he was an astronaut he flew planes for the Navy during the Korean War. He tested many new planes, including one that broke the sound barrier. Neil Armstrong was also courageous. During his first space mission, his spaceship's capsule spun out of control, and he had to guide the capsule to an emergency splashdown.
   b. *Binti Jua:* Animals can be heroes, too. On August 16, 1996, a 3-year-old child climbed into a gorilla exhibit at Brookfield Zoo near Chicago and fell to the bottom of the exhibit. A female gorilla, Binti Jua, carefully picked up the child and, screening him from the other gorillas, carried him to the zookeeper's door, where he was rescued by zoo personnel.
   c. *Martin Luther King, Jr.:* Martin Luther King, Jr. was a civil rights leader. He lived during a time in the United States when black citizens did not have the same rights as white citizens. He did not agree with this and thought he could make a difference in the world by becoming a minister. Dr. King believed he could change people's minds about segregation and that he could do this peacefully. He led a march to Washington, D.C., where he gave his famous "I have a dream" speech.
3. After each video or summary, ask your students the following questions:
   a. Who was the hero?
   b. What did the hero do?
   c. What makes him or her a hero?
4. Add your students' answers to those from the brainstorm session in Activity 1.

Optional Activity

If you feel that additional examples would help your students more fully grasp the qualities that make a hero, complete the following.

1. Ask the students to follow along as you read Handout: The Insect Hero and Handout: Mr. Bones to the Rescue. At logical points throughout each story, stop and ask, "Who is the hero? What did he do? What makes him a hero?"

2. If you need additional examples, you can create similar stories based on your students' interests.

ACTIVITY 3
Hero Qualities Worksheet

  Group or Individual Activity

🕐 **~5–10 minutes**

Materials

Not Included

*   Whiteboard or chart paper
*   Dry/wet erase markers or markers

Included

*   Handout: Hero Qualities

Instructions

1. Distribute Handout: Hero Qualities to students (one per student or per group).
2. Have students complete the handout as a group or individually. They can complete the handout independently, or you can read the questions aloud. Students can indicate by thumbs up or thumbs down whether they agree or disagree with each item. Based on students' answers, select questions to explore why students responded the way they did.

ACTIVITY 4
Heroes Game

Group Game

~5–10 minutes

Materials

Not Included

There are no materials for this lesson.

Included

There are no materials for this lesson.

Instructions

This game is adapted from a popular children's drama activity and encourages flexibility. The leader calls out a key phrase (e.g., "Scramble," "Strike a pose," "Go"), and students arrange their bodies in one of several prescribed poses (e.g., on all fours to resemble a dog, arms outstretched to simulate an elephant's trunk). If two students choose the same body position, they are asked to be flexible and assume another position.

1. Explain that you will be playing a game together.
2. Assign each hero a body position. For example, arms pointed above the head could represent Neil Armstrong's spaceship; arms bent under the armpits could represent Binti Jua the gorilla, and hands clasped together could simulate unity for Martin Luther King Jr.'s work with civil rights. You can also include heroes that the students have selected if they have already done so.
3. Choose a phrase that will signal each student to assume one of the hero's body positions. Say the phrase. If two students choose the same body position, one student must be flexible and change his or her position. Praise students for their ability to be flexible.
   a. You can provide increased student support by assigning one student to pick his or her pose first. This reduces the number of students who are asked to be flexible.
4. Repeat the game multiple times. If you have too few students to make the game interesting, have an adult participate.
5. Remind students about the movie poster project. Ask them to think about the individual they would like to choose as their hero, and tell them to choose their heroes before the following session, if they haven't already chosen their hero.

The Insect Hero

LESSON 1 HANDOUT

Mr. Proboscis knew everything there was to know about butterflies and insects. He studied them and worked in the butterfly garden at his zoo.

The Blue Morpho butterfly

One day he read that South America was going to have a season of unusually cold weather. "Oh, horrors!" he thought. "This is a calamity. The stunning Blue Morpho butterflies, the Postman butterflies, and the Julia butterflies can't survive the cold!"

Mr. Proboscis thought about a plan to help save the butterflies. "Aha! I've got it! I will take a group of my entomologist friends who study insects with me to South America, and we will work together to save those beautiful creatures. Even though I've never been to South America, I will try it."

Mr. Proboscis got on the phone and called all of his friends.

The Julia butterfly

The Postman butterfly

He bought them first-class airline tickets to South America and booked them all rooms at the fanciest hotel, called the Cocoon Hotel. They told him, "Mr. Proboscis, you always think about others. You are a great friend. Thanks a million!"

When Mr. Proboscis and his friends landed in South America, they gathered their building supplies and built a heated glass butterfly garden. They built it all together!

Then they took their nets and insect-finding instruments. They chased butterflies together and put them in the new butterfly garden.

They stood in the warm garden, feeding old bananas, apples, and papayas to the Postman butterflies, the Julia butterflies, and the Blue Morpho butterflies. All of the butterflies fluttered around them, landing on their hands and hats as if to say, "Thank you! You worked together to save us."

Written by Naomi Baum; reprinted by permission.

Movie Poster Example

LESSON 1 HANDOUT

INVENTIONS THAT ELECTRIFIED THE WORLD

My Hero, Benjamin Franklin

Brave, Dedicated, Hardworking, Flexible

G | **GENERAL AUDIENCES**
ALL AGES ADMITTED

LESSON 1 HANDOUT

Hero Qualities

Directions

Read the statements below.

Circle the word *agree* next to each statement that matches your opinion of what makes a hero.

Circle the word *disagree* next to each statement that does not match your opinion of what makes a hero.

1.	A hero is brave and strong.	Agree	Disagree
2.	A hero is caring and thoughtful.	Agree	Disagree
3.	A hero is selfish.	Agree	Disagree
4.	A hero is never frightened.	Agree	Disagree
5.	A hero wants to be rewarded for his or her actions.	Agree	Disagree
6.	A hero makes mistakes.	Agree	Disagree
7.	A hero is never silly.	Agree	Disagree
8.	A hero is dishonest.	Agree	Disagree
9.	A hero puts others before himself or herself.	Agree	Disagree
10.	A hero stands up for himself or herself.	Agree	Disagree
11.	A hero never gets angry.	Agree	Disagree
12.	A hero is always popular.	Agree	Disagree

LESSON 1 HANDOUT

Mr. Bones to the Rescue

Mr. Bones worked at the National Museum of Natural History in Washington, D.C. He was in charge of the new dinosaur exhibit. He was so proud of how real the dinosaurs looked.

"Wait a minute," Mr. Bones said one day. "Where is our brontosaurus? It's missing!"

Suddenly, Mr. Bones remembered something odd he had seen the day before: a small brown stick coming out of the janitor's pocket.

Mr. Bones thought, "That was weird. Maybe it wasn't a stick. Maybe it was a bone!"

The next day, he went to the janitor's closet and found the missing brontosaurus there.

The police arrested the janitor.

The museum threw a party for Mr. Bones.

"Mr. Bones, now our museum is great again. Thanks!" And they all gave him a high five.

Written by Naomi Baum; reprinted by permission.

Lesson 2 Who Is Your Hero?

 PURPOSE

This lesson is designed to help students identify a hero and create concrete connections with the hero, then apply those connections to flexibility and day-to-day choice making. There is one activity in this lesson.

Materials Required for All Activities

 Not Included

At least two computers with access to a printer *or* materials to make posters:

- Poster board
- White paper (one sheet per student)
- Crayons or markers
- Glue
- Additional art supplies as needed

Included

- Handout: Movie Poster Example: Benjamin Franklin (from Lesson 1)
- Handout: Hero Movie Poster Checklist (Internet) *or* Handout: Hero Movie Poster Checklist (Art Project)
- Internet link to create movie poster

Generalization

School Integration

- Continue with the School Integration activities from Lesson 1.
- Refer to students' heroes throughout the day.
- Refer to students' heroes when addressing flexibility goals and behaviors. For example, you might say to a student while making a plan for a game for recess, "_____ (insert hero's name) always has a Plan B. What is your Plan B?" When a student is having difficulty with a math problem, you might ask, "What would Harry Potter do?"
- Place a visual of students' heroes in key places, such as on a student's desk or on the cover of his or her notebook. Students may have ideas for where the visual can go.
- Talk with other team members (other teachers, the occupational therapist, the speech therapist) about students' heroes so that everyone on the team can integrate the heroes where appropriate.

Home Integration

There is no Home Extension for Lesson 2.

Modifications

For Older Students

- Use language and media that engage your students.
- Consider allowing the student to complete the handout or internet research individually.

ACTIVITY 1

Hero Identification and Development

<svg></svg> **Individual Activity**

<svg></svg> **~30 minutes**

Materials

Not Included

At least two computers with access to a printer *or* materials to make posters:

- Poster board
- White paper (one sheet per student)
- Crayons or markers
- Glue
- Additional art supplies as needed

Included

- Handout: Movie Poster Example: Benjamin Franklin (from Lesson 1)
- Handout: Hero Movie Poster Checklist (Internet) *or* Handout: Hero Movie Poster Checklist (Art Project)
- Internet link to create movie posters

Instructions

1. Review the qualities of a hero from Lesson 1, Activity 1, referring to the brainstorming activity, and Lesson 1, Activity 3, referring to the hero's qualities activity.
2. Ask students to share their chosen heroes.
3. Use Handout: Movie Poster Example: Benjamin Franklin to review the information that should be included on students' posters.
4. You may choose to have students make their posters by using a poster-creating web site or by using art supplies.
   a. If students will create their posters using the web site, go to http://bighugelabs.com/flickr/poster.php and demonstrate how to use it. Have students follow the directions on Handout: Hero Movie Poster Checklist (Internet).
   b. If students will create their posters using art supplies, have them follow the directions on Handout: Hero Movie Poster Checklist (Art Project).
5. Have students create their movie posters.

LESSON 2 HANDOUT

Hero Movie Poster Checklist (Art Project)

To complete your movie poster, you will need these supplies:

- 1 piece of poster board
- 1 piece of white paper (if you want to draw your hero)
- Crayons or markers
- Glue
- Any extra supplies to make your movie poster special

My Hero, Benjamin Franklin
Brave, Dedicated, Hardworking, Flexible

INVENTIONS THAT ELECTRIFIED THE WORLD

G GENERAL AUDIENCES ALL AGES ADMITTED

1. Go online and select a picture of your hero, or draw a picture of your hero on the white paper. Glue the picture in the middle of your poster.

2. Write your movie title near the top of your poster.

3. Write the name of your social skills group as the movie's presenter.

4. Think of a sentence that describes what makes your hero a hero, and write it where "Inventions that Electrified the World" is located.

   Examples: He helps people in need. He uses his power for good. Her inventions have changed our lives.

5. Think of four adjectives (describing words) to describe your hero, and write them where "Brave, Dedicated, Hardworking, Flexible" is located.

   Examples: brave, kind, loving, friendly, flexible

6. Write the director's name and the names of the people starring in your movie.

   Examples: Juan, Asia, Miss Simpson

7. Write the name and job of anyone else you would like mentioned on your poster.

   Examples: Jessica and Michael, camera crew

8. Give your movie a rating. Remember, you want everyone to have the chance to see your movie.

   Examples: G, PG, PG-13

9. What date will your movie be available to the public? Write that date in the bottom right section of the poster.

   Example: April 2

LESSON 2 HANDOUT

Hero Movie Poster Checklist (Internet)

1. Go online and select a picture of your hero.

2. Save the picture to the desktop. *Make sure you save the picture as a JPEG. Remember what you name the file.*

3. Go to http://bighugelabs.com/flickr/poster.php

4. Upload the picture you saved.

5. Choose a style for your poster.

   Examples: Light (fades to white), Dark (fades to black), Neutral (no fade)

6. Choose a title font and color.

   Examples: Classic, Fancy, Earthquake

7. Think of a title for your movie, and type it under "Movie title."

   Examples: My Hero, Benjamin Franklin; Harry Potter to the Rescue

8. Think of a sentence that describes what makes your hero a hero, and type it under "Tagline 1."

   Examples: He helps people in need. He uses his power for good. Her inventions have changed our lives.

9. Think of four adjectives (describing words) to describe your hero, and type them under "Tagline 2."

   Examples: brave, kind, loving, friendly, flexible

10. Type in the director's name and the names of the people starring in your movie under "Acting credits (at top)."

    Examples: Juan, Asia, Miss Simpson

11. Type in the name of your social skills group and anyone else you would like mentioned on your poster under "Production credits (at bottom)."

    Examples: Jessica and Michael, camera crew

12. Give your movie a rating. Remember, you want everyone to have the chance to see your movie.

    Examples: G, PG, PG-13

13. What date will your movie be available to the public? Type that date under "Release date."

    Example: April 2

14. Click **CREATE** to see what your poster looks like. If you need to make changes on your poster, *do not click* **BACK**. Instead, click **EDIT POSTER**.

15. Save your poster, and write down where you saved it.

Lesson 3 Hero Movie

 PURPOSE

This lesson is designed to solidify each student's understanding of how heroes can aid in developing flexibility. It also brings students' discoveries together in order to amplify their learning. There is one activity in this lesson.

Materials Required for All Activities

Not Included

- Videocamera (if available)
- Completed movie posters from Lesson 2

Included

- Handout: Snow Day Dilemma Hero Movie
- Handout: Video Game Decision Hero Movie
- Handout: Hero Movie Premiere Interview
- Home Extension 8 and Home Signoff

Generalization

School Integration

Continue generalization activities from Lessons 1 and 2.

Home Integration

- Upon completion of the lesson, send home a copy of Home Extension 8 and Home Signoff.
- Send home copies of students' work produced in Topic 4.
- If possible, send home copies of any video footage of students.

Modifications

For Older Students

Select and modify the hero movie script in a way that appeals to students' interests and is age appropriate.

ACTIVITY 1
Hero Movies

 **Role Play**

⏱ **~30 minutes**

Materials

Not Included

- Videocamera (if available)
- Completed movie posters from Lesson 2

Included

- Handout: Snow Day Dilemma Hero Movie
- Handout: Video Game Decision Hero Movie
- Handout: Hero Movie Premiere Interview
- Home Extension 8 and Home Signoff

Instructions

1. Have students present their hero movie posters. Ask each student to highlight who his or her hero is, what makes the hero a hero, and why the student wants to be like his or her hero.

2. Decide whether all students will be in all hero movies (i.e., you will repeat them, usually best for younger students or students who benefit from repetition) or whether each of the three hero movies will be completed only once by two students and yourself while the others watch (usually best for older students). Explain to students that they will have the opportunity to star in a hero movie as their hero and/or be interviewed as their hero.

3. For *hero movies:* Each student should have a chance to act as the hero at least once. You should act as an additional character in the hero movie. (The contents of Handout: Video Game Decision Hero Movie can be altered to highlight specific games that your students enjoy.)

   a. Introduce one hero movie.

   b. Have students practice and then present their hero movie, playing the part of their hero. (If possible, record the hero movie on video.)

   c. After the hero movie, ask, "What did _____ do that made him [or her] a hero?"

   d. Introduce the second hero movie.

   e. Have students practice and present their second hero movie. (If possible, record the hero movie on video.)

   f. After the hero movie, ask, "What did _____ do that made him [or her] a hero?"

4. For *interviews:* Each student will have the opportunity to play the interviewer and the hero. Hand the interviewer a copy of the questions. You can also add props if you wish, such as a microphone. The first time there is an interview, students should use Questions A. The second time, students should use Questions B. In Question 6 of Questions B, *movie* could be replaced with *blocks, game, ice cream flavor,* and so forth.

5. Review Home Extension 8 with students.

LESSON 3 HANDOUT

Video Game Decision Hero Movie

Setting:
This hero movie takes place in a home.

Characters:
1. Sam or Susie (friend who lives at the home) (S)
2. Rob or Rachel (friend going to Sam or Susie's home) (R)
3. Hero (H)
   _____ Name of the hero

S: (looks excited, pretends to look out the front door) I can't wait for my friend to get here. I have the whole day planned out. First, we'll play Mario on my Wii. Then, we'll go outside, and then we'll have peanut butter for lunch. It's going to be great!

(Hears a knocking sound)

S: (looks excited) He [or she] is here! (runs and opens the door) What's up?

R: (looks excited) Not much. How are you?

S: (talking fast) Great. I have our whole day planned. First, we'll play my favorite Mario video game. Then, we'll go outside, and then—

R: (looks nervous) Wait, I don't like Mario. My favorite video game is Wii Sports. Can't we play that?

S: (looks frustrated) No, the plan is to play Mario. I want to play my favorite game. Wii Sports is my second favorite game.

R: Well, fine, if you won't play Wii Sports, then I won't play anything at all.

S: Fine, we'll sit here and do nothing all day. (sits down in a chair, crosses arms, and looks away)

R: Fine, that's what we'll do. (sits down in a chair, crosses arms, and looks away)

S and R: (look bored, sigh)

H: (comes into the room, clears throat) Excuse me, but it seems to me we have a problem that needs fixing!

S and R: (look excited and say together) _____ [hero's name], is it really you?

H: Yes, it certainly is! And as the master of _____ [word that describes your hero], I cannot sit by and watch you waste this wonderful play date.

S: Yeah, but I want to play Mario.

R: I want to play Wii Sports.

H: We have a real dilemma on our hands! It sounds like the two of you are stuck, but not to fear...I have just the answer!

S: I don't know about this.

H: My solution will guarantee that you both get to do exactly what you want. We need to come up with a compromise. Are you ready?

S and R: Yeah!

H: Okay. The goal is that you have fun with each other. Your Plan A, to play only your chosen game or to do nothing, does not seem like it will help you accomplish your goal. I think that if you go with Plan B you will be much happier.

R: What is Plan B?

H: In Plan B you both get to play the games you like. You will play Mario for 20 minutes and then Wii Sports for 20 minutes. This way you accomplish your goal to have fun with each other, and you will still have more than enough time to go outside and eat lunch.

B: I love this plan! _____ [hero's name], do you want to play, too?

H: Sure, let's go!

LESSON 3 HANDOUT

Snow Day Dilemma Hero Movie

Setting:
This hero movie takes place in a home.

Characters:
1. Johnny (brother) or Jenny (sister) (J)
2. Bobby (brother) or Betty (sister) (B)
3. Hero (H)
   _____ Name of the hero

J: (looks excited, pretends to look out the window) I can't believe how much snow is out there. I can't wait to go outside and go sledding!

B: (walks into the room and looks excited) Did you see all of that snow? I can't wait to go outside and have a snowball fight.

J: (looks confused) Snowball fight, no way! This is the best day to go sledding.

B: (looks frustrated) Are you kidding? The best, coolest thing to do on a snow day is to have a snowball fight!

J: (looks nervous) Wait, if you don't come with me, then who will help me build a huge jump?

B: (looks frustrated) Well, if you don't come with me, then who will I throw snowballs with?

J: Well, fine, if you won't go sledding with me, then I won't play anything at all.

B: Fine, we'll sit here and do nothing all day. (sits down in a chair, crosses arms, and looks away)

J: Fine, that's what we'll do. (sits down in a chair, crosses arms, and looks away)

J and B: (look bored, sigh)

H: (comes into the room, clears throat) Excuse me, but it seems to me we have a problem that needs fixing!

J and B: (look excited and say together) _____ [hero's name], is it really you?

H: Yes, it certainly is! And as the master of _____ [word that describes your hero], I cannot sit by and watch you waste this incredible snow day.

J: Yeah, but I want to go sledding.

B: I want to have a snowball fight.

H: We have a real dilemma on our hands, but not to fear...I have just the answer!

J: I don't know about this.

H: My solution will guarantee that you both get to do exactly what you want. But you are going to have to be flexible. Are you ready?

J and B: Yeah!

H: Okay, here it is. You have 2 hours until your mom wants you home for lunch. For the first hour you will go sledding, and for the second hour you will have a snowball fight. How does that sound?

J: Compromises rock!

B: I love this plan! _____ [hero's name], do you want to come with us?

H: Sure, let's go!

LESSON 3 HANDOUT

Hero Movie Premiere Interview

Questions A

Participants:

(I) Interviewer: _____

(H) Hero: _____

Interviewer: *Welcome the audience and introduce the movie. Ask the hero the following questions. (You are welcome to add additional questions to your interview.)*

1. What makes you a great hero in this movie?
2. How do you save the day in your movie?
3. Who do you think should watch this movie?
4. Would you consider doing a sequel?
5. Why do you think so many people look up to you as a hero?
6. If you saw two kids arguing over what Wii game to play, how would you help them be flexible and solve their problem?
7. Is there anything else you want audiences to know?

Hero Movie Premiere Interview

Questions B

Participants:

(I) Interviewer: _____

(H) Hero: _____

Interviewer: *Welcome the audience and introduce the movie. Ask the hero the following questions. (You are welcome to add additional questions to your interview.)*

1. What makes you a great hero in this movie?
2. How do you save the day in your movie?
3. Who do you think should watch this movie?
4. Would you consider doing a sequel?
5. Why do you think so many people look up to you as a hero?
6. If you saw two kids arguing over which movie to go see, how would you help them be flexible and solve their problem?
7. Is there anything else you want audiences to know?

TOPIC
4

Home Extension 8

Summary: During the past three lessons, students have worked on identifying a hero and developing a connection with that hero to support the use of flexibility strategies.

There are several things you can do at home to help your child learn as fully as possible. The more experiences a student has outside the classroom, the better he or she is able to learn and apply that learning.

1. Review your child's handouts to develop an understanding of your child's selected hero.

   a. Handout: Hero Qualities shows the qualities your child has identified as important in a hero. Use these qualities as conversation starters to explore why your child chose this particular hero.

   b. You will also find a copy of your child's movie poster featuring his or her hero. Ask your child to explain the elements of the poster and why he or she chose to include them.

2. Begin to make connections between your child's hero and your child's daily life. For example, you might say, "I wonder what [insert name of child's hero] would do in this situation."

3. If you have or have had a personal hero or mentor, share with your child who that is. Discuss the reasons that person has been important to you.

4. With your child, complete Home Extension: The Making of a Personal Hero. Your child may dictate his or her answers to you.

Home Extension:
The Making of a Personal Hero

My personal hero is _____

1. What do I want in a hero? (Check all that apply.)

   __ Smart   __ Brave

   __ Talented   __ Flexible

   __ Strong   __ Honorable

   __ Athletic   __ Honest

   __ Funny   __ Other: _____

2. The qualities I admire in my hero are

   _____
   _____
   _____

3. I hope to be like my hero by

   _____
   _____
   _____

TOPIC
4

Home Signoff

Date sent home: _____

I have read
Home Extension _____

_____
Parent signature

Please return this page to
the social skills teacher by _____.

Extensions

Generalization

School Integration

- As opportunities for flexibility arise throughout the day, talk about the ways one of the heroes you have discussed might respond to such opportunities.
- Refer to students' heroes throughout the day, especially when addressing flexibility goals and behaviors.
- Place a visual of students' heroes in key places, such as on a student's desk or on the cover of his or her notebook.
- Talk with other team members (other teachers, the occupational therapist, the speech therapist) about students' heroes so that everyone on the team can integrate the heroes where appropriate.

Home Integration

- Upon completion of Lesson 3, send home a copy of Home Extension 8 and Home Signoff, including the attached Home Extension: The Making of a Personal Hero.
- Send home copies of the students' work completed during this topic.

Materials for Home

- Home Extension 8 and Home Signoff
- Copies of work produced by students (movie poster, Handout: Hero Qualities)
- Copies of recorded hero movies, if possible

REFERENCE

Ylvisaker, M., McPherson, K., Kayes, N., & Pellett, E. (2008). Metaphoric identity mapping: Facilitating goal setting and engagement in rehabilitation after traumatic brain injury. *Neuropsychological Rehabilitation, 18*(5–6), 713–741.

TOPIC
5

Why Be Flexible?

SPECIAL INSTRUCTIONS: The core goal of these lessons is to help students establish intrinsic motivation for being flexible. Although it is important to implement each component of this topic, you can modify the activities as necessary to better meet your students' needs. When implementing the lessons, use examples from students' experiences whenever possible.

Summary: This topic stresses intrinsic motivation for helping students to be flexible. In these two lessons, students explore how flexibility creates positive feelings and puts them in charge of outcomes. This topic includes explicit instruction, continued use of critical flexibility vocabulary, and an opportunity to examine outcomes that are possible when students are flexible and when they are not. The final lesson will most likely require at least two sessions, so plan accordingly.

Prerequisite skills: Understanding of the meaning of flexibility (Topic 1), familiarity with flexibility vocabulary (Topic 2)

Related skills: Intrinsic motivation, self-concept, goal setting

OUTCOME—CRITERIA FOR MASTERY

1. The student identifies the positive feelings that result from being flexible.
2. The student identifies the outcomes that will occur when he or she is flexible.

TOPIC BACKGROUND AND RATIONALE

Like all individuals, students with ASD respond best when their motivation level is high. However, implicit social motivation (i.e., the knowledge that a teacher is happy when the student does well or that by developing the reputation of being a flexible student, the teacher would be happier with the student and/or more likely to grant privileges) does not always work for those with ASD the same way it does for those without ASD. Therefore, it is important to explicitly teach the advantages of flexibility for achieving concrete goals that are meaningful to the individual student. Finding the right incentives to support learning is one of the crucial first steps in teaching students new skills. To effect behavioral change over time, it is important to establish and explicitly demonstrate how flexibility gives students more control and results in positive outcomes.

Lesson 1 The Advantages of Flexibility

 PURPOSE

This lesson will help students establish intrinsic motivation for being flexible by exploring, through concrete experiences, how being flexible can get them what they want and give them more independence. This lesson includes four activities.

Materials Required for All Activities

 ***Not Included***

- Whiteboard or chart paper
- Dry/wet erase markers or markers
- Video clip of a student reacting negatively to being stuck (optional)
- Die
- Game tokens (e.g., BINGO chips, coins)

 Included

- Visual: How Does It Feel?
- Handout: What to Do When What I Want Is Impossible
- Educator Script: What to Do When What I Want Is Impossible
- Handout: My Two Choices
- Educator Script: My Two Choices
- Visual: Group Flexibility Chant
- Flexibility Freeway Game Board
- Flexibility Freeway Game Cards (cut out ahead of time)
- Educator Guide: Flexibility Freeway Game Rules
- Home Extension 9 and Home Signoff

Generalization

School Integration

- When students are having a difficult time or come to a roadblock in naturally occurring situations throughout the day, use the image of the mud puddle to help them visualize what happens when they are stuck. Use the image of a bridge to help them visualize how to avoid the mud puddle by building a bridge over it.
- Reinforce students' demonstration of flexibility, highlighting what they were able to do as a result of their flexibility and what they would have lost if they had remained rigid and become stuck. Be sure to point out instances in which a student's flexibility increases his or her choices or independence.

Home Integration

Upon completion of Lesson 1, send home a copy of Home Extension 9 and Home Signoff.

Modifications

For Older Students

Create your own student scenarios and use examples from situations that have occurred in the classroom. Instead of the mud and bridge metaphor offered in the first lesson, your students may be more responsive to being stuck on a level in a video game and finding a way out or having a computer freeze and finding someone to fix the computer. The chants and group sayings will likely feel childish to your older students. Consider omitting them and using additional examples if students need further assistance understanding key concepts. You can use your students' recent experiences or examples from popular media, highlighting those sources most popular among your students (e.g., movies, books).

ACTIVITY 1
The Facts of Life

👥 **Group Discussion**

🕐 **~5–10 minutes**

Materials

Not Included

- Whiteboard or chart paper
- Dry/wet erase markers or markers

Included

There are no included materials for this activity.

Instructions

1. Ask students to reflect on the vocabulary words from Topic 2, and ask for volunteers to share ways their hero has helped them be more flexible (e.g., making compromises, having a Plan B).

2. Explain that students are going to learn more about how being flexible is helpful to them. Explain that there are certain things in life that are always true, and these are sometimes called *facts of life.* One fact of life is that what we want is not always possible.

3. Ask the students, "Has there ever been anything that you wanted that you could not get?" Be prepared to share your own examples to help students think of some. Student examples might include not being able to have the snack they wanted; not being able to do something in the order they wanted to do it in; and not being able to play a game they wanted to play, see a movie they wanted to see, sit in a certain seat, or hang out with a certain friend.

4. Ask probing questions to illustrate the point that there are certain things we cannot change.
   a. If the game we want is broken, can we play it?
   b. If the food we want is sold out, can we buy it?
   c. If the seat we want is taken, can we sit in it?
   d. If the restaurant we want to go to is closed, can we go in it?

5. Write the following on the whiteboard: *Sometimes what I want is impossible.* Have the students repeat this several times. It can be fun to make it a cheer, with everyone raising their hands as you all say, "Impossible!"

6. Tell students that every time there is something they want that is not possible to have, they have two choices, and *they* are in charge of those choices. In the next activity, they will explore these two choices.

LESSON 1

ACTIVITY 2

What to Do When What I Want Is Impossible

👥 **Group Activity**

🕐 **~5–10 minutes**

Materials

Not Included

- Whiteboard or chart paper
- Dry/wet erase markers or markers
- Video clip of a student reacting negatively to being stuck (optional)

Included

- Visual: How Does It Feel?
- Handout: What to Do When What I Want Is Impossible
- Educator Script: What to Do When What I Want Is Impossible

Instructions

1. Explain to students that you are going to talk about the choices they have when they can't get something they want. Present Visual: How Does It Feel?

2. Refer to the image of the mud on Visual: How Does It Feel? and ask, "How does it feel to get stuck in mud? How would you feel if you were walking along and you got stuck in this thick, ooey, gooey, messy mud?" Possible answers include *angry, frustrated, messy,* and *mad.* On Visual: How Does It Feel?, record students' answers around the puddle of mud shown.

3. Refer to the image of the bridge over the mud on Visual: How Does It Feel? and ask, "How does it feel to find a way around a big puddle of mud?" Possible answers include *relieved, happy,* and *excited.* On Visual: How Does It Feel? record students' answers around the bridge over the mud.

4. Ask students to think about a time when they might get "stuck in the mud" (e.g., they can't have the snack they wanted, they can't play the game they wanted to play, they have to go to bed). You'll likely get several examples of students *not* getting something they want, so highlight, "Those are all great examples, and I notice that we tend to get stuck in the mud when we can't get what we want or what we want is impossible." This would be a good place to show a video clip of a student who is stuck and having a tantrum or for the teacher to role-play what this situation might look like.

5. Review Handout: What to Do When What I Want Is Impossible with students. Use Educator Script: What to Do When What I Want Is Impossible as a guide. Color in the student version using the example provided or one from your students' experience.

6. Emphasize the following to students: Sometimes what I want is *impossible* (have students put their hands in the air), but if I am flexible I get something I want and I can feel good (have students bring their hands over their heart).

ACTIVITY 3
Stuck in the Mud or Flexible?

Group Discussion
~5–10 minutes

Materials

Not Included

- Whiteboard or chart paper
- Dry/wet erase markers or markers

Included

- Visual: How Does It Feel?
- Handout: My Two Choices (at least one copy per group and one for the teacher)
- Educator Script: My Two Choices
- Visual: Group Flexibility Chant

Instructions

1. Explain to students that they are going to practice thinking of different choices when what they want is not possible.

2. Reference Handout: My Two Choices and say, "Let's look at our first choice. We are going to call the first choice *stuck in the mud.*" Then, gesture to the second column with the picture of the bridge and say, "This is our second choice, which we'll call *flexible.* The picture of the bridge reminds us that when we're flexible, it's like a bridge that we can go over and avoid getting stuck in the mud." Gesture toward Visual: How Does It Feel? (from Activity 2) and remind students of all the negative feelings associated with being stuck and all the positive feelings associated with being flexible.

3. Reference Educator Script: My Two Choices and use the scenario written at the top to demonstrate completing Handout: My Two Choices. Begin by reading the scenario out loud to students and then ask the questions as prompted on the educator script. The educator script also provides some examples of answers that you can use to help prompt your students if needed.

4. Working with the group, use one copy of Handout: My Two Choices and together practice filling out the two columns with one of the following:
   a. The example from your earlier conversation
   b. An example that you provide
   c. An example from students' experience
   d. Something students saw in a favorite television show

5. Continue as a group and ask students to answer the questions at the bottom of Handout: My Two Choices. After students answer these questions, be sure to highlight that being flexible may not have gotten them all that they wanted, but it got them *much* more than getting stuck. Make a strong point of how getting stuck can actually make things happen that they *don't* want, and getting part of what they want is always better than getting *none* of what they want or something they *don't* want.

6. Show Visual: Group Flexibility Chant and say, "When I'm flexible, I'll get part, and I'll feel good in my heart." Have students repeat it.

ACTIVITY 4
Lesson Summary

 Group Activity

🕐 **~10–15 minutes**

Materials

Not Included

- Game tokens
- Die

Included

- Flexibility Freeway Game Board
- Flexibility Freeway Game Cards (cut out ahead of time)
- Educator Guide: Flexibility Freeway Game Rules
- Home Extension 9 and Home Signoff

Instructions

1. Summarize what the students have learned, and reiterate the following: Sometimes what I want is *impossible*, but if I am flexible I get something I want and feel good.
2. State the following phrases. After each one, have students give you a thumbs-up if they agree with the statement or a thumbs-down if they disagree.
   a. I can always get everything I want.
   b. Sometimes what I want is *impossible*.
   c. Being flexible helps me get something I want.
   d. Being flexible feels better than being stuck.
3. Have students play the Flexibility Freeway board game, in which they have the chance to make flexible choices. Review Educator Guide: Flexibility Freeway Game Rules before beginning.
4. Review Home Extension 9 with students.

LESSON 1 EDUCATOR SCRIPT

TOPIC
5

What to Do When What I Want Is Impossible

Every time I want something, there are three possible outcomes.

Let's say I would like to play outside with my friends for recess. What could happen?

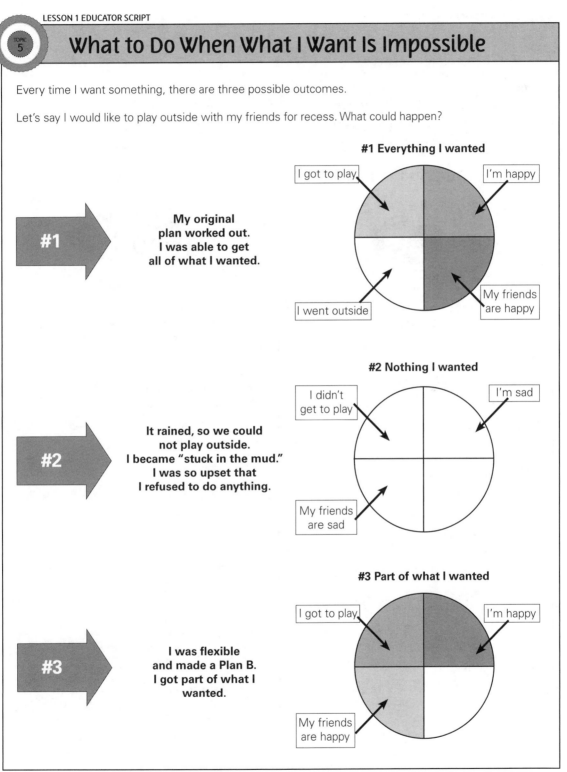

#1 Everything I wanted

I got to play

I'm happy

I went outside

My friends are happy

#1

My original plan worked out. I was able to get all of what I wanted.

#2 Nothing I wanted

I didn't get to play

I'm sad

My friends are sad

#2

It rained, so we could not play outside. I became "stuck in the mud." I was so upset that I refused to do anything.

#3 Part of what I wanted

I got to play

I'm happy

My friends are happy

#3

I was flexible and made a Plan B. I got part of what I wanted.

My Two Choices

Educator: I am very hungry. I am going to go to McDonald's with my family for a delicious hamburger. We start driving to McDonald's and hear on the radio that McDonald's is closed today.

- If I choose to get stuck in the mud, what will happen?

- If I choose to be flexible, what are my options? How will I feel? What will happen?

Stuck in the mud	Flexible

Stuck in the mud	**Flexible**
No food Bad mood Angry Hungry	Went to Wendy's Got food Was happy Enjoyed time with my family Made my parents proud of me
Did I get what I wanted? No	Did I get something I wanted? Yes

When I'm stuck, I

- Miss fun things

- Don't get anything I want

- Am not with people I like

- Am upset

- Am angry

- Do not earn all my points

Bring stuck might also result in

- Getting in trouble

- Wasted time

- Possibly missing part of lunch and recess or play time

When I'm flexible, I

- Get something I want

- Don't miss any part of the day

- Feel better

- Get to stay with people I like

- Get bonus points, etc.

> You will write your students' answers as they provide them.
>
> Keep this sheet as a ready reference during the activity. You can use it to get a conversation going if your students are struggling.

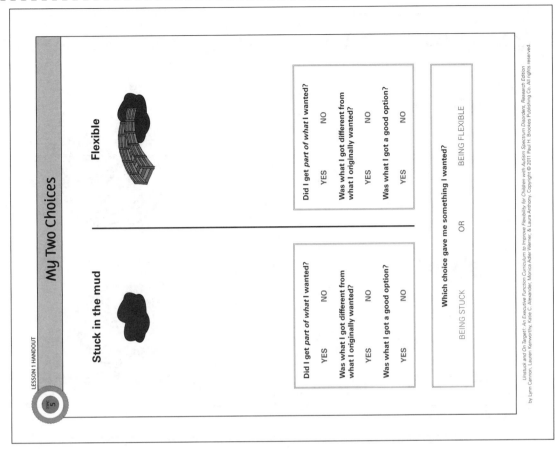

LESSON 1 HANDOUT

My Two Choices

Stuck in the mud

Flexible

Did I get *part of what I wanted?*

YES   NO

Was what I got different from what I originally wanted?

YES   NO

Was what I got a good option?

YES   NO

Did I get *part of what I wanted?*

YES   NO

Was what I got different from what I originally wanted?

YES   NO

Was what I got a good option?

YES   NO

Which choice gave me something I wanted?

BEING STUCK   OR   BEING FLEXIBLE

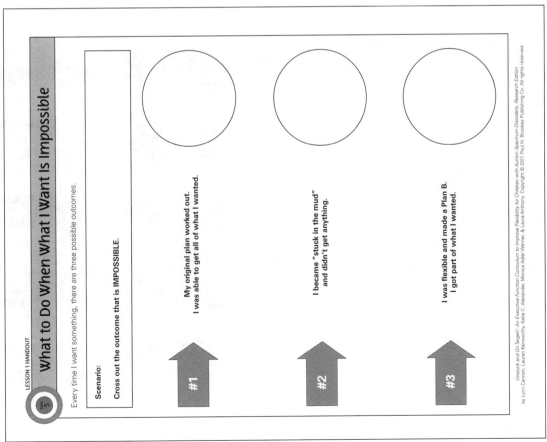

LESSON 1 HANDOUT

What to Do When What I Want Is Impossible

Every time I want something, there are three possible outcomes.

Scenario:

Cross out the outcome that is IMPOSSIBLE.

#1   My original plan worked out. I was able to get all of what I wanted.

#2   I became "stuck in the mud" and didn't get anything.

#3   I was flexible and made a Plan B. I got part of what I wanted.

How Does It Feel?

STUCK

FLEXIBLE

Group Flexibility Chant

When I'm flexible I'll get part...

and I'll feel good in my heart.

FLEXIBILITY FREEWAY GAME CARDS

STUCK IN THE MUD!

I would love some chicken nuggets. McDonald's is closed until 3:00 P.M. How can I be flexible and still reach my goal to eat chicken nuggets?

STUCK IN THE MUD!

I want to write, but the point on my favorite pencil is broken. How can I be flexible and still reach my goal to use my favorite pencil?

STUCK IN THE MUD!

I want to play with Sam. He is playing with John. How can I be flexible and still reach my goal to play with Sam?

STUCK IN THE MUD!

I really want to swing on the swings. Right now all of the swings are taken. How can I be flexible and still reach my goal to swing on the swings?

STUCK IN THE MUD!

I want to talk about video games, but my friends want to talk about dinosaurs. How can I be flexible and still reach my goal to talk about video games?

STUCK IN THE MUD!

I want to watch SpongeBob SquarePants, but my mom wants me to clean my room. How can I be flexible and still reach my goal to watch SpongeBob?

STUCK IN THE MUD!

I want to play outside, but I have to do my homework. How can I be flexible and still reach my goal to play outside?

STUCK IN THE MUD!

I want to go first in the board game, but my friend rolled the higher number. How can I be flexible and still reach my goal to go first in a game?

STUCK IN THE MUD!

I want to play baseball, but my friends are already playing basketball. How can I be flexible and still reach my goal to play baseball?

STUCK IN THE MUD!

I want to play with blocks, but my friends are playing a board game. How can I be flexible and still reach my goal to play with blocks?

FLEXIBILITY FREEWAY GAME CARDS

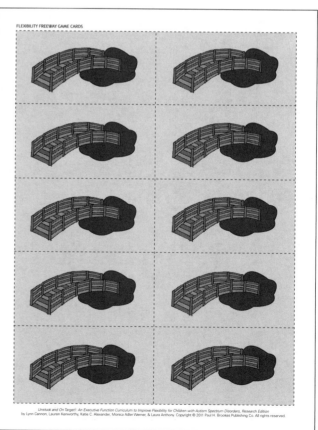

FLEXIBILITY FREEWAY GAME CARDS

DETOUR!
I wanted a hot dog for lunch, but there are none left. Since I can't always get what I want, how can I be flexible and get something else I can feel good about?

DETOUR!
I wanted to play on the computer, but they are all being used. Since I can't always get what I want, how can I be flexible and get something else I can feel good about?

DETOUR!
I wanted to talk about airplanes, but my friend doesn't. Since I can't always get what I want, how can I be flexible and talk about something else I can feel good about?

DETOUR!
I wanted to watch a movie, but it is time for bed. Since I can't always get what I want, how can I be flexible and get something else I can feel good about?

DETOUR!
I wanted to go first in the game of Tag. Since I can't always get what I want, how can I be flexible and get something else I can feel good about?

DETOUR!
I wanted to play video games, but it is time to do my homework. Since I can't always get what I want, how can I be flexible and get something else I can feel good about?

DETOUR!
I wanted a vanilla ice cream cone, but the store is out of vanilla. Since I can't always get what I want, how can I be flexible and get something else I can feel good about?

DETOUR!
I wanted to read the dinosaur book, but my friend is looking at it. Since I can't always get what I want, how can I be flexible and get something else I can feel good about?

DETOUR!
I wanted to play outside for recess, but it is too cold. Since I can't always get what I want, how can I be flexible and get something else I can feel good about?

DETOUR!
I wanted to answer the teacher's question, but she called on my classmate first. Since I can't always get what I want, how can I be flexible and get something else I can feel good about?

FLEXIBILITY FREEWAY GAME CARDS

FLEXIBILITY FREEWAY GAME CARDS

STOPLIGHT!
TRUE OR FALSE?
If I have a temper tantrum when I don't get what I want, people will want to help me come up with a plan to help me get something else I can feel good about.

STOPLIGHT!
TRUE OR FALSE?
I can always get everything I want.

STOPLIGHT!
TRUE OR FALSE?
I am in charge of my choice to be stuck in the mud or be flexible.

STOPLIGHT!
TRUE OR FALSE?
If I am stuck in the mud, I will not get anything I can feel good about.

STOPLIGHT!
TRUE OR FALSE?
Sometimes what I want is not possible.

STOPLIGHT!
TRUE OR FALSE?
Even if the thing I want is not available, it feels better to get something else I want than to be stuck in the mud and get nothing at all.

STOPLIGHT!
TRUE OR FALSE?
Being flexible helps me get something I want.

STOPLIGHT!
TRUE OR FALSE?
When I can't get what I want, I should yell and cry. If false, what should I do instead?

STOPLIGHT!
TRUE OR FALSE?
Being flexible feels better than being stuck.

STOPLIGHT!
TRUE OR FALSE?
When I can't get what I want, I have two choices. What are they?

FLEXIBILITY FREEWAY GAME CARDS

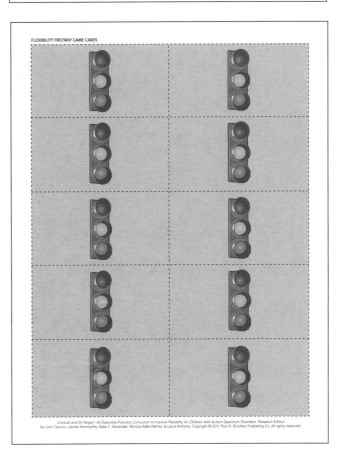

LESSON 1 EDUCATOR GUIDE

5

Flexibility Freeway Game Rules

Goal

For each player to reach End of the Freeway at space 50 on the board.

Directions

1. Everyone starts at Space 1 on the game board.

2. Take turns rolling the die and moving the corresponding number of spaces.

3. If you land on a mud puddle with a bridge, pick up a bridge card. Read the scenario. If you can identify a plan for how to be flexible and continue to work toward the goal on the card, you can go over the bridge and to the next space. If you cannot come up with a flexible solution, you are "stuck in the mud" until your next turn. You may move on your next turn.

4. If you land on a mud puddle with a detour sign, pick up a detour card. Read the scenario. If you recognize that you can't always get what you want but can identify a plan for how to be flexible and work toward a new goal that you feel good about, you can follow the detour sign to a new space. If you cannot come up with a flexible solution, you are "stuck in the mud" until your next turn. You may move on your next turn.

5. If you land on a stoplight, pick up a stoplight card. Read the scenario. If you answer the question correctly, you can move ahead to the next space. If you do not answer the question correctly, stay where you are until your next turn.

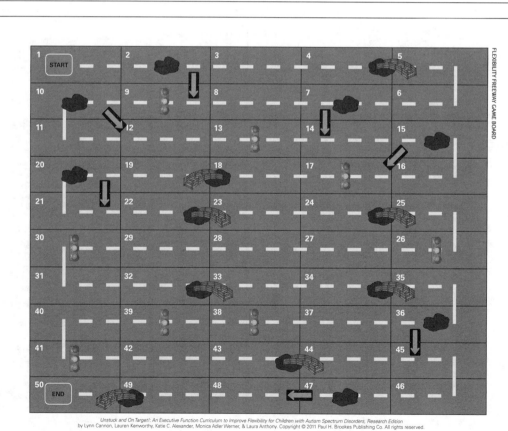

FLEXIBILITY FREEWAY GAME BOARD

Home Extension 9

Summary: During the course of Topic 5, students have worked on identifying how being flexible benefits them. Students have learned that what they want is not always possible. Students learned that every time there is something that they want that is not possible, they have two choices: to become stuck (represented by the image *stuck in the mud*) or to be flexible (represented by the image *build a bridge over the mud puddle*). Through concrete examples and games, students focused on the mantra "What I want is not always possible, but if I am flexible I get something I want and I feel good." During the final lesson, students will explore the powers (e.g., more independence, trust) that they gain from parents and teachers when they demonstrate flexibility.

There are several things you can do at home to help your child learn as fully as possible. The more experiences each student has outside the classroom, the better he or she is able to learn and apply that learning.

1. Review your child's handouts.

2. Highlight times when your child is flexible. Discuss the impact of his or her flexibility (he or she is happier, people around him or her are happier, he or she is in charge of consequences). Share times when you are flexible or stuck and discuss the impact of your choices. Compare the choice to be flexible with the choice to be stuck. Highlight opportunities that exist because your child was flexible.

3. Complete the Flexibility Feels…Scale with your child. Review the scenarios. Have your child rate how each scenario makes him or her feel by marking an X in the corresponding box (10 = feeling great; 1 = feeling lousy). Your child can choose a different symbol to record his or her feelings for the remaining scenarios.

4. Possible extension: Think of a time when you, your child, or your family had to be flexible. How did each stage of that process make the family feel?

Home Signoff

Date sent home: _____

I have read
Home Extension _____

_____
Parent signature

Please return this page to
the social skills teacher by _____

HOME EXTENSION 9 *(continued)*

Flexibility Feels...Scale

10	
9	
8	
7	
6	
5	
4	
3	
2	
1	

Directions: Read the scenario. Stop and think how you would feel in that situation.

You and your family have been looking forward to going out for a special pizza dinner all week.

Rate how you feel about your special dinner.

As you get close to the restaurant you realize it is closed. You can't believe this is happening. You start yelling in the car and you tell your parents you refuse to eat anywhere!

What choice did you make—to be stuck or to be flexible?

You are so upset that your parents drive home and skip the special dinner altogether.

Rate how you would feel if you were stuck and had to miss the special dinner altogether.

Let's say you made a different choice: You decide to drive to another great restaurant and get Mexican food instead.

Rate how you would feel if you were flexible.

Bonus: Think of a time when you, your parents, or your family chose to be flexible. Think about how you felt. Record it on the scale.

(page 2 of 2)

Lesson 2 Being Flexible Can Make Good Things Happen

 PURPOSE

The purpose of this lesson is to illustrate that when students are flexible, they gain power and increase the likelihood that other people will recognize their flexibility. As a direct result, students are more likely to earn preferred, positive experiences. In other words, flexibility increases the likelihood of positive outcomes, such as increased privileges. The students apply this concept to the creation of a video game that follows the same principles. There are three activities in this lesson.

Materials Required for All Activities

 Not Included

- Whiteboard or chart paper
- Dry/wet erase markers or markers
- Marbles
- Jar or other container to hold marbles, preferably something transparent
- Chart paper

 Included

- Educator Script: Flexibility Gives You Power Scenarios
- Video Game Cards (need to be cut before you begin the lesson)
- Educator Script: Video Game Introduction
- Handout: Gamers Inc. Mission Letter
- Handout: Quest 1 Example
- Educator Guide: Quest 1 Example
- Handout: Power Brainstorm
- Handout: Quest 1
- Handout: Quest 2
- Handout: Quest 3
- Handout: Quest 4
- Educator Script: Marble Jar: Flexible Reputation Scenarios

Generalization

School Integration

- When a student gains a new privilege or an accommodation is made in the student's favor, highlight for the student how his or her flexibility in the past made it possible for you to grant these privileges now.
- Students can continue to plan their video game by creating additional scenarios, additional levels, and so forth.

Home Integration

There is no Home Extension for Lesson 2.

Modifications

For Older Students

Older students may also enjoy creating the framework for a video game. Consider beginning the lesson with real images or documentaries that show the making of a video game. Older students may enjoy more complex video game themes and story lines.

ACTIVITY 1
Flexibility Powers

👥 **Group Activity**

🕐 **~5 minutes**

Materials

Not Included

- Whiteboard or chart paper
- Dry/wet erase markers or markers

Included

- Educator Script: Flexibility Gives You Power Scenarios

Instructions

1. Briefly review the activities from Lesson 1 by reading the following statements and having students give you a thumbs-up if they agree with the statement or a thumbs-down if they disagree.
   a. It is possible to always get everything I want.
   b. It always feels better to be flexible than to be stuck.
   c. Sometimes what I want is not possible.
   d. What I want is not always possible.
2. Ask students to think of a video game that has a quest, journey, or challenge that has to be met. Make sure each child can think of an example, and ask one student to describe a game. Ask additional questions about the game: What is the name of the game? What is the object of the game? What happens as the characters pass through the different levels? Are there special powers or abilities that help the characters reach their goals? How do the characters get those powers? Are there bonus points or special prizes in the game?
3. Tell the students that being flexible can help them gain "powers," or privileges, just like the characters in a video game gain powers.
4. Ask: "What powers do you think you earn from being flexible?" (Answers may include earning more privileges, having more independence, earning greater trust from teachers and parents, having classmates enjoy being around them, and making a choice for themselves instead of having an adult tell them what to do.)
5. Read aloud the scenarios in Educator Script: Flexibility Gives You Power Scenarios. After reading each one, ask students what powers the students in the scenarios might gain from being flexible. Record their answers on the whiteboard.

ACTIVITY 2
Flexibility Video Game

👥 **Group Activity**

🕐 **~45–60 minutes**

Materials

Not Included

- Whiteboard or chart paper
- Dry/wet erase markers or markers

 ### *Included*

- Video Game Cards (need to be cut before you begin the lesson)
- Educator Script: Video Game Introduction
- Handout: Gamers Inc. Mission Letter
- Handout: Quest 1 Example
- Educator Guide: Quest 1 Example
- Handout: Power Brainstorm
- Handout: Quest 1
- Handout: Quest 2
- Handout: Quest 3
- Handout: Quest 4

Instructions

Remember that this lesson will likely require more than one session, so plan accordingly. This lesson has multiple steps. It will be helpful to go through the whole lesson and review all of the handouts before starting instruction.

1. Students will create the storyboard for a video game that concretely reveals how flexibility increases the likelihood of desirable events occurring. Use Educator Script: Video Game Introduction to coach the students through the creation of their own video game storyboard.
2. Have students work through the creation of the storyboard using the handouts.

ACTIVITY 3
Flexible Reputation

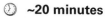 **Group Activity**
🕐 **~20 minutes**

Materials

Not Included

- Marbles (or similar objects; several for each student)
- Jar or other container to hold marbles, preferably something transparent (one for each student)
- Chart paper
- Markers

Included

- Educator Script: Marble Jar: Flexible Reputation Scenarios

Instructions

The idea for students to understand in this lesson is that when they are repeatedly flexible, they develop a flexible reputation. People start to think of them as flexible and are then more likely to give them privileges ("powers") based on the repeated flexibility.

1. Review the specific powers Star Commander Bex gained because of his flexibility.
2. Have students brainstorm situations in which they have had to be flexible. (You may use prompts to elicit answers, such as dinner, dessert, video game, computer game, waiting in line, standing in line, order of playing a game, or selecting a game.) Record their answers on chart paper.
3. Tell students that when they are repeatedly flexible over a period of time, they develop a reputation for being flexible. Make sure students understand the meaning of reputation: "Your behavior gives people certain thoughts about you—it forms your reputation. When you have a certain reputation, people start to treat you in a certain way." Give some examples: 1) someone who always says please and thank you—polite; 2) someone who loves to run around, constantly moving—energetic; and 3) someone who likes to talk with people and play games with others—friendly.
4. Help students make the connection between reputation and how people treat them. Record these thoughts visually to support student comprehension. For example,
   a. Friendly reputation → people want to be around you and play games with you
5. Ask students to brainstorm how people will treat them differently if they have a flexible reputation. Use examples that are meaningful to *your* students. For example,
   a. Was flexible when dessert was not available → an extra treat the following day
   b. Went to bed at bedtime instead of watching my favorite movie → able to stay up late the next day
   c. Let a classmate go first in line → teacher puts me first next time
6. Remind students that reputations develop over time. As they follow the scenarios you are going to read, they will watch a flexible reputation develop.
7. Hand out a small container and a handful of marbles to each student. Marbles represent flexible acts. The accumulation of marbles represents a growing flexible reputation.

continued

8. Read the scenarios aloud from the Educator Script: Marble Jar: Flexible Reputation Scenarios. If the fictional student was flexible, have students place a marble in their container. If the fictional student was not flexible, no marble goes in the container. Pause as indicated on Educator Script: Marble Jar: Flexible Reputation Scenarios to probe students' understanding of flexibility, reputation, and when it is okay to choose not to be flexible.

9. Repeat this activity as many times as necessary to ensure student comprehension.
    a. If students are forthcoming with personal examples, you can use those as scenarios.
    b. Create a fictional student who chooses not to be flexible more often than to be flexible. What type of reputation is this student developing?

10. At the end of the activity, review how the reputation was developed. What privileges did the student likely earn as a result of his or her flexible reputation? When is it okay not to be flexible?

Flexibility Gives You Power Scenarios

Scenario 1

Jimmy loves pizza. He would like to eat pizza every night. His parents decided that the family would have special pizza night every Friday.

Another tradition in Jimmy's family is that whoever has a birthday gets to pick his or her favorite meal to have for dinner. This Friday is Jimmy's sister's birthday. Jimmy recognized how special his sister's birthday was and decided to be flexible and not get upset about missing "Pizza Friday."

What are some powers Jimmy might gain from his parents for being so flexible?

Scenario 2

Sarah went to see the new *Transformers* movie with her mom and her friend Ben. When they got to the theater, they found out that the movie was sold out. Sarah was disappointed that she couldn't see *Transformers,* but she didn't want her fun time with her friend to end just because their first plan didn't work out. Sarah decided that she would be flexible and select another movie.

What are some powers Sarah might gain from her parents for being so flexible?

LESSON 2 EDUCATOR SCRIPT

Video Game Introduction

Setting the Stage

Educator: Creating a video game is hard work, and there are many steps.

One of the first things video game creators have to do is make a plan for the characters who will be in their video game. These are some of the things you will need to think about:

- What will the goal be?
- What obstacles will the characters face?
- What powers will they gain? How many levels will there be?

We are going to imagine that we work for Gamers Inc. They have asked us to create a plan for a video game in which the main character, Star Commander Bex, gets special powers by being flexible. The character will need these special powers to win the game and save his home planet.

1. *Distribute copies of Handout: Gamers Inc. Mission Letter, and read the letter to the group.*

Educator: The main character in this video game is Star Commander Bex, and his home planet, X-F1, is almost destroyed from hundreds of years of pollution.

To save his planet and win the game, Star Commander Bex has to complete at least four quests.

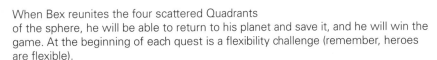

When he successfully completes each quest, he gets a Quadrant of the planet-healing sphere that will renew his home planet.

When Bex reunites the four scattered Quadrants of the sphere, he will be able to return to his planet and save it, and he will win the game. At the beginning of each quest is a flexibility challenge (remember, heroes are flexible).

2. *Show students Handout: Quest 1 Example.*

Educator: We must come up with the flexible and the stuck things that Star Commander Bex might do on each quest.

3. *Use Educator Guide: Quest 1 Example to demonstrate how this works.*

(page 1 of 2)

Video Game Introduction

Building the Video Game

Step 1: Powers

Educator: We also must decide what powers Star Commander Bex will get when he solves a quest flexibly. These are very important because the quests get harder and harder, and Star Commander Bex will need extra powers to succeed. This handout lists some ideas for special powers. Let's look at them and then decide what powers we want Star Commander Bex to be able to earn on his quest.

1. *Show students Handout: Power Brainstorm. Refer to the examples listed, then have students come up with their own special powers to list.*

Step 2: Quest Story Boarding

Educator: Listen to the first quest Star Commander Bex will go on.

2. *Reread Handout: Quest 1 with students.*
3. *Show a flexible card.*

Educator: What would Star Commander Bex do if he were flexible?

4. *Record student answers. Glue the flexible card under the quest to begin a flowchart, as shown on Handout: Quest 1 Example.*
5. *Show students a yellow power card.*

Educator: Which power will Star Commander Bex gain? (Students will use this power to accomplish the next quest).

6. *Glue the yellow power card to the flowchart.*
7. *Show a stuck card*

Educator: What would Star Commander Bex do if he were stuck?

8. *Glue the stuck card to the flowchart.*
9. *Read and glue the mud card to the flowchart.*

Educator: Decide what Star Commander Bex will do to become unstuck.

10. *Glue the flexible option card to the flowchart.*
11. *Draw arrows between all the cards on the flowchart.*
12. *Repeat these steps for all four quests..*

FLEXIBLE OPTION
Students will come up with the flexible option.

(page 2 of 2)

LESSON 2 HANDOUT

Quest 1 Example

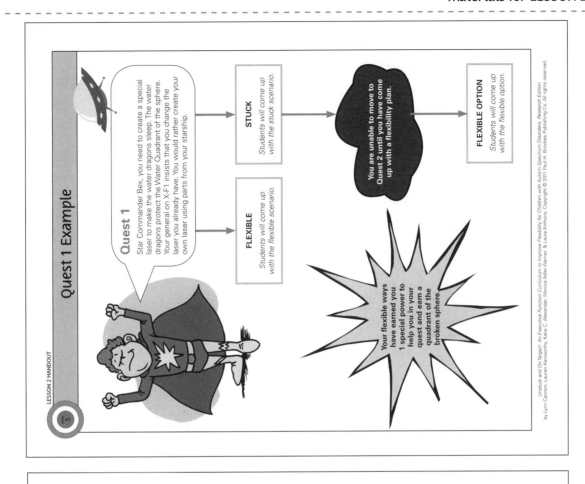

Quest 1

Star Commander Bex, you need to create a special laser to make the water dragons sleep. The water dragons protect the Water Quadrant of the sphere. Your general on X-F1 insists that you change the laser you already have. You would rather create your own laser using parts from your starship.

FLEXIBLE
Students will come up with the flexible scenario.

STUCK
Students will come up with the stuck scenario.

You are unable to move to Quest 2 until you have come up with a flexibility plan.

FLEXIBLE OPTION
Students will come up with the flexible option.

Your flexible ways have earned you 1 special power to help you in your quest and earn a quadrant of the broken sphere.

LESSON 2 HANDOUT

Gamers Inc. Mission Letter

To: Students at _____ School

From: Gamers Inc. Headquarters

Your mission:

Many galaxies away, there is a large planet that is being destroyed by hundreds of years of pollution. This planet, X-F1, has only one hope for renewal: a planet-healing sphere that long ago was shattered into four pieces that have been scattered across the galaxy. These pieces are the Water Quadrant, the Fire Quadrant, the Air Quadrant, and the Earth Quadrant.

The leaders of X-F1 have identified one hero who is able to find the pieces of the sphere: Star Commander Bex. He is the smartest, strongest, and fastest being on his home planet. He is also the best pilot of the fastest, most indestructible starship, the Galactic Bolt. With this ship, Star Commander Bex will begin a journey across the galaxy to save his home planet, X-F1.

Gamers Inc. is asking you to do the following:

1. Come up with flexible solutions so that Star Commander Bex doesn't get stuck, which would put his quests and possibly his whole mission in danger.

2. Choose the items that he will earn and use to find the Quadrants of the sphere and save his planet.

VIDEO GAME CARDS

YELLOW POWER CARD — Your flexible ways have earned you 1 special power to help you in your quest and earn a quadrant of the broken sphere.	**MUD CARD** — You are unable to move to Quest 2 until you have come up with a flexibility plan.
YELLOW POWER CARD — Your flexible ways have earned you 1 special power to help you in your quest and earn a quadrant of the broken sphere.	**MUD CARD** — You are unable to move to Quest 3 until you have come up with a flexibility plan.
YELLOW POWER CARD — Your flexible ways have earned you 1 special power to help you in your quest and earn a quadrant of the broken sphere.	**MUD CARD** — You are unable to move to Quest 4 until you have come up with a flexibility plan.
YELLOW POWER CARD — Your flexible ways have earned you 1 special power to help you in your quest and earn a quadrant of the broken sphere.	**MUD CARD** — You are unable to move to the next quest until you have come up with a flexibility plan.
FLEXIBLE OPTION	**STUCK**

VIDEO GAME CARDS

FLEXIBLE OPTION	**STUCK**
FLEXIBLE OPTION	**STUCK**
FLEXIBLE OPTION	**STUCK**
FLEXIBLE	**FLEXIBLE**
FLEXIBLE	**FLEXIBLE**

LESSON 2 HANDOUT

Power Brainstorm

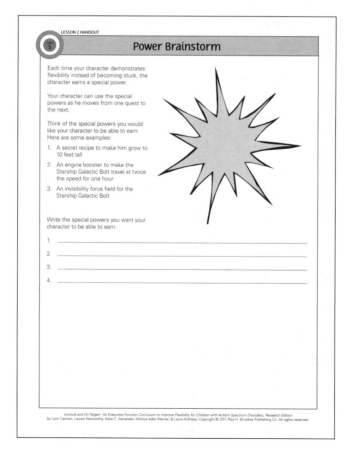

Each time your character demonstrates flexibility instead of becoming stuck, the character earns a special power.

Your character can use the special powers as he moves from one quest to the next.

Think of the special powers you would like your character to be able to earn. Here are some examples:

1. A secret recipe to make him grow to 10 feet tall
2. An engine booster to make the Starship Galactic Bolt travel at twice the speed for one hour
3. An invisibility force field for the Starship Galactic Bolt

Write the special powers you want your character to be able to earn.

1. _____
2. _____
3. _____
4. _____

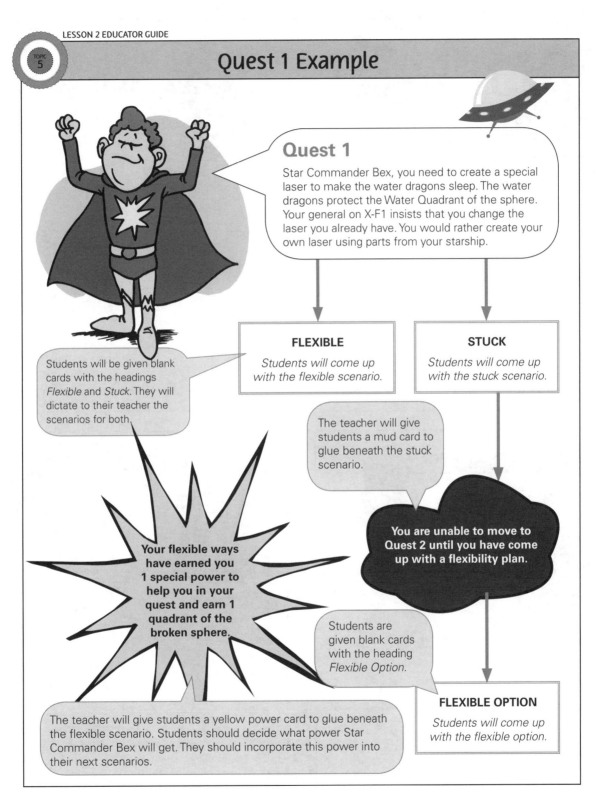

LESSON 2 EDUCATOR GUIDE

Quest 1 Example

Quest 1

Star Commander Bex, you need to create a special laser to make the water dragons sleep. The water dragons protect the Water Quadrant of the sphere. Your general on X-F1 insists that you change the laser you already have. You would rather create your own laser using parts from your starship.

FLEXIBLE

Students will come up with the flexible scenario.

STUCK

Students will come up with the stuck scenario.

Students will be given blank cards with the headings *Flexible* and *Stuck*. They will dictate to their teacher the scenarios for both.

The teacher will give students a mud card to glue beneath the stuck scenario.

You are unable to move to Quest 2 until you have come up with a flexibility plan.

Your flexible ways have earned you 1 special power to help you in your quest and earn 1 quadrant of the broken sphere.

Students are given blank cards with the heading *Flexible Option.*

The teacher will give students a yellow power card to glue beneath the flexible scenario. Students should decide what power Star Commander Bex will get. They should incorporate this power into their next scenarios.

FLEXIBLE OPTION

Students will come up with the flexible option.

Quest 1

Star Commander Bex, you need to create a special laser to make the water dragons sleep. The water dragons protect the Water Quadrant of the sphere. Your general on X-F1 insists that you change the laser you already have. You would rather create your own laser using parts from your starship.

Quest 2

Star Commander Bex, you must create a shield to protect you from the volcanic planet that is home to the Fire Quadrant of the sphere. You believe that the metal from the Dwarven Planet V-Dar will be the most powerful, but that planet is too far away.

Quest 3

Star Commander Bex, you discover that a huge storm protects the Air Quadrant of the sphere, which is hidden deep in the storm cloud. You must find a way to make it safely through the storm. Your starship's engine has become too weak to speed through the storm.

Quest 4

Star Commander Bex, you love to work with your trusted friend Commander Dash. Unfortunately, Dash is sick and won't be able to accompany you on your final quest to get the Earth Quadrant of the sphere, which is protected by constant earthquakes on its cavernous home planet.

LESSON 2 EDUCATOR SCRIPT

Marble Jar: Flexible Reputation Scenarios

Students place one marble in their jar for each flexible act. Pause at the italicized text to reflect on how the student's behavior is helping to develop reputation.

1. My favorite ice cream was sold out, so I had to order pie.

2. The swings were taken on the playground, so I went on the slide.

3. The computer was out of batteries, so I played a board game.

4. I knew my friend loved to be first in line, so I went second.

5. I couldn't find the blue marker, so I used the green one instead.

> *How does your jar look now? Based on how full your jar is,*
> *what type of a reputation does this student have? Why?*

6. My sister was watching a movie, so I used the computer instead.

7. I was going to have toast, but we were out so I chose to have cereal instead.

8. I wanted to read the new Harry Potter book, but it was checked out of the library so I chose a science fiction book.

9. My friend didn't want me to play with one of my classmates. I told him I didn't want to leave my classmate out, and I included my classmate in my game anyway.

> *Was the student flexible here? Why not? Do you think it was okay for him to choose not*
> *to be flexible? (Yes, sometimes you need to stand up for what you believe in.) What did*
> *this do to his reputation? (His jar is still very full, so he still has a flexible reputation.)*

10. I wanted a chocolate bar, but only Skittles were available. I chose to eat the Skittles even though they're not my favorite.

11. I was going to go outside to play, but it started raining. I told my teacher that I had wanted to play outside, and I got stuck thinking about how much I had wanted to play outside. My teacher tried to help me get unstuck, but it was too hard. I was so stuck that I couldn't do a Plan B and missed playing inside during recess time. Then, I was stuck because I didn't get to play, and I felt so upset that my teacher suggested that I take a break. After my break, I felt a little better, but it was harder to do my work. So, I have more homework than usual from my science class.

12. I wanted the chair closest to the door, but when I got in the room, my classmate had already taken it. I sat in another chair.

> *How does your jar look now? Highlight that even though this student got really*
> *stuck and didn't get his work done that his overall reputation is preserved. This is*
> *a good opportunity to reiterate that we all make mistakes, and that it is okay and*
> *we can learn from those mistakes. Based on how full your jar is, what type of a*
> *reputation does this student have? Why? What sorts of privileges (powers) do*
> *you think the student might get because he has such a flexible reputation?*

13. My favorite teacher was absent today, so I did math with the substitute.

Marble Jar: Flexible Reputation Scenarios

14. I play a board game every afternoon with my friend. He has gone first in the game for the last six days. He wanted to go first today. I told him I thought it would be fair if I was allowed to go first today.

15. My friend promised me that he would bring my favorite comic book back to school with him today, but he forgot it. I got so stuck thinking about how much I had wanted to read it today that I told my teacher I wasn't going to do any of my morning work. My teacher helped me, but I didn't have time to do my math work this morning because it took me so long to get unstuck.

> *How does your jar look now? Again highlight that even though this student had a difficult time that his overall reputation is still one of being a flexible student. Based on how full your jar is, what type of a reputation does this student have? Why? What sorts of privileges (powers) do you think the student might get because he has such a flexible reputation?*

16. A new student joined my classroom, so I had to change math groups.

17. My teacher wanted to rearrange the seats in the classroom. She put my desk in the last row. I told her I could not see the board from there, and asked if it would be possible to keep my old seat up front.

18. I was looking forward to doing our classroom presentations on traveling in communities in the United States. I had prepared a great presentation on light rail transportation in large cities. Right before it was my turn, our teacher told us that we had run out of time and we would finish our presentations the next day. I got so stuck thinking about how I had wanted to do my presentation today that I yelled out that I hate running out of time. I also yelled at my friend who had just presented because it felt like it was her fault. My teacher reminded me of the classroom rules, so I apologized. I still wish that I could have given my presentation on the first day.

> *How does your jar look now? Based on how full your jar is, what type of a reputation does this student have? Why? What sorts of privileges (powers) do you think the student might get because he has such a flexible reputation?*

19. We had a 2-hour delay at school because of snow, and we were not able to have music, my favorite class. I felt really upset about that and yelled out that I was so mad at the snow storm and the delay in school. My teacher reminded me that I should keep a calm voice. I asked her if we could come up with a Plan B. She reminded me that we would have music next week, and she promised me that we could listen to music during our indoor recess.

Continue with examples until you think the students understand the development and positive consequences of a flexible reputation. They should also understand the importance and validity of standing their ground in some cases and that in the end this rigidity does not negatively affect a flexible reputation.

Extensions

Generalization

School Integration

- When students are having a difficult time or come to a roadblock in naturally occurring situations throughout the day, use the image of the mud puddle to help them visualize what happens when they are stuck. Use the image of a bridge to help them visualize how to avoid the mud puddle by building a bridge over it.
- Reinforce students' demonstration of flexibility, highlighting what they were able to do as a result of their flexibility and what they would have lost if they had remained rigid and become stuck.
- When a student gains a new privilege or an accommodation is made in the student's favor, highlight for the student how his or her flexibility in the past made it possible for you to grant these privileges now.

Home Integration

Upon completion of Lesson 1, send home a copy of Home Extension 9 and Home Signoff, including the attached Flexibility Feels…Scale.

Materials for Home

- Home Extension 9 and Home Signoff

Your Goals
Getting What You Want

SPECIAL INSTRUCTIONS: The core goal of these lessons is to help students identify what goals are and how to set and achieve goals. Although it is important to introduce the concept of goals and the Goal-Plan-Do-Check (GPDC) script, please modify the activities as necessary to better meet the needs of your students.

Summary: In this topic, students learn the definition of *goal*, how to establish a goal, and how to make a plan for obtaining a goal. This topic sets forth an empirically supported approach to skill acquisition called Goal-Plan-Do-Check (GPDC).

Prerequisite skills: Understanding of the meaning of flexibility; familiarity with flexibility vocabulary; understanding of the value of flexibility with reference to a personal hero

Related skills: Core language comprehension, ability to identify concrete goals

OUTCOME—CRITERIA FOR MASTERY

1. The student defines *goal*.
2. The student identifies a goal.
3. With minimal prompts, the student applies the GPDC script to structure a multiple-step task.

TOPIC BACKGROUND AND RATIONALE

This topic introduces a fundamental script that underlies many of the activities in *Unstuck and On Target!* It is a generic and widely applicable self-regulatory/problem-solving script that provides a template for approaching a problem, situation, or project. The first part of this script is the introduction of the concept of a goal. Making the definition of *goal* explicit is a very important step for students on the autism spectrum because they can easily over-focus on details and lose sight of the main reason for, or goal of, their activity. In this topic, students are taught a standard operating procedure for reaching goals known as the GPDC. GPDC breaks down any activity into small, achievable chunks, helping the student to focus on the right goal from the beginning. It promotes flexibility by encouraging the development of a plan, revision of the plan, and development of an alternative plan (Plan B). Students are encouraged to try things out (their plan) and then go back and check on the success of the plan. This provides a prompt for the self-monitoring that is often difficult for them. An additional virtue of this approach is that the focus is on the plan, not on the student's difficulties; therefore, a breakdown in the situation can be blamed on an unhelpful plan rather than on the student. A primary focus of this curriculum is to scaffold students in their efforts to be flexible using the GPDC template. Students learn that the failure of Plan A does not have to be debilitating because there is always a Plan B.

Lesson 1 Setting and Achieving Goals Using Goal-Plan-Do-Check

PURPOSE

This lesson helps students define *goal*. In addition, this lesson introduces GPDC. Students will learn that more than one plan is often needed and that when a plan does not work, it is okay. What is needed is simply a different plan. There are three activities in this lesson.

Materials Required for All Activities

Not Included

- Whiteboard or chart paper
- Dry/wet erase markers or markers
- Video clip: Pink Panther, "Think Before You Pink" (6 minutes, 30 seconds)

Included

- Home Extension 10 and Home Signoff

Generalization

School Integration

- As often as possible, begin framing a student's actions in terms of his or her goal. For example, if a student is working to complete a handout in class, say, "So your goal is to finish this handout in class so that you don't need to take it home as homework." Similarly, highlight the actions of others in terms of goals.
- It is critical to embed GPDC language throughout the day once students have learned what each word in *Goal-Plan-Do-Check* represents (e.g., "What is your goal?" "Tell me about your plan." "Okay, if Plan A doesn't work out, what will you do for Plan B?").

Home Integration

Upon completion of Lesson 1, send home a copy of Home Extension 10 and Home Signoff.

Modifications

- For older students, consider the inclusion of more complex goals and activities.
- All students will require initial instruction in GPDC and exploration of this template. Use examples to make it as salient as possible.

Tips for the Educator

- As GPDC is taught, introduce a consistent color coding that will reinforce the concept (e.g., Goal = Blue, Plan = Green, Do = Orange, Check = Red). Use this color scheme consistently in visuals.
- Several themes are critical to the successful use of GPDC:
  a. Plans need to be specific.
  b. Some plans that seem like they will work really well do not. That is why it is important for students to learn to check the plan to see if it is working and if the goal is being achieved.
  c. Because some plans will not work, students should always be prepared to shift to a Plan B.
  d. Emphasize that good planning is not about getting it right the first time but about changing the plan when needed.

ACTIVITY 1
What Is a Goal?

☆ **Presentation**

🕑 **~5 minutes**

Materials

Not Included

- Whiteboard or chart paper
- Dry/wet erase markers or markers

Included

There are no included materials for this activity.

Instructions

The first part of this lesson presents students with a basic definition of *goal*.

1. Write the following definition on the whiteboard or a sheet of chart paper: *A goal is something that you want or need to do.*
2. To the basic definition, add the following and discuss: *A goal can be something that you want to do, something that you know how to do but want to do better, or something that you want to learn to do.*
3. Under the definition, write at least five different examples of goals and discuss them. Possibilities include the following:
    a. Goals in the classroom (something students are earning together)
    b. Goals of the school
    c. Daily personal goals, such as going to a movie
    d. Goals from students' heroes (refer to Topic 4 and the following goal bank for ideas)
4. Keep this list posted for Activity 2.

Hero Goal Bank

- SpongeBob SquarePants: Save King Neptune
- The Tick: Bring justice
- Bart Simpson: Make people laugh
- Spider-Man: Save Mary Jane
- Superman: Protect innocent people
- Batman: Protect Gotham City from crime
- Wonder Woman: Protect people
- Supergirl: Help Superman protect others
- Albert Einstein: Contribute to the science of physics
- Abraham Lincoln: Keep the United States together and end slavery
- Martin Luther King, Jr.: Create equal rights for all people
- Rosa Parks: Support civil rights
- Bill Gates: Create a computer operating system
- Luke Skywalker: Lead the Rebel Alliance
- Obi-Wan Kenobi: Train Jedi Knights
- Yoda: Lead the Jedi

ACTIVITY 2
GPDC Description, Part 1

▤ **Video and Discussion**
◷ **~15 minutes**

Materials

Not Included

- Whiteboard or chart paper
- Dry/wet erase markers or markers
- List from Activity 1
- Video clip: Pink Panther, "Think Before You Pink"
  (6 minutes, 30 seconds)

Included

There are no included materials for this activity.

Instructions

1. Ahead of time, search the Internet for the Pink Panther video clip "Think Before You Pink." Bookmark it for students to view.

2. Explain to students that once they decide what they want to do (their goal), they must decide *how* they are going to do it (their plan). Write the following on the whiteboard or chart paper. Use a different color for the goal and the plan, colors that you will use consistently throughout this topic.
   a. *Goal: what you want to do*
   b. *Plan: how you will do it*

3. Inform students that they are about to watch a video of the Pink Panther trying to meet his goal. Show the video clip. As they watch, have students determine how many plans the Pink Panther tries.

4. At the conclusion of the video, ask the following questions:
   a. What was the Pink Panther's goal? (to cross the street)
   b. Did the Pink Panther use one plan or more than one plan? (Respond to students' answers.)
   c. Can anyone tell how many plans the Pink Panther used? (There were 12 attempts!)
   d. Can anyone name some of the Pink Panther's plans? (walk, follow the silly directions on the walk/don't walk sign, pretend to be a little old woman, fly while wearing an eagle suit, pole jump, use rocket propulsion, charge as a knight on a horse, walk a tightrope above the street, shoot out of a cannon, build a bridge from one window to another above the street, and pretend to be a mother cat leading her kittens across the street)

5. Explain that it is not enough to have just one plan—Plan A. Students need to have at least one other plan—Plan B. In fact, they may need many plans.

6. Underneath what you wrote in Step 2, write the following:
   a. *Start with a Plan A and a Plan B.*
   b. *You may need many plans.*

7. Be sure to emphasize to each student that he or she is a capable plan maker. The failure of a plan is not the failure of a person.

8. Keep what you have written in sight for Activity 3.

ACTIVITY 3
GPDC Description, Part 2

⭐ **Presentation**

🕐 **~10 minutes**

Materials

Not Included

- Whiteboard or chart paper
- Dry/wet erase markers or markers
- List from Activities 1 and 2

Included

- Home Extension 10 and Home Signoff

Instructions

1. Explain that once students decide what they want to do (their goal) and how they are going to do it (their plan), they must do it. To help students understand this concept, use the analogy of planning a trip. They first decide where they are going, then they plan which routes they will take or how they will get there, and then they go on the trip.

2. Ask, "How will you know whether or not the plan/trip route worked?" Students should respond that they would know it worked if they arrive at the correct place.

3. Explain that the key is to check, or evaluate, a plan: "Once you have tried your plan, you must stop and think about whether it helped you get where you want to go."

4. Continue adding to the list from Activities 1 and 2. Under *You may need many plans,* write,
   a. *Do: Try your plan.*
   b. *Check: Stop and think. Did my plan work? Do I need to try a different plan?*

5. Review Home Extension 10 with students.

Home Extension 10

Summary: During this lesson, students have learned the definition of a goal and how to work toward a goal through a strategy called Goal-Plan-Do-Check (GPDC). GPDC is a problem-solving script that helps students address a problem, situation, or project. GPDC builds on the strengths of students with autism spectrum disorders (ASD) by systematically breaking down an activity into small, achievable chunks and helps the student focus and sustain efforts toward meeting the specified goal.

In addition to supporting problem solving, GPDC promotes flexibility, self-monitoring, and self-esteem.

- **Flexibility:** GPDC process requires that students try out and revise plans as necessary, creating alternative plans (Plan B),

- **Self-monitoring:** Students must continuously monitor the results of their efforts in order to effectively "check" their plans.

- **Self-esteem:** When things do not work out, the focus is on the plan and not on the student's difficulties. The inadequacies of Plan A are not about the person being "bad" or incapable but reflect the need for a new plan, and students learn that they are capable of generating many plans and achieving success.

Goal-Plan-Do-Check
Goal: Decide on something you want to do (have a friend over for a playdate, get an *A* on your test).
Plan: Make a plan for how you will do it.

Start with a Plan A and a Plan B. Sometimes you need more than one plan to reach your goal.

Do: Try your plan.
Check: Stop and think about how your plan is working.

What is a goal? A goal is something that you want or need to do.

Why is this lesson important? Students with ASD have a cognitive style that lends itself to a focus on details rather than the overall meaning or reason for their activity. Explicit instruction on goals and meeting goals helps students with ASD adjust for this cognitive style and improve their effectiveness.

There are several things you can do at home to help your child learn as fully as possible. The more and varied experiences each student has outside the classroom, the better he or she is able to learn and apply that learning.

1. Review the definition of *goal* with your child.

2. Provide examples of your own goals, large and small.

3. Use GPDC to give your child an example of how you set and work tow

4. Use the GPDC language as often as possible at home. For example, s
   The goal is to buy groceries. With your child, think about each step yo
   your goal. The first few steps of the plan might look like this:

   a. Plan what we want to eat next week

Source: Ylvisaker (2006).

Home Signoff

Date sent home: _____

I have read
Home Extension _____

_____
Parent signature

Please return this page to
the social skills teacher by _____

HOME EXTENSION 10 *(continued)*

Home Extension 10

Home Extension Reflections

Upon completion of the Home Extension, please have your child complete this form and return it to school. If needed, your child may dictate his or her answers to you.

What goal did you talk about?

_____

_____

What do you think is the best part of the plan you talked about?

_____

_____

_____

Do you have any advice for your parent(s) to improve upon GPDC technique?

_____

_____

_____

(page 3 of 3)

HOME EXTENSION 10 *(continued)*

Home Extension 10

b. See if we already have those things at home.

c. Make of list of the things we want to eat that we do not have.

5. Here is another example: Say your child wants to watch his or her favorite TV show at 8:00 P.M. tonight. Ask your child, "Is that your goal?" "What should your plan be to achieve that goal?" The first few steps of the plan might look like this:

   a. Complete math homework by 6:00 P.M.

   b. Eat dinner and load dishwasher by 7:00 P.M.

   c. Take shower.

During the next lessons, students will begin to practice Goal-Plan-Do-Check.

(page 2 of 3)

Lesson 2 GPDC Application and Practice

 PURPOSE

Students practice using GPDC to solve problems and obtain goals that are meaningful to them. This guided practice is critical to fostering the routine use of GPDC. In addition to guided practice, it is essential that teachers embed GPDC language in every routine of the day. There are two activities in this lesson; one is optional.

Materials Required for All Activities

Not Included

- Whiteboard or chart paper
- Dry/wet erase markers
- Cereal
- Milk
- Bowl
- Spoon
- Paper towels

Included

There are no included materials for this lesson.

Generalization

School Integration

- Continue with the generalization activities from Lesson 1, embedding GPDC language as frequently as possible.
- When students encounter problems or need to develop goals during their everyday routines, use GPDC to approach the situation. Ask a student, "What is your goal?" and begin to guide the student through developing his or her GPDC. Emphasize the importance of making a Plan B. As the student begins to demonstrate proficiency with this approach, fade the level of prompting.

Home Integration

There are no Home Extensions for this lesson.

Modifications

- Because the purpose of this lesson is to help students apply GPDC to a routine activity with which they are familiar, select an activity that best matches your comfort and students' familiarity and interests. In addition, it should be an activity that is destined to yield humorous results along the way (such as pouring milk—just a little—outside the bowl). Any number of activities would satisfy the objective of this lesson.
- If dietary restrictions prevent you from using cereal, making a sandwich is a good alternative.

Tips for the Educator

This lesson will most likely result in some degree of mess. Prepare students who are distressed by such circumstances in advance of the activity.

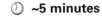

GPDC Practice (Optional)

👥 **Group Activity**
🕐 **~5 minutes**

Materials

Not Included

- Whiteboard or chart paper
- Dry/wet erase markers or markers

Included

There are no included materials for this activity.

Instructions

This activity is optional and can be included if you feel that your students need an additional example.

1. Explain that students can look at every situation, determine what their goal is, make a plan for how to do it, do it, and check or reflect on how it went.
2. Use the example of going to the movies. First, elicit discussion about what the goal is. Write the goal on the board. Examples include the following:
   a. *To go see a movie*
   b. *To go to the movies and have fun*
3. Discuss what the plan should be. Write the plan on the board. One example follows:
   a. *Decide what movie to see.*
   b. *Invite a friend.*
   c. *Decide what time to arrive.*
   d. *Decide whether you want to buy tickets beforehand.*
   e. *Decide whether you want to buy a snack.*
4. Pretend to carry out (do) the event. Have the students close their eyes and picture themselves going through the sequence of events that they have planned.
5. Tell the students that a very important part of the process is to check how the plan went. Ask them how they thought the plan went.
6. Next, ask them to close their eyes and picture the event with something going wrong. For example, suppose they get the movie theater and the movie they want to see is sold out. What would they do? Do they have a Plan B?
7. Ask students whether there is anything they would do differently the next time they plan this trip.

ACTIVITY 2
GPDC Practice

👥 **Group Activity**
🕐 **~30 minutes**

Materials

Not Included

- Whiteboard or chart paper
- Dry/wet erase markers or markers
- Cereal
- Milk
- Bowl
- Spoon
- Paper towels (in case of a milk spill)

Included

There are no included materials for this activity.

Instructions

This is intended as a playful way to try GPDC and refine the students' approach to problem solving.

1. Briefly review GPDC. Introduce this activity by stating, "Today we will practice using Goal-Plan-Do-Check to make a bowl of cereal." Ask how many students know how to make cereal.
2. Show the students all of the ingredients.
3. Ask them to tell you what the goal is. Write it on the board.
4. Ask them to tell you what they think the first step in the plan should be. Write the step on the board. Have them continue giving you the steps, and record them in order on the board.
5. When they believe they have given you all the steps, explain that you are now going to *do* their plan. Follow the steps on the board *exactly*. If the step says to put the cereal in the bowl, put the box of cereal in the bowl (without opening it).
6. Continue carrying out the plan until you have done all the steps.
7. Ask students to *check*—decide how their plan worked. Have them use the following scale.

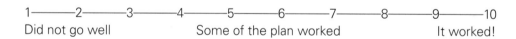

1———2———3———4———5———6———7———8———9———10
Did not go well   Some of the plan worked   It worked!

8. Ask them whether any part of the plan needs to be fixed. Next to the original plan, write *Plan B*. Tell them that sometimes when checking, they might decide that they need a Plan B, which will bring them back to the plan stage.
9. Go through each step again, rewriting the steps that worked and amending the steps that need to be changed.
10. *Do* the new plan by following the steps on the board. This time it should work.
11. Then *check*—have students use the scale and discuss how the new plan went.

1———2———3———4———5———6———7———8———9———10
Did not go well   Some of the plan worked   It worked!

12. To summarize the activity, highlight the students' flexibility in generating another plan and their expertise at plan making.

Lesson 3 GPDC Application and Practice

 PURPOSE

In Lesson 3, students continue to practice GPDC. The student identifies a goal that he or she needs to address in the context of the school day and develops a plan to begin working toward it using Mission Possible. The student will select at least one teacher (not an instructor of this intervention protocol) to whom he or she will teach GPDC and invite to assist with his or her Mission Possible (i.e., goal). In addition to this critical guided practice, it is essential that teachers embed GPDC language in every routine of the day. There are two activities in this lesson.

Materials Required for All Activities

Not Included

- Whiteboard or chart paper
- Dry/wet erase markers or markers

Included

- Handout: What Is Your Goal? (one per student)
- Educator Script: What Is Your Goal?
- Handout: Mission Possible (one per student/distribute to selected teachers at the end of the lesson)
- Educator Script: Mission Possible
- Classroom Extension 4
- Home Extension 11 and Home Signoff

Generalization

School Integration

- Ensure that students provide their selected teacher with a copy of Handout: Mission Possible as well as Classroom Extension 4.
- Continue with the generalization activities from Lesson 1 and 2, embedding GPDC language as frequently as possible.
- Students should work on their Mission Possible (i.e., goal) every day. This is best accomplished by assigning a time when students can address it and receive teacher support. Students should have selected a goal relevant to the school day, so time for practice should be a natural selection.

Home Integration

Upon completion of the lesson, send home a copy of Home Extension 11 and Home Signoff.

Modifications

- Older students may respond better to simply referring to their work on personal goals as *My Goal* or something similar rather than *Mission Possible*.
- There may be value in informing students that young adults and adults set goals and work toward them continuously. Normalizing goal acquisition can be a powerful way to support older students.

LESSON 3

What Is Your Goal?

    👤 **Individual Activity**
    🕐 **~15 minutes**

Materials

Not Included

- Whiteboard or chart paper
- Dry/wet erase markers or markers

Included

- Handout: What Is Your Goal? (one per student)
- Educator Script: What Is Your Goal?

Instructions

The objective of this activity is to help students begin to think about their goal. Students should focus on a goal that is personally meaningful but is also something that requires improvement at school. At the conclusion of this activity, each student should have an identified goal.

1. Rewrite the definition of *goal* from Lesson 1.
2. Distribute Handout: What Is Your Goal? to students to help them brainstorm possible goals. Have them work on their handouts individually. *Some students will require moderate one-to-one support from the educational team.* Refer to Educator Script: What Is Your Goal? for examples of student goals.
3. Upon completion of the handout, each student should have one goal that will be the first he or she will address in Activity 2.

Mission Possible

    👤 **Individual Activity**
    🕐 **~15 minutes**

Materials

Not Included

- Students' goals from Lesson 1

Included

- Handout: Mission Possible (one per student/distribute to selected teachers at the end of the lesson)
- Educator Script: Mission Possible
- Home Extension 11 and Home Signoff

Instructions

1. Review GPDC with students.
2. Distribute Handout: Mission Possible. Students should begin working on this handout independently, but most will require one-to-one teacher support to complete it.
3. Have each student select at least one of his or her other teachers to whom the student will teach GPDC and invite to participate in his or her Mission Possible (i.e., goal). Write that teacher's name at the top of each student's handout.
4. Inform students of when they are scheduled to work on their Mission Possible with the teacher they select.
5. As needed, plan times in the student's day to provide a naturally occurring opportunity to practice his or her Mission Possible.
6. Once students begin creating and testing their plan, work with them to refine the plan or use a Plan B as needed.
7. Regularly implement and evaluate the plan.
8. Provide selected teachers a copy of Handout: Mission Possible.
9. Review Home Extension 11 with students.

LESSON 3 EDUCATOR SCRIPT

TOPIC
6

What Is Your Goal?

Directions

1. You are going to decide on a goal that you want to start working on at school. Choose the one that means the most to you. If you like more than one, your teacher can help you choose the first one that you will work on.

2. Circle the goals that you would like to work on.

3. Place a star next to the goal that you'll start with.

> In this teacher's edition of the student handout, we provide examples of the kinds of specific goals that will be the most helpful. It is critical that each student's goal be narrow in focus, specific, and attainable in the short term. If a student chooses a long-term goal, help him or her narrow the goal to one of its steps or components.

- I want to be a good friend.

  I want to say at least one kind thing to one friend.

  I will cooperate with my friends when we work together in class.

  I will greet my classmates with happiness and respond to their greetings.

- I want to be a good student.

  I want to be a good student and memorize my multiplication facts.

  I will practice my 5s tables three times a day (homeroom, relaxation, and homework).

- I want more privileges or freedom.

  I want to earn 5 minutes of free time at the end of the day.

- Others?

1._____

_____

_____

2._____

_____

_____

LESSON 3 HANDOUT

6

What Is Your Goal?

Directions

1. You are going to decide on a goal that you want to start working on at school. Choose the one that means the most to you. If you like more than one, your teacher can help you choose the first one that you will work on.

2. Circle the goals that you would like to work on.

3. Place a star next to the goal that you will start with.

- I want to be a good friend.
- I want to be a good student.
- I want more privileges or freedom.
- Others?

1._____

_____

_____

2._____

_____

_____

LESSON 3 EDUCATOR SCRIPT

Mission Possible

Name: _____ Date: _____

Teacher to share Mission Possible with: _____

> It can be helpful to include a picture or an icon of the student's hero on this worksheet.

Goal: *What do you want to do?*
_____
_____
_____

> Start with student's goal from Lesson 1. Upon mastery of that goal, continue to introduce new goals that are meaningful to the student.

Plan A: *How do you want to do it?*
_____
_____

Plan B: *How*
_____

> You may find that you can use one handout across several attempts, making revisions as necessary. However, it may be useful to print one copy with the goal already written, so that there is less work to do as the student progresses.
>
> Once a plan is working, copy a sheet that has the working plans already written to continue decreasing the amount of work required. Working on a computer template can also be helpful.
>
> You may also find it helpful to provide one number for each line to guide students (e.g.,1 on the first line, 2 on the second).
>
> Creating a plan requires a fine balance. It cannot be so detailed that there are 30 steps to the plan, but the plan needs to be specific enough that the student can follow it. If the student appears to be either too specific or not specific enough in his or her plan, provide guidance in sculpting the plan.

Do: *When*
_____

Check: *How did it go? (circle one)*

1———2———3———4———5———6———7

Did not go well   Some of it worked

LESSON 3 HANDOUT

Mission Possible

Name: _____ Date: _____

Teacher to share Mission Possible with: _____

Goal: *What do you want to do?*
_____
_____
_____

Plan A: *How do you want to do it?*
_____
_____

Plan B: *How do you want to do it if Plan A does not work?*
_____
_____

Do: *When do you want to try out your plan?*
_____
_____

Check: *How did it go? (circle one)*

1——2——3——4——5——6——7——8——9——10

Did not go well   Some of the plan worked   It worked!

Classroom Extension 4

TOPIC 6

Teacher: _____ **Student initials:** _____ **Date:** _____

Summary: Students are learning a problem-solving script known as Goal-Plan-Do-Check.

What is Goal-Plan-Do-Check?
Goal-Plan-Do-Check is a simple, systematic approach to goal selection and accomplishment. It is empirically supported to help individuals improve problem solving and skill acquisition.

What difference will this make in the classroom?
Students who are able to solve problems independently are better able to participate successfully and independently in your class.

What should I do to help my student(s)?
The following must be implemented across settings/classes and teachers for students to fully learn and apply the concept of Goal-Plan-Do-Check (also called Mission Possible). It requires simply integrating a few key words and phrases and dedicating a little extra time to helping students apply it in your class.

- As often as possible, use the phrase "What is your goal?" to help students maintain goal clarity and goal-directed persistence.

- When there is a time to address your student's Mission Possible, guide him or her through the application of the plan that has been developed.

- When a student has a consistent difficulty, it may be helpful to use Goal-Plan-Do-Check to approach the difficulty. Please help protect the student from too many Missions and use a triage approach if there are several difficulties worthy of targeting. In the beginning, address one goal at a time, progressing to no more than about three.

- In the beginning, students will have difficulty generating Goal-Plan-Do-Check during a problem situation, but with practice, this will become easier.

- Students have learned that they frequently will need a Plan A and a Plan B and sometimes many other plans. Please encourage this contingency plan approach in your class. It will help your students be flexible in anticipation of potential breakdowns in the original plan.

- Students will need reminders to make goals and plans specific and that plans should be added to gradually.

Key words and phrases
- Identify/label the issue (e.g., "Is this your goal?" "What is your goal?" "Do you have a plan?" "What is your plan?" "Do you have a Plan B?").

- Offer a strategy (e.g., "Maybe we can…").

- Offer general reassurance and reinforcement (e.g., "That was great!" You're doing a great job with your plan; I think it's working!" "I can see that you're working on your goal!").

Begin using this problem-solving approach immediately. Use it to frame how you might approach a solution to a given problem, narrating aloud your goal and your plan.

Home Extension 11

Summary: During this lesson, students have continued to practice Goal-Plan-Do-Check (GPDC). Please see Home Extension 10 for more details about GPDC.

There are several things you can do at home to help your child learn as fully as possible. The more experiences each student has outside the classroom, the better he or she is able to learn and apply that learning.

1. Complete Mission Possible Home with your child. You will also find a script called "Home Teacher Script" for your child's use in teaching you how to establish a GPDC that you can approach together at home. Using this script, your child will pretend to be the teacher while you pretend to be the student. This kind of role reversal is an incredibly powerful teaching tool for children.

2. Use the GPDC language as often as possible at home. For example, say you need to go shopping. The goal is to buy clothes. With your child, think about each step you need in your plan to achieve your goal. The first few steps of the plan might look like this:

   a. Plan what we want to wear next week

   b. See if we already have those things at home.

   c. Make of list of the things we want to wear that we do not have.

3. Here is another example. Say your child wants to play video games after lunch. Ask your child, "Is that your goal?" "What should your plan be to achieve that goal?" The first few steps of the plan might look like this:

   a. Complete English homework by 10:00 A.M.

   b. Eat lunch by 11:00 A.M.

   c. Ask brother to use video game system.

We are getting ready to start a new topic that will include more strategies for improving flexibility. Please stay tuned.

Home Signoff

Date sent home: _____

I have read
Home Extension _____

_____
Parent signature

Please return this page to
the social skills teacher by _____

HOME EXTENSION 11 (continued)

Mission Possible Home

Date: _____

Goal: *What do you want to do?*

1. Go to the grocery store to get groceries for the family.
2. Prepare a snack for the family.
3. Go on a playdate.
4. Get ready in the morning.

Plan A: *How do you want to do it?*

_____
_____
_____

Plan B: *How do you want to do it if Plan A doesn't work?*

_____
_____
_____

Do: *When do you want to try out your plan?*

_____
_____

Check: *How did it go? (circle one)*

1   2   3   4   5   6   7   8   9   10

Did not go well   Some of it worked   It worked!

(page 3 of 3)

Unstuck and On Target!: An Executive Function Curriculum to Improve Flexibility for Children with Autism Spectrum Disorders, Research Edition
by Lynn Cannon, Lauren Kenworthy, Katie C. Alexander, Monica Adler Werner, & Laura Anthony. Copyright © 2011 Paul H. Brookes Publishing Co. All rights reserved.

HOME EXTENSION 11 (continued)

Home Teacher Script

Do this at home with a parent. You get to be the teacher and help your parent fill out Mission Possible Home. Please use this script to help you.

STEP 1:

Teacher: "What do you want to do? We get to pick one of these goals to work on at home!"

Read the goals on Mission Possible Home with your parent. Then, wait for your parent to choose a goal to work on.

STEP 2:

Teacher: "That's a great pick! Now we need to make a plan together. Let's start with the first step and think about what we should do next. Try to make it as specific as you can, and I'll help, too."

Work with your parent to create a Plan A. Ask your parent to write out the plan on Mission Possible Home.

STEP 3:

Teacher: "You know what? It's not enough to make a Plan A. You also need a Plan B just in case Plan A doesn't work like you want it to. Let's think about something that could get in the way of our plan working like something we need is missing. Can you think of anything? Let's think of a Plan B that would help us get around that problem and still meet our goal."

Work with your parent to create a Plan B. Ask your parent to write out the Plan B on Mission Possible Home.

STEP 4:

Teacher: "When do you want to try your new plan?"

Write down when you will try it. Write this in the *Do* section on Mission Possible Home.

Once you have tried your plan, remember to check it!

(page 2 of 3)

Unstuck and On Target!: An Executive Function Curriculum to Improve Flexibility for Children with Autism Spectrum Disorders, Research Edition
by Lynn Cannon, Lauren Kenworthy, Katie C. Alexander, Monica Adler Werner, & Laura Anthony. Copyright © 2011 Paul H. Brookes Publishing Co. All rights reserved.

Extensions

Generalization

School Integration

- As often as possible, begin framing a student's actions in terms of his or her goal. Similarly, highlight the actions of others in terms of goals. Embed GPDC language throughout the day once students have learned what each word in *Goal-Plan-Do-Check* represents.
- When students encounter problems or need to develop goals during their everyday routines, use GPDC to approach the situation.
- Upon completion of Lesson 3, Activity 2, students should provide their selected teacher with a copy of Handout: Mission Possible as well as Classroom Extension 4.
- Assign a time when students can address their Mission Possible (i.e., goal) every day and receive teacher support

Home Integration

- Upon completion of Lesson 1, send home a copy of Home Extension 10 and Home Signoff, including the attached Home Extension Reflections.
- Upon completion of Lesson 3, send home a copy of Home Extension 11 and Home Signoff, including the attached Home Teacher Script and Mission Possible Home.

Materials for Home

- Home Extension 10 and Home Signoff
- Home Extension 11 and Home Signoff

Reference

Ylvisaker, M. (2006). *Tutorial: Self-regulation/executive function routines after TBI.* Available on The Brain Injury Association of New York State web site: http://www.projectlearnet.org/tutorials/sr_ef_routines.html

Scripts That Help You Be Flexible

SPECIAL INSTRUCTIONS: The core goal of these lessons is to help students make a habit of using three specific flexibility scripts. Although it is important to teach and practice each of these scripts, please modify the activities as necessary to better meet your students' needs.

Summary: The goal of Topic 7 is to teach students three self-regulatory scripts that, combined with the previously introduced GPDC, give students a set of cognitive routines for behaving flexibly. The three scripts are Big Deal/Little Deal, Choice/No Choice, and Handling the Unexpected. These scripts are practiced repeatedly, reinforced visually, and incorporated into multiple activities at school and at home so that they become automatic for students, teachers, and parents.

Prerequisite skills: Understanding of the meaning of flexibility; familiarity with flexibility vocabulary; understanding of the value of flexibility with reference to a personal hero and concrete social-emotional goals

Related skills: Core language comprehension, ability to participate in group discussion and activities

OUTCOME—CRITERIA FOR MASTERY

1. With minimal adult prompts, the student applies the Big Deal/Little Deal script to evaluate a situation and respond accordingly.
2. With minimal adult prompts, the student applies the Choice/No Choice script to evaluate a situation and accept a requirement.
3. With minimal adult prompts, the student applies the Handling the Unexpected script to do or accept something unusual.

TOPIC BACKGROUND AND RATIONALE

Flexibility is a self-regulation skill. Self-regulation is established through internalized self-talk, and students with ASD need explicit instruction in self-regulatory self-talk about how to be flexible. Students will not internalize these critical self-regulatory scripts unless the scripts 1) become a habit for teachers and parents in their interactions with students, 2) are practiced repeatedly, and 3) are visually reinforced. This topic is designed to teach difficult-to-learn flexibility skills in a format that is specifically tailored to the cognitive strengths and weaknesses typically found among students with ASD. The rationale for each of the three scripts is as follows:

- The Big Deal/Little Deal self-regulatory script helps students distinguish what is important from what is not important so that they can be less anxious about situations of lesser importance and take seriously situations of greater importance. It also gives students a strategy for changing a big deal into a little deal when possible. This script should be useful to help students 1) break a perseverative set, 2) avoid negative behaviors when staff need to move beyond a matter that is truly unimportant, 3) avoid negative interactions with other students over minor provocations and generate a repair for the situation, and 4) engage in something important when they would prefer not to.

- With the Choice/No Choice self-regulatory script, students learn to 1) distinguish what is within their power to change and what is not, 2) break a perseverative set and stop trying to influence something they cannot change, and 3) identify when their contribution is necessary to an activity.

- The Handling the Unexpected script gives students a step-by-step approach to adjusting to the unexpected. Children with ASD rely on very consistent routines and become upset when change occurs or their expectations are violated. Because they need routine, it is useful to specifically teach them strategies for handling unexpected violations of routine.

Lesson 1 Big Deal/Little Deal

 ## PURPOSE

Students, teachers, and parents learn the Big Deal/Little Deal script and incorporate it into their daily conversation. There are three activities in this lesson.

Materials Required for All Activities

Not Included

- Whiteboard or chart paper
- Dry/wet erase markers or markers
- Marker
- Masking tape

 ### Included

- Educator Script: Big Deal/Little Deal
- Big Deal/Little Deal Cards (print double-sided on card stock)
- Visual: Big Deal/Little Deal 1–10 Scale
- Classroom Extension 5
- Home Extension 12 and Home Signoff

Generalization

School Integration

Distribute Classroom Extension 5 and Educator Script: Big Deal/Little Deal to all teaching staff so teachers can implement strategies when working with students.

Home Integration

Upon completion of Lesson 1, send home a copy of Home Extension 12 and Home Signoff. Home Extension 12 includes Big Deal/Little Deal for parents to read and complete with their child. Giving the student the role of teacher is a useful way to reinforce the material.

Modifications

For older students, use activities that are more age appropriate and that cater to their interests. Students may be interested in analyzing Big Deal/Little Deal in terms of their hero's life, historical events, or scientific discoveries.

ACTIVITY 1
Big Deal/Little Deal Introduction

☆ **Presentation**

🕐 **~5–10 minutes**

Materials

Not Included

- Whiteboard or chart paper
- Dry/wet erase markers or markers

Included

- Educator Script: Big Deal/Little Deal

Instructions

This lesson introduces students to the basic definition of *big deal/little deal* and a general script to apply the concept when the opportunity presents itself.

1. Review an earlier activity about being flexible. Say, "I am going to make a few statements. After each one, I want you to give me a thumbs-up if you agree, or a thumbs-down if you disagree."
   a. It is possible to always get everything I want.
   b. It always feels better to be flexible than to be stuck.
   c. Sometimes what I want is not possible.
   d. What I want is not always possible.
2. Ask students if anyone would like to volunteer to talk about how their Mission Possible is going. This would be a helpful place for you to talk about a goal that you are working toward and how your plan is going.
3. Use Educator Script: Big Deal/Little Deal to introduce students to this critical phrase.
4. As you go through the script, record salient points and examples on the whiteboard.

ACTIVITY 2
Big Deal/Little Deal Practice

👥 **Group Activity**

🕐 **~5–10 minutes**

Materials

Not Included

- Whiteboard or chart paper
- Dry/wet erase markers or markers

Included

- Big Deal/Little Deal Cards (print double-sided on card stock)

Instructions

In this activity, students practice applying their new knowledge.

1. Give each student one Big Deal/Little Card. One side of the card should say "Big Deal," and the other should say "Little Deal."
2. Read the following scenarios, and ask students to vote on each one using one of the cards. Is it a big deal or a little deal?
   a. You break your leg.
   b. There is nothing at all to eat in your house for a week.
   c. You are not picked to be first in line for an activity.
   d. You cannot sit where you want during lunch.
   e. The lunch menu changes at the last minute.
   f. Art is canceled because the teacher is sick.
   g. Your pet dies.
   h. Your friend gets ahead of you in line, and you get so upset that you hit him.
   i. Your teacher asks you to revise an essay that you wrote.
   j. You fail a subject because you refuse to revise your work.
   k. Your friend believes in the Loch Ness Monster, but you do not.
   l. Your classmate supported a presidential candidate that you oppose.
3. Keep a tally of votes on the whiteboard, and discuss disagreements.
4. Generate additional examples from your experiences with students, and invite students to offer scenarios. Review at least 10 scenarios.

ACTIVITY 3
Converting Big Deals to Little Deals

👥 **Group Activity**

🕐 **~5–10 minutes**

Materials

Not Included

- Marker
- Masking tape

Included

- Visual: Big Deal/Little Deal 1–10 Scale
- Home Extension 12 and Home Signoff

Instructions

1. Introduce the idea that some things that are a big deal can be changed into a little deal, but some cannot. The death of a student's pet is a big deal that cannot be turned into a little deal; a student needs time and the support of family and school to get over this type of situation.

2. But some big deals *can* be turned into little deals. For example, if a student works really hard on an essay and even adds pictures, and then the essay gets stepped on by mistake and torn, that feels like a big deal to the student. But if a teacher can help the student print out a new copy of the essay, the big deal can be turned into a little deal.

3. Place a long piece of masking tape on the floor in an area with plenty of space. Write the numbers 1–10 along the tape.

4. Post Visual Big Deal/Little Deal 1–10 Scale so all students can see it. Read the following scenarios one at a time, and ask students to stand on the number on the masking tape that shows how big a deal each scenario is to them. (Explain ahead of time that these are personal opinions; situations feel different to every person.)

    a. You lose your homework.
    b. You break your pencil.
    c. You cannot go outside for recess because it is raining.
    d. Your pet dies.
    e. You stub your toe.
    f. You have a fight with your friend.
    g. You cannot have dessert.
    h. You lose $20.
    i. You trip and fall down the stairs.
    j. You get a C on your science test.
    k. The computer crashes before you can save your work.

5. After you have read several scenarios, ask students to identify how they would make each big deal into a little deal. Then, have them move to the number that represents this little deal.

6. Review Home Extension 12 with students.

Big Deal/Little Deal

As you highlight major points, record them on the whiteboard.

Little Deal

A little deal is something that

- Can be mildly annoying
- You can ignore
- Requires a small change in plans
- Does not really change anything important
- Is a temporary problem
- You can put up with to get something else you really want

Discuss big deal ideas that are important for friends to agree on (e.g., respect for each other) as well as little deal ideas about which friends or classmates can agree to disagree.

Highlight examples, including some involving yourself:

- I wanted to pack a ham sandwich for lunch this morning, but my husband/wife ate all the ham! At first I started to get angry, and then I decided this was really a little deal and that I could make myself a cheese sandwich, which I also like.
- Sam's friend John believes that T-Rex dinosaurs were the fiercest of all, but Sam disagrees. At first, he gets angry and does not want to play with John, but then he decides that this is a little deal because they can agree to disagree and still have fun together.

Big Deal

A big deal is something that

- You cannot get over quickly
- You cannot ignore
- You cannot develop an alternative for
- Changes something really important for a long time
- Means you lose something you cannot get back
- Is worth standing up for (you may need to review this phrase with students)

Highlight examples:

- Use heroes that students have selected—Rosa Parks thought that having to always sit at the back of the bus was a big deal. Obi-Wan Kenobi thought that stopping Darth Vader from dominating the universe was a big deal.
- Use concrete examples that are meaningful to students—getting all their points for good behavior is a big deal because it earns them something they want. Keeping a friend is a big deal. Finding a way to have fun with Plan B when Plan A has failed is a big deal.

LITTLE DEAL	LITTLE DEAL
LITTLE DEAL	LITTLE DEAL
LITTLE DEAL	LITTLE DEAL
LITTLE DEAL	LITTLE DEAL
LITTLE DEAL	LITTLE DEAL

BIG DEAL	BIG DEAL
BIG DEAL	BIG DEAL
BIG DEAL	BIG DEAL
BIG DEAL	BIG DEAL
BIG DEAL	BIG DEAL

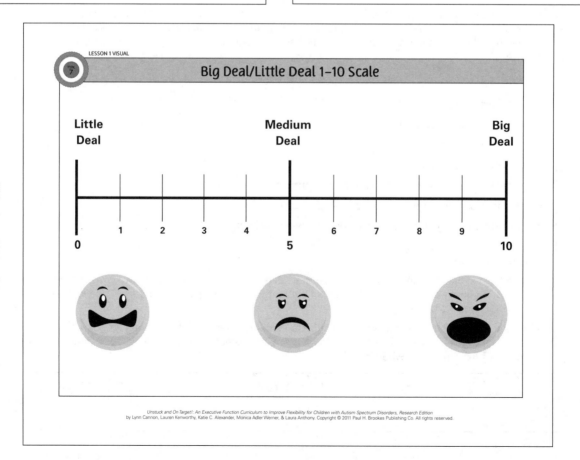

LESSON 1 VISUAL

Big Deal/Little Deal 1–10 Scale

Classroom Extension 5

Teacher: _____ Student initials: _____ Date: _____

Summary: Students are learning a self-regulatory script called Big Deal/Little Deal to help them behave flexibly.

What is Big Deal/Little Deal? The Big Deal/Little Deal script helps students distinguish what is important from what is not important so that they can be less anxious about situations of lesser importance and take seriously situations of greater importance. It also provides students with a framework for changing what feels like a big deal into a little deal.

What difference will this make in the classroom? Students who are able to distinguish what is important from what is not important are better able to participate successfully and independently in school activities. Students who have a vocabulary for labeling a big deal can seek help to address the problem, or turn it into a little deal, without resorting to disruptive behaviors.

What should I do to help my student(s)?

1. Use the phrase *big deal/little deal* to frame students' viewpoints about events.

2. Initially, use the Big Deal/Little Deal script at times when a student is not upset to avoid creating negative associations with this script from the beginning.

3. When a student encounters a disappointment, an unwanted request for a change in behavior, or an irritating behavior in another student, educational staff can ask the student if it is a big deal or a little deal. This will only be successful if staff respect student responses. The Big Deal/Little Deal script is not meant to allow adults to impose their own viewpoint that specific events or requests are little deals, when students report that they are big deals. Rather, the script is meant to allow teaching staff to help students automatically access the concept that not everything is a big deal and that students can decide how much they care about specific events or requests and respond appropriately.

4. When a student has identified something as a big deal, ask the student whether the big deal can be made into a little deal, and provide suggestions if appropriate.

5. Highlight the Big Deal/Little Deal script in your own actions and reactions to events and demands. Praise students when they do the same.

Key words and phrases

- Ask students to identify/label an issue (e.g., "Is this is a big deal or a little deal?").

- If students are uncertain how to label the issue, scaffold their response (e.g., "This is just a little deal because we can _____").

- When something is a big deal to the student, prompt problem solving (e.g., "Can we make this into a little deal? What if we _____?").

- As staff and students become familiar with this script, it should also be used in an abbreviated version whenever appropriate. Staff or students can simply ask, "Is this a big deal or a little deal? Can we change it to a little deal?"

Source: Ylvisaker (2006).

Home Extension 12

Summary: Your child is learning to use the words *big deal* and *little deal* as a quick reminder that some things are more important than others.

Why is this important? The purpose of this phrase is 1) to help students distinguish what is important from what is not important, so that they can be less anxious about little deals and take big deals seriously; 2) to help them break out of a repetitive, stuck idea; 3) to help them avoid negative behaviors when it is time to move beyond something that really is unimportant; 4) to help them avoid negative interactions with other students over minor provocations; and 5) to get them to engage in something important at a time when they would prefer not to.

We hope that you will use this phrase at home, too. Here are some guidelines:

- Identify or label the issue as being a big deal or a little deal: "This is a big deal…" or "This is not a big deal…" "This is just a little deal—this is not important."

- State the reason: "This is just a little deal because we can _____."

- Offer a strategy: "Maybe we can _____."

- Respect your child's view of what makes a big deal. The Big Deal/Little Deal script does not mean that adults insist that specific events or requests are little deals when children report that they are big deals.

There are several things you can do at home to help your child learn as fully as possible. The more experiences each student has outside the classroom, the better he or she is able to learn and apply that learning.

1. Coach your child as indicated above.

2. As you and your child become familiar with this script, you can simply ask, "Is this a big deal or a little deal?"

3. If something is a big deal to your child, discuss whether or not it can be made into a little deal. Offer suggestions for how this might be done.

4. Complete Big Deal/Little Deal with your child. Your child has been asked to help *you* complete this to reinforce his or her understanding of big and little deals (the child is teaching you the concept; you, the parent, are the student; the child is the teacher). As you know, your child will learn these concepts best by teaching them to someone else—in this case, you!

During the next lesson, we will talk about choices.

Source: Ylvisaker (2006).

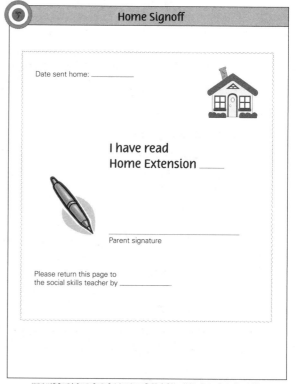

Home Signoff

Date sent home: _____

I have read
Home Extension _____

_____
Parent signature

Please return this page to
the social skills teacher by _____

Home Extension 12

Big Deal/Little Deal

Use red/green to draw lines from the phrase *Big Deal* to all the items that are big deals. Use red/green to draw lines from the phrase *Little Deal* to all the items that are little deals.

You cannot get over quickly

Is mildly annoying

Does not really change anything important

Big Deal

You cannot ignore

Requires a small change in plans

You cannot develop an alternative for

Is worth fighting for

You can ignore

Little Deal

Changes something really
important for a long time

Means you lose something
you cannot get back

Is a temporary problem

(page 2 of 2)

Lesson 2 Choice/No Choice

 PURPOSE

Students, teachers, and parents learn the Choice/No Choice script and incorporate it into their daily conversation. There are two activities in this lesson.

Materials Required for All Activities

Not Included

- Whiteboard or chart paper
- Dry/wet erase markers or markers

Included

- Educator Script: Choice/No Choice
- Choice/No Choice Cards (print double-sided on card stock)
- Classroom Extension 6
- Home Extension 13 and Home Signoff

Generalization

School Integration

Distribute Classroom Extension 6 and Educator Script: Choice/No Choice to all teaching staff so that educators can implement key strategies when working with students.

Home Integration

Upon completion of Lesson 2, send home a copy of Home Extension 13 and Home Signoff.

Modifications

For older students, include activities that are age appropriate and that cater to their interests. Students may be interested in analyzing Choice/No Choice in terms of their heroes' lives, historical or current events, or politics.

ACTIVITY 1
Choice/No Choice Introduction

☆ **Presentation**
~5–10 minutes

Materials

Not Included

- Whiteboard or chart paper
- Dry/wet erase markers or markers

Included

- Educator Script: Choice/No Choice

Instructions

This lesson introduces students to the basic definition of choice/no choice and a general script to apply the concept when the opportunity presents itself.

1. Use Educator Script: Choice/No Choice to introduce students to this critical phrase.
2. As you go through the script, record salient points and examples on the whiteboard.

ACTIVITY 2
Choice/No Choice Practice

👥 **Group Activity**
~5–10 minutes

Materials

Not Included

- Whiteboard or chart paper
- Dry/wet erase markers or markers

Included

- Choice/No Choice Cards (print double-sided on card stock)

Instructions

In this activity, students practice applying their new knowledge.

1. Print the Choice/No Choice Cards double-sided on card stock. Cards say "Choice" on one side and "No Choice" on the other side. You should have a total of 10 cards. Give each student a Choice/No Choice card.
2. Read the following scenarios, and ask students to vote on each one using the card. Is it a choice or no-choice situation?
   a. You are trying to decide whether to order pizza or fried chicken for lunch.
   b. You need to use the restroom.
   c. It is your job to hand in your class's lunch orders each day to the main office. You have earned enough points to cash in.
   d. You have a new language arts teacher.
   e. You and a classmate have free time.
   f. It is your job to complete a group project by putting everyone's work on a poster board for display.
   g. The fire drill goes off.
   h. You are trying to decide whether to wear your red shirt or your blue one.
   i. The stoplight for walkers says Don't Walk.
   j. Students have to learn to read.
   k. You want to buy a candy bar, and the cashier asks for $1.09.
   l. You are trying to decide who to invite over for a playdate.
   m. Your mom tells you that it is time to go to the doctor's office.
3. Keep a tally of votes on the whiteboard, and discuss disagreements.
4. Generate additional examples from your experiences with students, and invite students to offer scenarios. Review at least 10 scenarios.
5. Review Home Extension 13 with students.

LESSON 2 EDUCATOR SCRIPT

Choice/No Choice

As you highlight major points, record them on the whiteboard.

Choice

A choice occurs when

- There are multiple ways to solve a problem
- There is more than one option for what to do next
- There are different, equally correct ways to do something
- You are asked for your opinion

Highlight the following examples:

- Mary's teacher asks her to solve three long division problems in any way she thinks works best.
- Luke Skywalker can choose to join his father on the dark side.
- Martha can choose a chocolate chip cookie or a sugar cookie.
- Jack can go to a movie and then have dinner or have dinner and then go to a movie.
- Sara's mom can make pasta or potatoes for dinner.

Generate additional examples that are salient for your students.

No Choice

A no-choice situation occurs when

- There is only one correct way to do something
- There is a specific requirement that a specific thing be done
- There is only one acceptable option
- Something is required by law or the rules of the school or house
- Something specific has to occur at a specific time

Highlight the following examples:

- If you make a certain income from your job, you have to pay taxes.
- You must eat to live.
- Children are required by law to go to school.
- When a child is sick, he or she must stay home.
- You must feed an animal that you are taking care of, or it could die.

Classroom Extension 6

Teacher: _____ Student initials: _____ Date: _____

Summary: Students are learning a self-regulatory script called Choice/No Choice to help them behave flexibly.

What is Choice/No Choice? Choice/No Choice helps students distinguish what is within their power to control and what is not. It gives students and teachers a phrase that allows them to automatically access the concept that some situations and expectations are given and there is no point in resisting them, whereas others do offer a choice. It also helps students decide when they are performing a necessary or essential function that they need to complete, or that others are depending on them to complete, versus an activity that they can freely choose to stop.

What difference will this make in the classroom? Students who are able to distinguish between what is within their power to control and what is not are better able to accept what is beyond their control, less disruptive, and less likely to get stuck on resisting something that is inevitable.

What should I do to help my student(s)?

1. As often as possible, use the phrase *choice/no choice* to frame students' viewpoints about events.

2. Initially, use the Choice/No Choice script at times when a student is not upset to avoid creating negative associations with this script from the beginning.

3. Label Choice situations more frequently than you label No Choice situations.

4. Highlight the Choice/No Choice script in your own actions and reactions to events and demands. Praise students when they do the same.

Key words and phrases

- Identify/label the issue (e.g., "You have a choice here" or "You know this is a no-choice situation").

- State the reason (e.g., "This is a no-choice deal because _____").

- Develop a strategy (e.g., "What is a way we can get through this?").

- As staff and students become familiar with this script, it should also be used in an abbreviated version whenever appropriate. Staff or students can simply ask, "Is this Choice or No Choice?"

Source: Ylvisaker (2006).

Home Extension 13

Summary: Your child is learning to use the words *choice/no choice* as a quick reminder that some situations and expectations are not negotiable and there is no point in resisting them, but others do offer a choice.

Why is this lesson important? The purpose of this is to help children 1) distinguish what is within their power to change and what is not; 2) cease a repetitive, stuck behavior and stop trying to influence something that cannot change; and 3) identify when their contribution is necessary for an activity and they have to carry it out.

We hope that you will use this phrase at home, too. Here are some guidelines:

- Identify or label the issue as offering a choice or no choice: "You have a choice here" or "You know this is a no-choice situation."

- State the reason: "This is a no-choice deal because _____."

- Develop a strategy: "What is a way we can get through this?"

- Label choice situations more frequently than you label no-choice situations.

- Use the no-choice label at times when your child is not upset. It is important to avoid creating negative associations with this idea from the beginning.

There are several things you can do at home to help your child learn as fully as possible. The more experiences each student has outside the classroom, the better he or she is able to learn and apply that learning.

1. Coach your child as indicated above.

2. As you and your child become familiar with this script, you can simply ask, "Is this a choice or no choice?"

3. Complete Choice/No Choice. Your child has been asked to help you complete it, and it reinforces the meaning of *choice* and *no choice*. As you know, your child will learn these concepts best by teaching them to someone else—in this case, you! (So you are the student in this homework and your child is the teacher.)

During the next lesson, we will talk about routines.

Source: Ylvisaker (2006).

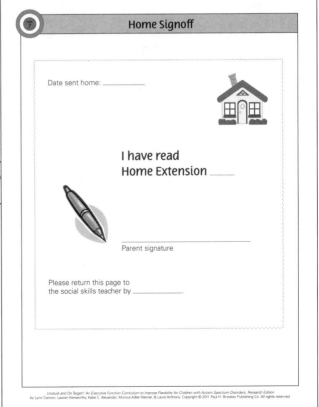

Home Signoff

Date sent home: _____

I have read
Home Extension _____

_____
Parent signature

Please return this page to
the social skills teacher by _____.

Home Extension 13

Summary: Your child is learning to use the words *choice/no choice* as a quick reminder that some situations and expectations are not negotiable and there is no point in resisting them, but others do offer a choice.

Why is this lesson important? The purpose of this is to help children 1) distinguish what is within their power to change and what is not; 2) cease a repetitive, stuck behavior and stop trying to influence something that cannot change; and 3) identify when their contribution is necessary for an activity and they have to carry it out.

We hope that you will use this phrase at home, too. Here are some guidelines:

- Identify or label the issue as offering a choice or no choice: "You have a choice here" or "You know this is a no-choice situation."
- State the reason: "This is a no-choice deal because _____."
- Develop a strategy: "What is a way we can get through this?"
- Label choice situations more frequently than you label no-choice situations.
- Use the no-choice label at times when your child is not upset. It is important to avoid creating negative associations with this idea from the beginning.

There are several things you can do at home to help your child learn as fully as possible. The more experiences each student has outside the classroom, the better he or she is able to learn and apply that learning.

1. Coach your child as indicated above.

2. As you and your child become familiar with this script, you can simply ask, "Is this a choice or no choice?"

3. Complete Choice/No Choice. Your child has been asked to help you complete it, and it reinforces the meaning of *choice* and *no choice*. As you know, your child will learn these concepts best by teaching them to someone else—in this case, you! (So you are the student in this homework and your child is the teacher.)

During the next lesson, we will talk about routines.

Source: Ylvisaker (2006).

(page 1 of 2)

HOME EXTENSION 13 *(continued)*

Home Extension 13

Choice/No Choice

Use green to draw lines from *Choice* to all the items that are choices. Use red to draw lines from *No Choice* to all the items that are no-choice items.

Choice

- Paying taxes
- Choosing fruit in the store
- Playing Pokemon or Yu-Gi-Oh!
- Wearing a seatbelt
- Paying bills
- Getting your teeth cleaned
- Getting medical check-ups
- Taking or buying lunch
- Going to school
- Using Arial or Courier Font
- Handing in an assignment
- Participating in a fire drill
- Selecting paint colors

No Choice

- Buying gifts
- Taking out smelly trash
- Feeding a pet
- Learning to read

(page 2 of 2)

CHOICE/NO CHOICE CARDS

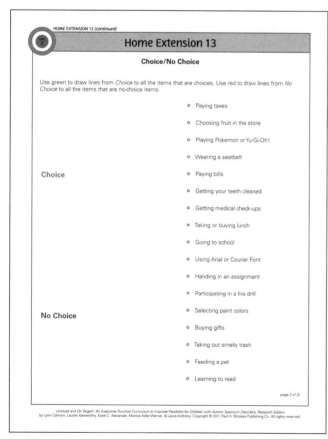

CHOICE	CHOICE
CHOICE	CHOICE
CHOICE	CHOICE
CHOICE	CHOICE
CHOICE	CHOICE

Lesson 3 Handling the Unexpected

 PURPOSE

Students, teachers, and parents learn the Handling the Unexpected script and incorporate it into their toolkit for accepting change. There are two activities in this lesson.

Materials Required for All Activities

 Not Included

- Whiteboard or chart paper
- Dry/wet erase markers or markers
- Game tokens
- Die

 Included

- Educator Guide: Handling the Unexpected Game Rules
- Handling the Unexpected Game Board
- Handling the Unexpected Game Cards (cut out ahead of time)
- Visual: Big Deal/Little Deal 1–10 Scale (from Lesson 1)
- Handout: Handling the Unexpected
- Classroom Extension 7
- Home Extension 14 and Home Signoff

Generalization

School Integration

Distribute Classroom Extension 7 and Handout: Handling the Unexpected to all teaching staff so that educators can implement key strategies when working with students. Handout: Handling the Unexpected may be used as often as necessary to help students adjust to a change in the classroom.

Home Integration

Parents of a student who is having difficulty adjusting to change will be highly motivated to use the Handling the Unexpected script if it is effective at school. Once the script has been implemented, send home a copy of Home Extension 14 and Home Signoff. Also send home a copy of Handout: Handling the Unexpected to inform parents of how the script is implemented and in what situations.

Note: Handout: Handling the Unexpected may be sent home again in the future if it is used in class to help the student adjust to a change.

Modifications

For older students, use activities that are more age appropriate and that cater to their interests.

ACTIVITY 1
Handling the Unexpected Introduction

⭐ **Presentation**

🕐 **~10 minutes**

Materials

Not Included

- Whiteboard or chart paper
- Dry/wet erase markers or markers

Included

There are no included materials for this activity.

Instructions

In this activity, students receive a basic introduction to handling the unexpected.

1. Ask your students: "Has anyone ever been mad or upset because things did not go as expected—for example, when there was a substitute teacher? That can feel like a really big deal, right?"

2. Have students offer examples, and record the main ideas on the whiteboard. Provide additional examples (e.g., Once a field trip to the zoo was canceled because of bad weather and I was really upset; I was so mad when I got sick the day before I was supposed to go whitewater rafting and the trip had to be canceled).

3. Ask students what helps turn a big deal into a little deal. Write their ideas on the whiteboard. Add your own ideas, too. Following are some examples:
   a. Being told in advance about the change
   b. Getting a 5-minute warning that you will have to stop doing something when you're having fun
   c. Taking a deep breath and remembering that you can be flexible
   d. Asking questions so you can learn exactly what will change and what will stay the same
   e. Knowing when the change will be over
   f. Knowing that there is a good reason for the change
   g. Thinking about what your hero would do

4. Keep this list. You may want to make a visual that you post in the classroom of some strategies to turn big deals into little deals.

ACTIVITY 2
Handling The Unexpected Exploration

👥 **Group Activity**

🕐 **~15–20 minutes**

Materials

Not Included

- Game tokens
- Die

Included

- Handling the Unexpected Game Rules
- Handling the Unexpected Game Board
- Handling the Unexpected Game Cards (cut out ahead of time)
- Visual: Big Deal/Little Deal 1–10 Scale (from Lesson 1)
- Home Extension 14 and Home Signoff

Instructions

1. Follow Educator Guide: Handling the Unexpected Game Rules to play the Handling the Unexpected game.
2. There are extra blank cards in Handling the Unexpected Game Cards so you or your students can add relevant scenarios if desired.
3. Review Home Extension 14 with students.

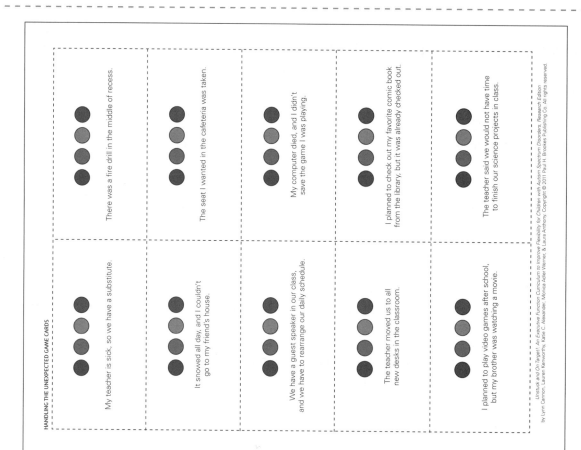

HANDLING THE UNEXPECTED GAME CARDS

There was a fire drill in the middle of recess.

The seat I wanted in the cafeteria was taken.

My computer died, and I didn't save the game I was playing.

I planned to check out my favorite comic book from the library, but it was already checked out.

The teacher said we would not have time to finish our science projects in class.

My teacher is sick, so we have a substitute.

It snowed all day, and I couldn't go to my friend's house.

We have a guest speaker in our class, and we have to rearrange our daily schedule.

The teacher moved us to all new desks in the classroom.

I planned to play video games after school, but my brother was watching a movie.

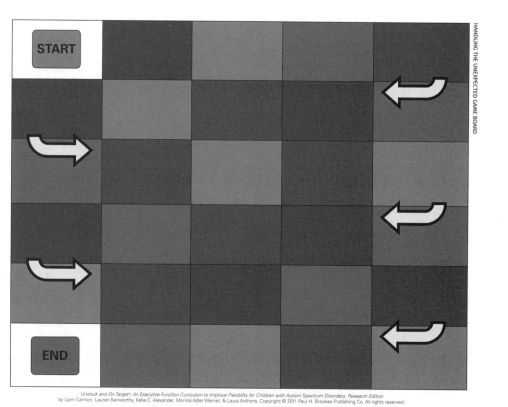

HANDLING THE UNEXPECTED GAME BOARD

START

END

Handling the Unexpected

LESSON 3 HANDOUT

7

Name of student: _____

Name of teaching staff: _____

Date: _____

What will change? Identify the change, ideally well in advance of the event.

_____

What will stay the same?

_____

Why is the change happening?

_____

PLAN: What might help me turn a big deal change into a little deal:

___ Practicing it in advance
___ Knowing when the change will be over
___ Reminding myself that I can be flexible; I have done it before
___ Knowing there is a good reason for the change
___ Thinking of how my hero would react to the change
___ Having a Plan B

CHECK: What actually helped me turn this change into a little deal:

___ Practicing it in advance
___ Knowing when the change will be over
___ Reminding myself that I can be flexible; I have done it before
___ Knowing there is a good reason for the change
___ Thinking of how my hero would react to the change
___ Having a Plan B

NOTE TO PARENTS: We wanted you to know that we used this handout in school today to help your child adjust to a change. The purpose of the Handling the Unexpected handout is to give students a specific step-by-step approach that they can take when they need to adjust to the unexpected. Our students rely on very consistent routines and become upset when change occurs or their expectations are violated. Because they need routine, it is useful to create a routine for handling the unexpected or a routine to accept change. This routine can be useful at home as well as at school.

Handling the Unexpected Game Rules

LESSON 3 EDUCATOR GUIDE

7

Goal: For each player to reach the end

How to Play the Game

1. Each player places a game token on Start.
2. Players take turns rolling the die and move the corresponding number of spaces.
3. Players take a game card, read the scenario, and follow the directions for the color they have landed on (see Game Card Key).

Game Card Key

(red circle)	**Turn it back!**	Rate the situation on the 1–10 scale then discuss the strategy you would use to turn it back into a little deal"
(green circle)	**Super friend to the rescue!**	Read the scenario and give advice to the group for how to handle the unexpected event.
(gray circle)	**Make a list!**	Read the scenario about the unexpected event. List two things that will stay the same and two things that will be different.
(dark circle)	**Act it out!**	Read the scenario about the unexpected event. Act out an inappropriate way to handle this unexpected event. Act out an appropriate way to handle this unexpected event.

Classroom Extension 7

TOPIC
7

Teacher: _____ Student initials: _____ Date: _____

Summary: Students are learning a self-regulatory script called Handling the Unexpected to help them behave flexibly.

What is the Handling the Unexpected script? This script provides students with a step-by-step approach to managing unexpected events, such as changes in routine, a substitute teacher, and so forth.

What difference will this make in the classroom? Students who have a specific routine for accepting change are less easily upset by the unexpected events that occur in any school setting, and therefore less disruptive in class.

What should I do to help my student(s)?

1. Use the Handling the Unexpected script and handout to work through an unexpected event *before* a student has become upset about the change. The entire worksheet may not be necessary for every student; use it as needed.

2. Realize that the Handling the Unexpected script and handout will be effective only if used as a helpful tool rather than a forced behavioral requirement.

3. As part of the script, remember to clarify for the student what will change and what will stay the same.

4. Post several copies of Handout: Handling the Unexpected in an easy-to-reach location.

Key words and phrases

- Identify the issue. Ideally, an event or a change in routine is identified well in advance (e.g., "Today we are going to do _____ a little differently").

- State the reason (e.g., "We need to be *flexible* because _____").

- Generate a strategy (e.g., "Let's practice the way we are going to do this today").

- Encourage students to use specific self-soothing/calming mantras during stressful changes (e.g., "I can be *flexible*. I have done it before" or "I don't like change, but this will be okay").

Home Extension 14

Summary: Your child is learning to use a step-by-step approach called Handling the Unexpected to manage the unexpected.

Why is this lesson important? Children with autism spectrum disorders rely on very consistent routines and become upset when change occurs or their expectations are violated. Because they need routine, it is useful to teach them specific strategies for handling unexpected changes in routine.

We hope that you will use the Handling the Unexpected script at home, too. Here are some guidelines:

- Identify the issue: "Today we are going to do _____ a little differently." Ideally, an unexpected event or a change in routine is identified well in advance.

- State the reason: "We need to be *flexible* because _____."

- Generate a strategy: "Let's practice the way we are going to do this today."

- Encourage your child to use specific self-soothing/calming mantras during stressful changes: "I can be *flexible*. I have done it before." "I don't like change, but this will be okay."

- Keep several copies of Handout: Handling the Unexpected in an easy-to-reach location. Use the handout anytime you need to work through a change with your child.

There are several things you can do at home to help your child learn as fully as possible. The more experiences each student has outside the classroom, the better he or she is able to learn and apply that learning.

1. Coach your child as indicated above.

2. As you and your child become familiar with this script, you can use Handout: Handling the Unexpected to help guide your child through a change.

Next, we will begin a new topic that teaches different levels of goals: those that are of high priority and those that are of lower priority. Stay tuned for more information!

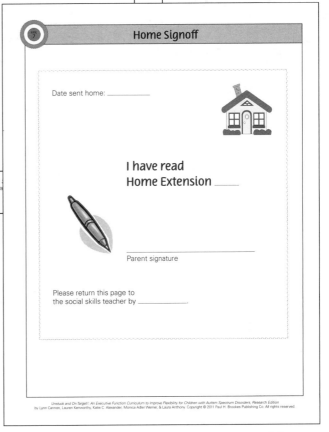

Home Signoff

Date sent home: _____

I have read
Home Extension _____

_____
Parent signature

Please return this page to
the social skills teacher by _____.

Extensions

Generalization

School Integration

- Upon completion of Lesson 1, distribute Classroom Extension 5 and Educator Script: Big Deal/Little Deal to all teaching staff.
- Upon completion of Lesson 2, distribute Classroom Extension 6 and Educator Script: Choice/No Choice to all teaching staff.
- Upon completion of Lesson 3, distribute Classroom Extension 7 and Handout: Handling the Unexpected to all teaching staff.

Home Integration

- Upon completion of Lesson 1, send home a copy of Home Extension 12 and Home Signoff, including the attached Big Deal/Little Deal.
- Upon completion of Lesson 2, send home a copy of Home Extension 13 and Home Signoff, including the attached Choice/No Choice.
- Upon completion of Lesson 3, send home a copy of Home Extension 14 and Home Signoff. Also send home a copy of Handout: Handling the Unexpected.

Materials for Home

- Home Extension 12 and Home Signoff
- Home Extension 13 and Home Signoff
- Home Extension 14 and Home Signoff
- Handout: Handling the Unexpected

Reference

Ylvisaker, M. (2006). *Tutorial: Self-regulation/executive function routines after TBI.* Available on The Brain Injury Association of New York State web site: http://www.projectlearnet.org/tutorials/sr_ef_routines.html

Journey to Target Island

SPECIAL INSTRUCTIONS: The core goals of these lessons are to help students review what goals are and learn how to prioritize large goals—often social or long term—over others. Although it is essential to introduce the concepts of goals, overarching goals, and choosing among goals, please modify the activities as necessary to better meet your students' needs. Throughout this topic, the large, overarching goal will be known as the Target Goal, or TG.

- -

Summary: In the three lessons of this topic, students build on their knowledge of goals by learning how to distinguish large, important goals from smaller, less important goals. The concept of a target goal is introduced, such as being a good friend. Students explore how to choose among two or more competing goals in favor of the more important, or target, goal.

Prerequisite skills: Understanding of the meaning of flexibility, familiarity with flexibility vocabulary, understanding of the value of flexibility with reference to a personal hero, understanding of the definition of a goal, ability to identify a personal goal

Related skills: Core language comprehension

- -

OUTCOME—CRITERIA FOR MASTERY

1. The student defines target goal and identifies a personal Target Goal (TG).
2. When presented with scenarios involving choice, the student identifies the TG and the smaller goals that are in conflict.

TOPIC BACKGROUND AND RATIONALE

Students on the autism spectrum often have difficulty intuiting what is most important in a situation. They can easily lose sight of the big picture amid small details. For this reason, it is important to introduce the concept of goals, or overarching aims, that may require several steps to achieve. In addition to learning what a goal is, students with ASD require explicit instruction in understanding that some goals are more important than others. They can easily become stuck and inflexible regarding small issues and as a result can derail social interactions. The concept of a TG is an important tool for helping students identify the most important goal in a given situation.

Lesson 1 What Is a Target Goal?

PURPOSE

This lesson provides students with a definition of a *target goal* (TG) and examples, a discussion of heroes, and a video clip on choosing a personal TG. There are two activities in this lesson.

Materials Required for All Activities

Not Included

- Whiteboard or chart paper
- Dry/wet erase markers or markers
- Video clip: Pink Panther, "In the Pink of the Night" (6 minutes, 7 seconds)

Included

- Handout: Target Island Introduction Story
- Visual: Target Island Goal
- Educator Guide: Target Island Goal

Generalization

School Integration

- As often as possible, begin framing a student's actions in terms of his or her TG versus other goals. For example, if a student is working to complete a handout in class, you might say, "So, your TG is to finish this handout in class, and your other [or "Whim Island"] goal is to talk to your friend. Let's make a plan to keep your TG and get to your other goal later."
- Similarly, highlight the actions of others in terms of TGs and other goals.

Home Integration

There is no Home Extension for Lesson 1.

Modifications

- Older students would benefit from the inclusion of more complex, competing TGs and other goals.
- Use activities that are more age appropriate for older students and that cater to their interests.

ACTIVITY 1
What Is a Target Goal?

☆ **Presentation**

🕐 **~10 minutes**

Materials

Not Included

- Whiteboard or chart paper
- Dry/wet erase markers or markers

Included

- Handout: Target Island Introduction Story
- Visual: Target Island Goal
- Educator Guide: Target Island Goal

Instructions

In this lesson, students review the basic definition of *goal* and learn the definition of *target goal*.

1. Read Handout: Target Island Introduction Story to students or have students read the story on their own.

2. Post Visual: Target Island Goal. Next to it, write the following definition: *A Target Goal is something that you want or need to do that is more important than anything else you may want to do at the same time.*

3. Explain that there is often much happening at the same time, so it is important to focus on the most important goal—the TG—at any point in time.

4. Use Educator Guide: Target Island Goal to direct your discussion about TGs. It provides a script to explore the idea of TGs and lesser goals using humorous examples from selected heroes. Modify this script and your discussion as necessary to make them relevant to your students.

5. Keep Visual: Target Island Goal posted for Activity 2.

ACTIVITY 2
Target Goal Example

📽 **Video and Discussion**
🕐 **~20 minutes**

Materials

Not Included

- Whiteboard or chart paper
- Dry/wet erase markers or markers
- Video clip: Pink Panther, "In the Pink of the Night" (6 minutes, 7 seconds)

Included

There are no included materials for this activity.

Instructions

1. Search the Internet to find the Pink Panther video clip titled "In the Pink of the Night." Bookmark it for students to view.
2. Inform the students that they are about to watch a video of the Pink Panther. He has a TG, but other goals keeping getting in the way. Ask students to think about what the Pink Panther's TG might be.
3. Have students watch the video.
4. At the conclusion of the video, ask the following questions and write the students' answers on the whiteboard:
   a. What was the Pink Panther's TG? (He wanted to catch the train on time, so he needed to get out of bed.)
   b. What were some of his other goals? (Possible answers include staying asleep, keeping the alarms quiet, silencing the bird, and eating breakfast.) Respond to students' answers.
5. Summarize for students that it can be really hard to balance a TG with other goals that also reflect something they want. In the video, the Pink Panther wanted more sleep, but he was really upset when he missed the train. Explain that the class will continue to work together to learn how to set a TG and achieve it even when other goals are desirable, too.

LESSON 1 HANDOUT

Target Island Introduction Story

The following story sets the scene for the Target Goal lessons and, hopefully, makes the topic of Target Goals more fun for your students. Read this story before introducing the definition for Target Island goals. If you like, try reading it in character, read it out loud more simply, or provide students a copy to read independently.

So, ye be searchin' for Target Island, eh? Many a new sailor has tried and failed—there be many a distraction about that can run the unwise sailor off course. These distractions be known as "Whim Islands." Ye know ye've found a Whim Island when it's filled with the things ye want, except for one thing—the one thing that can only be found on Target Island. That one thing—the most important thing—is the goal that is more important than anything else that ye be wantin' to do at any partic'lar point in time.

Once ye be knowin' the most important, target goal, chart yer course. Ye'll be seein' many a Whim Island, offering treasures that'll tempt ye off course. Ye must ignore them if ye hope to find Target Island and all its treasures. I wish ye fair winds and calm seas for smooth sailing, me mateys.

VISUAL: TARGET ISLAND GOAL

Whim Island

Whim Island

Whim Island

Target Island

Target Island Goal

Educator: Think about one of your heroes. What is his or her Target Goal?

You may use the Hero Goal Bank from Topic 6 (the names of actual people in this bank are reprinted below) to help students. They might answer with something like "protect the people" or "invent a cure." Using their responses, create a chart with each hero's name and TG on the whiteboard. See the chart that follows for an example.

Educator: But what if the hero wanted a donut? What if he stopped to get a donut instead of protecting the people? Part of being a hero is understanding that he may want a donut, but first, he must protect the people.

Explore other humorous examples of heroes' TGs and competing, less important goals—known as Whim Goals. Write down humorous examples of Whim Goals.

Example visual for Hero Target Goals and Whim Goals

Hero	Target Goals	Whim Goals
Firefighter	Protect people	Eat a donut
Benjamin Franklin	Invent the lightning rod	Have a picnic with a friend

Hero goal bank

- Albert Einstein: Contribute to the science of physics
- Abraham Lincoln: Keep the United States together and end slavery
- Martin Luther King, Jr.: Create equal rights for all people
- Rosa Parks: Support civil rights
- Bill Gates: Create a computer operating system

Provide at least five examples for students, and use actual student heroes when possible.

Lesson 2 Your Target Goals

 PURPOSE

This lesson further explores the concept of TGs and Whims (competing goals). The students explore these concepts concretely with an art activity that incorporates the Target Island visual. There are two activities in this lesson.

Materials Required for All Activities

 Not Included

- Whiteboard or chart paper
- Dry/wet erase markers or markers
- Scissors
- Marker
- Modeling clay
- Toothpicks/small flags
- Poster board
- Glue

 Included

- Handout: My Target Goal
- Island Project Cards
- Handout: Island Project Directions

Generalization

School Integration

- Continue with the generalization activities from Lesson 1.
- It is critical to embed TG language throughout the day once students have learned the associated concepts (e.g. ,"What is your TG?" "Is that your TG, or is that a Whim?" "Okay, so what is your plan for your TG?").

Home Integration

There is no Home Extension for Lesson 2.

Modifications

Consider an art or craft activity that is a better match for older students, such as having students create a comic strip that illustrates competing goals.

ACTIVITY 1
Target Goals and Whims (Other Goals)

☆ **Presentation**

⏱ **5 minutes**

Materials

Not Included

- Whiteboard or chart paper
- Dry/wet erase markers or markers

Included

- Handout: My Target Goal

Instructions

1. Review the definition of a TG as well as some of the examples from Lesson 1.
2. Provide students with additional examples of TGs and write them on the whiteboard. These examples should include those that are directly relevant to students' daily lives, such as the following:
   a. *To be a good friend*
   b. *To be a good student*
   c. *To become the CEO of a video game company*
   d. *To be president*
3. Provide students with additional examples of Whims (other goals), such as the following:
   a. *Eat the last cookie (instead of sharing)*
   b. *Play video games (instead of finishing homework)*
   c. *Talk to my friend during class*
4. Ask students to select a TG that they would like to work on. Each student should write down his or her TG on Handout: My Target Island.

ACTIVITY 2
Creating Target Island

👤 **Individual Activity**

⏱ **~15–20 minutes**

Materials

Not Included

- Scissors
- Marker
- Modeling clay
- Toothpicks/small flags
- Poster board
- Glue

Included

- Island Project Cards
- Handout: Island Project Directions

Instructions

The students remain together as a group for this activity, although each student should complete the activity individually.

1. Give Handout: Island Project Directions and other materials to each student. Have students complete Steps 1–3 of the directions.
2. Students create their own Target Island out of modeling clay (Step 4 of the directions). They write their TG and put it on the island (suggestions for doing so are given in Step 5 of the directions).
3. Students may decorate their Whim Island boards if they wish.
4. Students present their boards and Target Islands to their classmates.

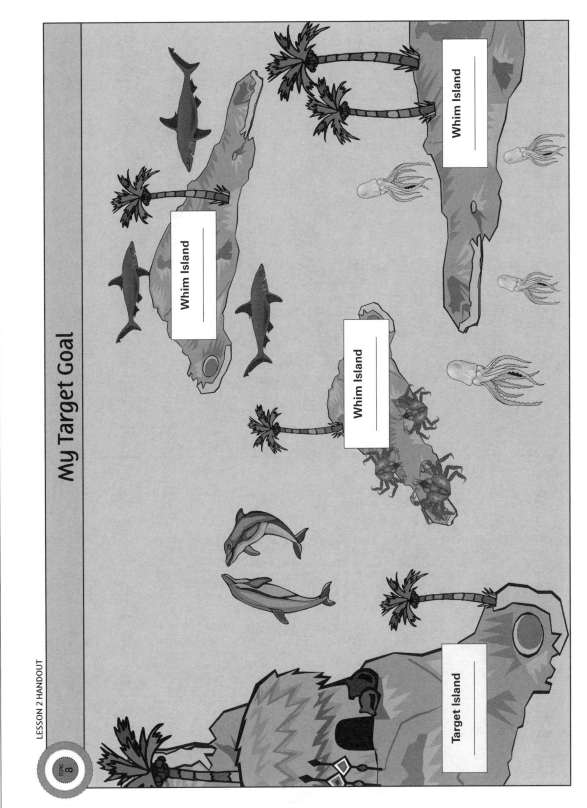

LESSON 2 HANDOUT

My Target Goal

Whim Island _____

Whim Island _____

Whim Island _____

Target Island _____

Unstuck and On Target!: An Executive Function Curriculum to Improve Flexibility for Children with Autism Spectrum Disorders, Research Edition by Lynn Cannon, Lauren Kenworthy, Katie C. Alexander, Monica Adler Werner, & Laura Anthony. Copyright © 2011 Paul H. Brookes Publishing Co. All rights reserved.

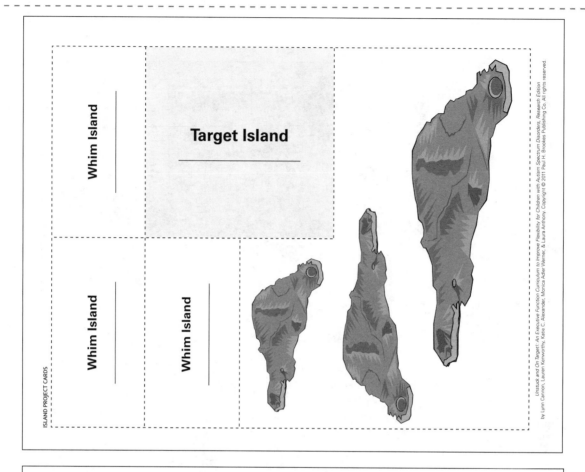

ISLAND PROJECT CARDS

Whim Island
_____

Target Island
_____

Whim Island
_____

Whim Island
_____

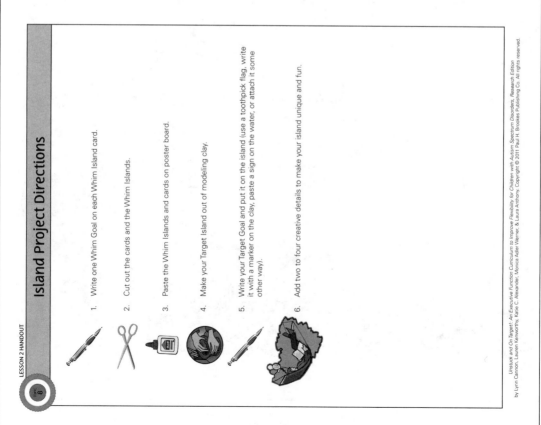

LESSON 2 HANDOUT

Island Project Directions

1. Write one Whim Goal on each Whim Island card.

2. Cut out the cards and the Whim Islands.

3. Paste the Whim Islands and cards on poster board.

4. Make your Target Island out of modeling clay.

5. Write your Target Goal and put it on the island (use a toothpick flag, write it with a marker on the clay, paste a sign on the water, or attach it some other way).

6. Add two to four creative details to make your island unique and fun.

Lesson 3 Conflicting Goals

 PURPOSE

In this lesson, students practice applying their knowledge of TGs and competing goals to play a game modeled after Chutes and Ladders. There is one activity for this lesson.

Materials Required for All Activities

 Not Included

- Game tokens (e.g., BINGO chips, coins)
- Die

 Included

- Up, Up, and Away Target Island Goals Game Board
- Educator Guide: Up, Up, and Away Target Island Goals Game Rules
- Drain Pipe Cards
- Wind Cards
- Home Extension 15 and Home Signoff

Generalization

School Integration

- Continue with the generalization activities from Lesson 1 and 2, embedding TG language as frequently as possible.
- Frame core activities of the day (e.g., class period, lunch, recess) in terms of the student's TG for that period. For example, before recess, you might remind a student that his or her TG is to be a good friend; another student might receive a reminder before math class that his or her TG is to be a good student. Depending on your students' understanding, you may need to review what it means to be a good friend or a good student.

Home Integration

Upon completion of Lesson 3, send home a copy of Home Extension 15 and Home Signoff.

Modifications

Modify this activity as needed for older students, keeping in mind that the objective is for students to apply their knowledge in a meaningful, hands-on, engaging activity. Activities may include creating a play or a video.

Target Goals in Action Board Game

👥 **Group Game**

🕐 **~20 minutes**

Materials

Not Included

- Game tokens (e.g., BINGO chips, coins)
- Die

Included

- Up, Up, and Away Target Island Goals Game Board
- Educator Guide: Up, Up, and Away Target Island Goals Game Rules
- Drain Pipe Cards
- Wind Cards
- Home Extension 15 and Home Signoff

Instructions

1. Using Educator Guide: Up, Up, and Away Target Island Goals Game Rules, go over the rules for playing the Up, Up, and Away Target Island Goals game. Modify the rules as needed to accommodate students' comfort level with competition and game playing. If winning and losing are difficult for your students, explain that there is no winner; all players must cross the finish line in any order.
2. Establish a way to decide who will go first.
3. Have students play the game.
4. Review Home Extension 15 with students.

LESSON 3 EDUCATOR GUIDE

Up, Up, and Away Target Island Goals Game Rules

Goal

For each player to cross the star at 50

How to play the game

1. Everyone starts at 1.

2. Take turns rolling the die and move the corresponding number of spaces.

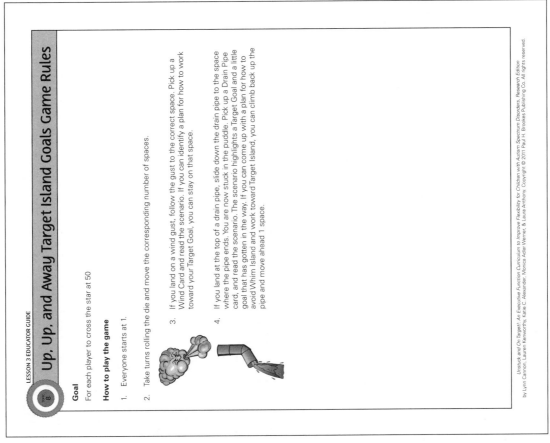

3. If you land on a wind gust, follow the gust to the correct space. Pick up a Wind Card and read the scenario. If you can identify a plan for how to work toward your Target Goal, you can stay on that space.

4. If you land at the top of a drain pipe, slide down the drain pipe to the space where the pipe ends. You are now stuck in the puddle. Pick up a Drain Pipe card, and read the scenario. The scenario highlights a Target Goal and a little goal that has gotten in the way. If you can come up with a plan for how to avoid Whim Island and work toward Target Island, you can climb back up the pipe and move ahead 1 space.

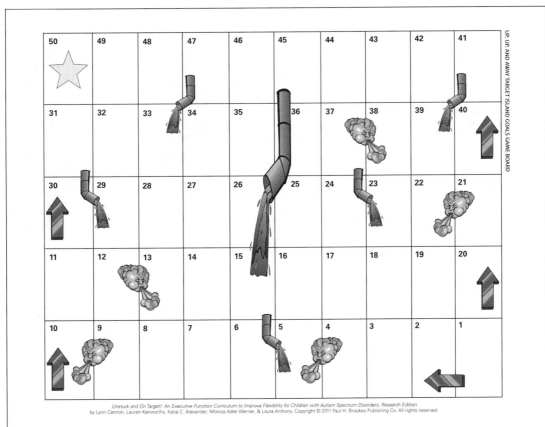

UP, UP, AND AWAY TARGET ISLAND GOALS GAME BOARD

DRAIN PIPE CARDS

My Target Goal is to be a good friend.
I can't wait to see the new vampire movie. I
know my friend doesn't like vampire movies,
but I bought us two tickets anyway.

My Target Goal is to get good grades.
I was supposed to study for my history
test after school. Instead of studying,
I decided to go outside and play basketball.

My name is Superman, and my Target Goal
is to protect people. Today I wanted to stay
home and watch my favorite movie instead
of go out and protect people.

I am SpongeBob SquarePants, and my
Target Goal is to save King Neptune.
I decided to take the day off and spend
time with Patrick at the Crusty Crab.

As Luke Skywalker, my Target Goal
is to lead the Rebel Alliance. I decided
to spend the day hanging out with
Princess Leah and R2-D2.

My name is Bill Gates. My Target Goal is
to create a computer operating system.
I decided to take a couple days
off work and play golf.

My Target Goal is to be a good friend.
I was feeling tired and didn't want to go
to my friend's house. I decided not to call
my friend, and I played video games by
myself instead.

My Target Goal is to get good grades, so
I can go to college. I decided I would rather
play video gam...

My name is Martin Luther King, Jr.
My Target Goal was to create equal
rights for all people. I decided that
I wanted to take a vacation.

My Target Goal is...
I am not supp...
during math cla...
friend about...
started talkin...

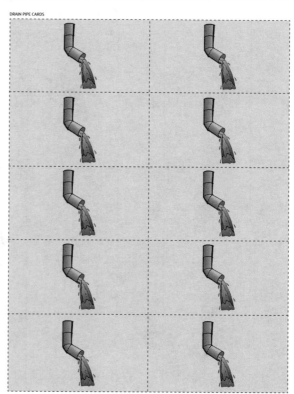

DRAIN PIPE CARDS

WIND CARDS

My Target Goal is to get good grades. I really want to play video games, but I have homework. I made a plan so that I can do both.
My plan is _____.

My Target Goal is to eat healthy. It is my friend's birthday, and I would like to have a cupcake and candy. I made a plan to have the cupcake but still work toward my Target Goal.
My plan is _____.

My name is Batman. My Target Goal is to protect Gotham City from evil. I am feeling really tired and need a nap. I made a plan, so I can get some rest and still save the city.
My plan is _____.

I am SpongeBob SquarePants. My Target Goal is to be the best fry cook in the ocean. Patrick wants me to come over for his birthday. I made a plan, so I can still work at the Crusty Crab but see my buddy as well.
My plan is _____.

My name is Obi-Wan Kenobi, and my Target Goal is to train the Jedi Knights. I found a new light saber that I want to try out. I found a way to try the new light saber without missing training time.
My plan is_____.

My Target Goal is to be a good friend. I really want to play basketball, but my friend really likes soccer. I made a plan to help me work toward my Target Goal.
My plan is _____.

My Target Goal is to be a good friend. I really want to see the new Harry Potter movie, but my friend is not allowed to see it. I made a plan to help me work toward my Target Goal.
My plan is _____.

My Target Goal is to be a flexible friend. My friend wants to play tag at recess, and I would like to swing. I made a plan to help me work toward my Target Goal.
My plan i_____.

My goal is to be a good student, so I can get a good job. I wanted to go to my friend's birthday party instead of doing my book report. I made a plan to help me work toward my Target Goal.
My plan is _____.

My Target Goal____ class. I really wan____ game during m____ help me work____ My plan i____

WIND CARDS

Home Extension 15

Summary: During this lesson, students have used crafts, games, and role-play activities to understand the importance of recognizing and working toward their most important goal, called a Target Goal.

What is a Target Goal? A Target Goal is something that your child wants or needs to do that is more important than anything else he or she may want to do at the same time. A Target Goal may be academic, such as getting a better grade in math; it may be social, such as being a good friend.

What is a Whim? A Whim is another, smaller objective your child may have that interferes with reaching his or her Target Goal. For example, your child's Target Goal may be to get a better grade in math, but his or her Whim might be to play a video game during homework time.

There are several things you can do at home to help your child learn as fully as possible. The more experiences each child has outside the classroom, the better he or she is able to learn a concept and apply that learning.

1. Use Target Goal and Whim language as often as possible during your child's daily activities. For example, you might ask your child, "Is that a Target Goal or are you stopping off on Whim Island?" if he or she is becoming distracted from the primary goal. You also might ask your child before he or she starts a project, "What is your Target Goal? Might there be some Whim Islands that would be distracting to you that we need to make a plan about?"

2. Complete the attached worksheet with your child. The goal of this worksheet is to problem-solve with your child about a goal that is important at home and to create a plan to achieve that goal. In this way, it is also a review of Goal-Plan-Do-Check.

In the next lesson, we will start a new topic about being a flexible friend.

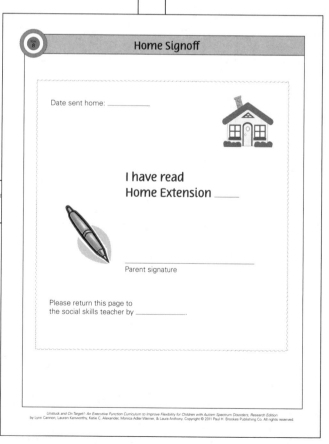

Home Signoff

Date sent home: _____

I have read
Home Extension _____

Parent signature

Please return this page to
the social skills teacher by _____

HOME EXTENSION 15 *(continued)*

TOPIC
8

Target Goals and Whims at Home

1. What is a goal that is important at home? (Examples: being a good sibling, being a good helper, doing specific chores)

_____

_____

2. With your child, define what that goal means specifically. (What does your child need to do? What is the description of that goal?)

_____

_____

3. What Whims typically get in the way of achieving the goal?

_____

_____

_____

4. What is your child's Plan A for achieving his or her goal and addressing the Whims?

_____

_____

5. What is your child's Plan B?

_____

_____

6. When will your child try his or her plan?

_____

Check: *How did it go? (circle one)*

1 ——— 2 ——— 3 ——— 4 ——— 5 ——— 6 ——— 7 ——— 8 ——— 9 ———10

Did not go well   Some of it worked   It worked!

(page 2 of 2)

Extensions

Generalization

School Integration

- As often as possible, begin framing a student's actions in terms of his or her TG versus other goals.
- Highlight the actions of others in terms of TGs and other goals.
- Embed TG language throughout the day once students have learned the associated concepts.
- Frame core activities of the day (e.g., class period, lunch, recess) in terms of the student's TG for that period.

Home Integration

Upon completion of Lesson 3, send home a copy of Home Extension 15 and Home Signoff, including the accompanying Target Goals and Whims at Home.

Materials for Home

- Home Extension 15 and Home Signoff

Being Flexible Makes You a Good Friend

SPECIAL INSTRUCTIONS: The core goal of these lessons is to help students establish intrinsic motivation for being flexible. Although it is important to implement each component of this topic, please modify the activities as necessary to better meet your students' needs. When implementing the lessons, use examples from students' everyday lives whenever possible.

Summary: The three lessons in this topic will help students establish motivation for being flexible. They will explore how flexibility empowers them to be a good friend, creates positive feelings, and puts them in charge of outcomes. This topic includes explicit instructions, continued use of the critical flexibility vocabulary, and an opportunity to examine outcomes that are possible when students are flexible and when they are not.

Prerequisite skills: Understanding of the meaning of flexibility, familiarity with flexibility vocabulary, understanding of the importance of flexibility

Related skills: Intrinsic motivation, self-concept, goal setting

OUTCOME—CRITERIA FOR MASTERY

1. The student identifies reasons that being flexible makes him or her a good friend.
2. The student identifies options for what to do if he or she disagrees with a friend.
3. The student identifies the outcomes that will occur when he or she is flexible.

TOPIC BACKGROUND AND RATIONALE

Like all individuals, children with ASD respond best when their motivation level is high. Implicit social motivation, however, is not always present. Therefore, it is important to explicitly teach the advantages of flexibility for achieving concrete social and emotional goals that are meaningful to the individual student. Finding the right incentives to support learning is one of the crucial first steps in teaching students new skills. Topics in this lesson identify ways to develop and use motivation as a tool to affect learning and behavior. To affect behavioral change over time, it is important to establish and explicitly demonstrate how students have control over their decisions and how flexibility results in positive outcomes.

Lesson 1 Flexibility Helps When Your Friend Makes a Mistake

 PURPOSE

This lesson will help students establish intrinsic motivation for being flexible by explicitly reviewing, through concrete experiences, why being flexible makes them a good friend when a friend makes a mistake. There are three activities in this lesson.

Materials Required for All Activities

 Not Included

- Whiteboard or chart paper
- Dry/wet erase markers or markers
- Craft sticks
- Two pipe cleaners
- Clock or stopwatch

Included

- Handout: Friend Pie Pieces (cut out before lesson; one set for each student)
- Educator Script: Friend Mistake Scenarios
- Handout: Teacher Mistake Scenarios
- Voting Cards (cut out before lesson; one set for each student)
- Educator Guide: Bulletin Board Example

Generalization

School Integration

- Distribute Educator Script: Friend Mistake Scenarios and Handout: Teacher Mistake Scenarios to all teaching staff.
- Start a bulletin board on reasons to be flexible; you will add to this board throughout the lessons in this topic (see Educator Guide: Bulletin Board Example).

Home Integration

There is no Home Extension for Lesson 1.

Modifications

Create mistake scenarios that reflect situations that have happened in your classroom.

ACTIVITY 1
Everyone Makes Mistakes

☆ **Presentation**

🕐 **~10 minutes**

Materials

Not Included

- Whiteboard or chart paper
- Dry/wet erase markers or markers
- Craft stick
- Two pipe cleaners

Included

There are no included materials for this activity.

Instructions

1. Say to students, "It is nice to have a friend." Ask students to give a thumbs-up if they agree with that statement.
2. Offer examples of things students like to do with their friends, and ask students for additional examples. Record them on the whiteboard, writing each in a box or bubble (see Figure 9.1). Following are some examples.
   a. Play games
   b. Have a serious conversation
   c. Laugh
   d. Have something in common
   e. Like to do the same things
3. Say, "Everyone makes mistakes." Ask students to give a thumbs-up if they agree with that statement.
4. Then, say, "Friends make mistakes sometimes." Ask students to give a thumbs-up if they agree with that statement.
5. Explain that all friends make mistakes. Ask students to share examples of ways a friend could make a mistake. Sometimes a friend
   a. Says something that hurts my feelings
   b. Behaves poorly
   c. Is too silly
   d. Is having a bad day
6. Record these answers on the whiteboard, placing the word *Mistake* in a box or bubble and all the examples in boxes or bubbles below *Mistake* (see Figure 9.1).
7. Ask, "Have you ever made a mistake?" Have students give a thumbs-up if they have ever made a mistake.
8. Give an example of a time you made a mistake (e.g., "My friend told me a secret one time. She asked me not to tell anyone, but I made a mistake and told our other friend. My friend was upset with me for having shared her secret").
9. To illustrate this example, draw an arrow from *share secrets* to *hurt feelings* as shown in the figure.
10. Ask the students for examples of when they made a mistake, and emphasize that everyone makes mistakes sometimes. Continue to draw arrows from a friendship description word to a mistake word.
11. Ask, "Does a friendship have to end if someone makes a mistake?" Explain that being flexible helps people to keep being friends even if someone makes a mistake. Emphasize again that everyone makes mistakes. Ask students to think about what happens if a friend makes a mistake and students are rigid about it.

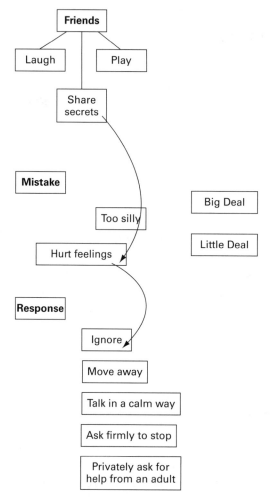

Figure 9.1. Example of discussion about friendship.

12. Write the name of two fictitious students on each side of the craft stick. Make up a scenario about how one student made a mistake. Ask, "If the other student decides to be rigid, what will happen to the friendship?" Demonstrate that the friendship will break by breaking the craft stick (see Figure 9.2).

13. Ask, "What if, instead of being rigid, the friend was flexible?" Show students two pipe cleaners and explain that each pipe cleaner represents one friend. Twist the pipe cleaners around each other. Explain that the twists represent the strength of their friendship—the friends have fun together, laugh at each other's jokes, and so forth.

Figure 9.2. Craft stick showing how friendship can break.

14. Say, "When one friend makes a mistake, it puts a strain on the relationship." Pull the pipe cleaners apart slightly to show this strain. Ask students whether the friendship broke. No, it did not break because these are flexible friends.

15. Ask, "What are some things you can do if your friend makes a mistake?" Record students' answers on the whiteboard in boxes or bubbles (see Figure 9.1). Here are some examples:

    a. Decide if it is important or not, and ignore it if it isn't.

    b. Privately get help from an adult.

    c. Talk it through in a calm way.

    d. Ask the friend firmly to stop.

16. Using an example of a mistake that is recorded on the whiteboard, ask students whether the mistake is a Big Deal or a Little Deal. Draw arrows from *Mistake* to *Big Deal* or *Little Deal*, then to different responses recorded. Refer back to the example about sharing your friend's secret.

17. Ask students how they resolved the mistakes they gave as examples. Record the information with an arrow.

ACTIVITY 2

Flexible Friendship Pie

 Group Activity

🕐 **~10 minutes**

Materials

Not Included

All materials for this activity are included.

Included

- Handout: Friend Pie Pieces (cut out before lesson; one set for each student)
- Educator Script: Friend Mistake Scenarios

Instructions

1. Hand out the precut Friend Pie Pieces, one set per student. (See the instructions at the top of Handout: Friends Pie Pieces.) Make sure students correctly separate the pieces of each pie.

2. Read each scenario from Educator Script: Friend Mistake Scenarios.

3. After each scenario, have students assemble the pie to show what the friends were doing, what mistake one friend made, whether the mistake was a Big Deal or a Little Deal, and how a flexible friend could respond.

    a. First piece: What were the friends doing?

    b. Second piece: What mistake did the friend make?

    c. Third piece: Decide if the mistake was a Big Deal or a Little Deal. (Emphasize that there is no right answer; everyone is allowed his or her opinion.)

    d. Fourth piece: Decide how the friend can be flexible and deal with the mistake. (Again, emphasize that there is no right answer; everyone is allowed an opinion, and there are multiple ways to be flexible.)

4. Once the pie is assembled, show students that if they continue around the circle, the piece following the fourth piece indicates how the friends can continue the things they were doing before the mistake.

Activity 3
Mistake Skits

Group Activity

~10 minutes

Materials

Not Included

- Clock or stopwatch
- Craft sticks (optional)

Included

- Handout: Teacher Mistake Scenarios
- Voting Cards (cut out before lesson; one set for each student)

Instructions

1. Make a copy of Voting Cards for each student. Prior to the lesson, cut out the *Fun/Mistake* card. Fold the card along the dotted line and tape the two sides together.
2. Cut out the five response cards. If you wish, you may tape each card to a craft stick. Hand out one set of the Voting Cards to each student.
3. Have one student act as the timekeeper.
4. Using the scenarios from Handout: Teacher Mistake Scenarios, the teacher and another adult act out playing together having fun and making mistakes. Every 30 seconds (or as appropriate) the timekeeper says, "Freeze," and students vote on what is happening by holding up a card that says *Fun* or *Mistake*.
5. If it is a mistake, students vote with a solution card:
   a. Ignore
   b. Move away
   c. Talk in a calm way (kind)
   d. Ask firmly to stop
   e. Privately get adult help
6. The teacher and adult should respond according to the solution(s) students choose.

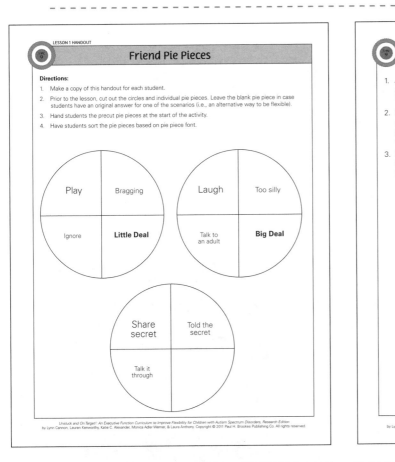

Friend Pie Pieces

LESSON 1 HANDOUT

Directions:

1. Make a copy of this handout for each student.

2. Prior to the lesson, cut out the circles and individual pie pieces. Leave the blank pie piece in case students have an original answer for one of the scenarios (i.e., an alternative way to be flexible).

3. Hand students the precut pie pieces at the start of the activity.

4. Have students sort the pie pieces based on pie piece font.

Circle 1: Play | Bragging | Ignore | **Little Deal**

Circle 2: Laugh | Too silly | Talk to an adult | **Big Deal**

Circle 3: Share secret | Told the secret | Talk it through

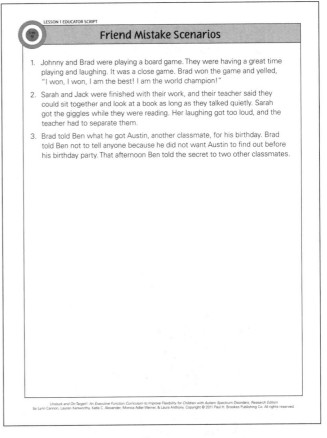

Friend Mistake Scenarios

LESSON 1 EDUCATOR SCRIPT

1. Johnny and Brad were playing a board game. They were having a great time playing and laughing. It was a close game. Brad won the game and yelled, "I won, I won, I am the best! I am the world champion!"

2. Sarah and Jack were finished with their work, and their teacher said they could sit together and look at a book as long as they talked quietly. Sarah got the giggles while they were reading. Her laughing got too loud, and the teacher had to separate them.

3. Brad told Ben what he got Austin, another classmate, for his birthday. Brad told Ben not to tell anyone because he did not want Austin to find out before his birthday party. That afternoon Ben told the secret to two other classmates.

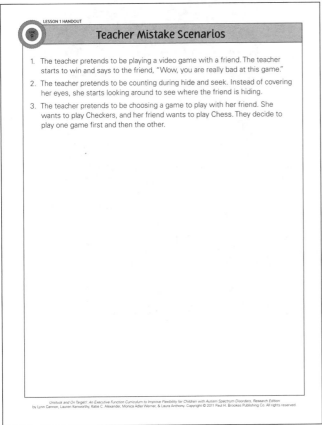

Teacher Mistake Scenarios

LESSON 1 HANDOUT

1. The teacher pretends to be playing a video game with a friend. The teacher starts to win and says to the friend, "Wow, you are really bad at this game."

2. The teacher pretends to be counting during hide and seek. Instead of covering her eyes, she starts looking around to see where the friend is hiding.

3. The teacher pretends to be choosing a game to play with her friend. She wants to play Checkers, and her friend wants to play Chess. They decide to play one game first and then the other.

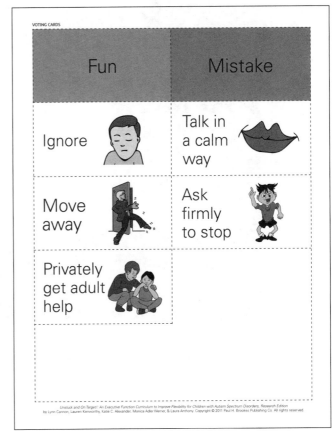

VOTING CARDS

Fun	Mistake
Ignore	Talk in a calm way
Move away	Ask firmly to stop
Privately get adult help	

Bulletin Board Example

The numbers to the left of the example indicate the order in which you should add information to the board.

Ideas for additions

- Students can help find pictures (from magazines, the Internet, or ones they have created) to support the messages on the board.

- Add a piece of uncooked spaghetti to illustrate rigidity and a rubber band to illustrate flexibility.

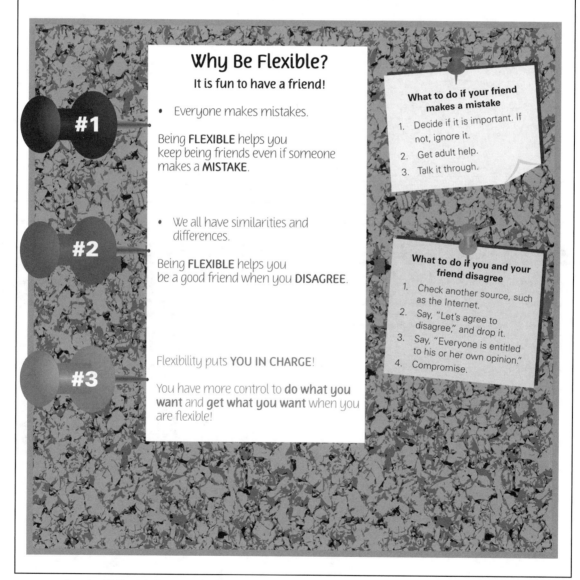

Why Be Flexible?
It is fun to have a friend!

- Everyone makes mistakes.

Being **FLEXIBLE** helps you keep being friends even if someone makes a **MISTAKE**.

- We all have similarities and differences.

Being **FLEXIBLE** helps you be a good friend when you **DISAGREE**.

Flexibility puts **YOU IN CHARGE**!

You have more control to **do what you want** and **get what you want** when you are flexible!

What to do if your friend makes a mistake

1. Decide if it is important. If not, ignore it.
2. Get adult help.
3. Talk it through.

What to do if you and your friend disagree

1. Check another source, such as the Internet.
2. Say, "Let's agree to disagree," and drop it.
3. Say, "Everyone is entitled to his or her own opinion."
4. Compromise.

Lesson 2 All Friends Have Similarities and Differences

 PURPOSE

This lesson will help students begin to recognize and appreciate the similarities and differences they have with their classmates and friends. There are three activities in this lesson.

Materials Required for All Activities

 ### Not Included

- Whiteboard or chart paper
- Dry/wet erase markers or markers
- BINGO chips (e.g., coins, buttons)

 ### Included

- Handout: My Similarities and Differences
- Handout: Flexy BINGO Cards
- Educator Script: Flexy Callout Sheet

Generalization

School Integration

- Distribute Handout: My Similarities and Differences to all teaching staff.
- Highlight the similarities and differences students and teachers have with one another. Note how these contribute to making the classroom a wonderful, exciting place to be.

Home Integration

There is no Home Extension for Lesson 2.

Modifications

Create scenarios that reflect situations that have happened in your classroom.

ACTIVITY 1
Everyone Disagrees Sometimes

⭐ **Presentation**
🕐 **5 minutes**

Materials

Not Included

- Whiteboard or chart paper
- Dry/wet erase markers or markers

Included

There are no included materials for this activity.

Instructions

1. Ask students if they have ever had a disagreement with someone. (If necessary, discuss what *disagreement* means.)
2. Ask students to give you a thumbs-up if they think everyone has disagreed with someone at some time.
3. Explain that all friends disagree at some time. The secret to staying friends even when you have a disagreement is to be *flexible*. Being flexible helps you be a good friend when you disagree. Write this on the board.
4. Acknowledge that we all have similarities and differences. Sometimes we will agree about an idea or about what to do, and sometimes we will disagree. Ask students, "Wouldn't this world be a boring place if we were all exactly the same? Thought the same? Dressed the same? Acted the same? Our differences make us unique and special and make this world a lot more fun."
5. Point out that there are many things that may make a student and his or her friend different:
   a. They may learn in different ways.
   b. They may dress in different ways.
   c. They may behave in different ways.
   d. They may believe different things (A student may think *Shrek the Third* is the best movie in the world, and a friend may not agree. A friend may think Geronimo Stilton is the best book character in the world, and the student may not agree.)

ACTIVITY 2
Similarities and Differences

👥 **Partner Activity**
🕐 **~15 minutes**

Materials

Not Included

- Whiteboard or chart paper
- Dry/wet erase markers or markers

Included

- Handout: My Similarities and Differences

Instructions

1. Draw a Venn diagram on the whiteboard for each pair of students (see Figure 9.3). Write each student's name next to one circle. If necessary, explain to students that either side of the diagram, where the circles do not overlap, is for things that are unique to each student; the middle section, or overlap, is for things they have in common with a friend.
2. Pass out Handout: My Similarities and Differences. Tell the students that they will be answering the questions aloud to create a Venn diagram that will show the similarities and differences between them and their partner. As students answer the questions, students or teachers can record the answers on the Venn diagram.

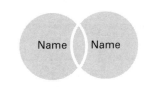

Figure 9.3. Venn diagram.

ACTIVITY 3
Flexibility Bingo

👥 **Partner Activity**
🕐 **~10 minutes**

Materials

Not Included

- BINGO chips (e.g., chips, buttons, coins)

Included

- Handout: Flexy BINGO Cards
- Educator Script: Flexy Callout Sheet

Instructions

1. To play Flexibility BINGO—or Flexy—pass out Handout: Flexy BINGO Cards and BINGO chips (e.g., chips, buttons, coins) to each student. All cards contain all of the items. Let students know that they will be playing blackout (i.e., playing until all items on their card have been covered up). (*Note:* Each student gets one Flexy BINGO Card—page 1 or page 2 of Handout: Flexy BINGO Cards.)
2. Use Educator Script: Flexy Callout Sheet to call clues. Students place chips on their card as in traditional BINGO.

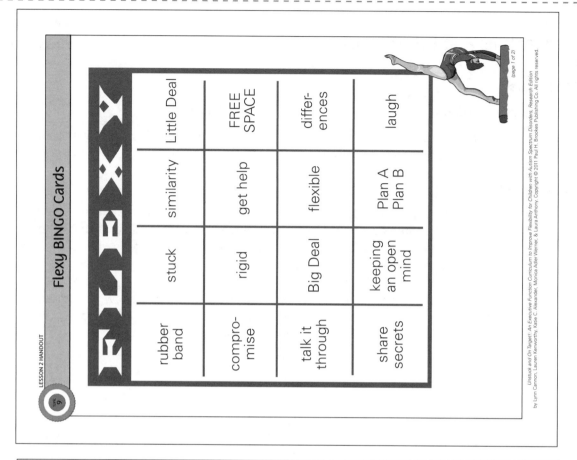

Unstuck and On Target!: An Executive Function Curriculum to Improve Flexibility for Children with Autism Spectrum Disorders, Research Edition by Lynn Cannon, Lauren Kenworthy, Katie C. Alexander, Monica Adler Werner, & Laura Anthony. Copyright © 2011 Paul H. Brookes Publishing Co. All rights reserved.

LESSON 2 HANDOUT

Flexy BINGO Cards

FLEXY

rubber band	stuck	similarity	Little Deal
compro-mise	rigid	get help	FREE SPACE
talk it through	Big Deal	flexible	differ-ences
share secrets	keeping an open mind	Plan A Plan B	laugh

(page 1 of 2)

LESSON 2 HANDOUT

My Similarities and Differences

1. What is my age?

2. What is my favorite color?

3. What is my favorite sport?

4. What is my favorite food?

5. What is my favorite time of day?

6. What is my favorite class?

7. Do I have a sister?

8. Do I have a brother?

9. What is the name of my school?

10. What is the name of my teacher?

Unstuck and On Target!: An Executive Function Curriculum to Improve Flexibility for Children with Autism Spectrum Disorders, Research Edition by Lynn Cannon, Lauren Kenworthy, Katie C. Alexander, Monica Adler Werner, & Laura Anthony. Copyright © 2011 Paul H. Brookes Publishing Co. All rights reserved.

LESSON 2 EDUCATOR SCRIPT

TOPIC
9

Flexy Callout Sheet

	Example		Answer
1.	My goal is to go to the movies. I decided that first I would check to see if *Transformers* was playing. If it wasn't, I would look for a different movie. I made a _____ and a _____.	1.	Plan A, Plan B
2.	This is something you do with your friends: Often you tell jokes to make your friends _____.	2.	laugh
3.	I am still friends with John even though he likes video games and I like computer games. Our _____ make us unique and special.	3.	differences
4.	A _____ is an example of a flexible object.	4.	rubber band
5.	This is something you do with your friends: You tell your friends things in private that are important and special to you.	5.	share secrets
6.	I wanted to listen to music, and my friend wanted to read a book. We decided to listen to music for 5 minutes and then read a book for 5 minutes. We made a _____.	6.	compromise
7.	Some problems are Big Deals, and some problems are Little Deals. I saw a classmate bullying another student and making him do something he did not want to do. This is a _____.	7.	Big Deal
8.	You get a new video game. The graphics are great. The game is fun to play, but you wish that there were more options for control of the character. The game is not all good, but it's not all bad. You are _____.	8.	keeping an open mind
9.	My friend and I had a disagreement. We didn't want to ruin our friendship over a silly disagreement, so we decided to sit down and talk about what happened. We decided to _____.	9.	talk it through
10.	My friend and I both love pizza. This is something we have in common. This is a _____.	10.	similarity
11.	I wanted to play checkers, but Sara wanted to play chess. We ended up not playing anything because we were _____ and could not come up with a compromise.	11.	stuck
12.	Some problems are Big Deals, and some problems are Little Deals. My friend forgot to say "excuse me" when he bumped my desk. This was a _____.	12.	Little Deal
13.	I wanted to focus on Mars for our science project, but my friend insisted that we focus on Jupiter. We could not reach an agreement, so it was time for us to _____.	13.	get help
14.	These are all examples of something or someone being _____: • Being able to do splits • Letting a friend go first in a game • A rubber band	14.	flexible
15.	These are all examples of something or someone being _____: • Refusing to play Connect 4 because I wanted to play cards • A craft stick • Black-and-white thinking (not keeping an open mind)	15.	rigid

 **Lesson 3 Flexibility Helps When You Disagree with Your Friend**

 PURPOSE

This lesson helps students establish intrinsic motivation for being flexible by explicitly reviewing, through concrete experiences, why being flexible makes them a good friend when they disagree. There are two activities in this lesson.

Materials Required for All Activities

 Not Included

- Whiteboard or chart paper
- Dry/wet erase markers or markers
- Die

Included

- Handout: What to Do When We Disagree (cut out before lesson)
- Handout: Flexibility Skits (cut out before lesson)
- Educator Guide: Flexibility Skit Frameworks
- Zinger Game Board
- Educator Guide: Zinger Game Rules (cut out game tokens before playing)
- Zinger Playing Cards (cut out before playing)

Generalization

School Integration

- Distribute Handout: What to Do When We Disagree to all teaching staff.
- Continue to add to the bulletin board (see Number 2 on Bulletin Board Example).

Home Integration

There is no Home Extension for Lesson 3.

Modifications

Create flexibility skit scenarios that reflect situations that have happened in your classroom.

ACTIVITY 1
When We Disagree

👥 **Group Activity**
🕐 **~15 minutes**

Materials

Not Included

- Whiteboard or chart paper
- Dry/wet erase marker or marker

Included

- Handout: What to Do When We Disagree (cut out before lesson)
- Handout: Flexibility Skits (cut out before lesson)
- Educator Guide: Flexibility Skit Frameworks

Instructions

1. Reemphasize that even the best of friends have disagreements sometimes. Being flexible helps you be a good friend when you disagree.
2. Take the cutout strips from Handout: What to Do When We Disagree and put them on the whiteboard. Depending on the level of your students, you can have them generate these independently and write them on the board.
3. On the whiteboard, draw a T chart and label it *Choices and Consequences*. On one side of the chart write *Positive Consequences;* on the other side write *Negative Consequences* (see Figure 9.4). If necessary, discuss the idea that consequences are what happen as a result of our choices.
4. Explain that when students have a disagreement, they always have two choices: a positive, flexible choice and a negative, rigid choice.
5. Hand out Flexibility Skit 1 (top half of Handout: Flexibility Skits). Students work to figure out the consequence of each choice. As an option, students can act out the scenarios to help reinforce the concepts.
6. Discuss the rigid choice. Talk about the consequence of this choice and how the friends would feel. Then, discuss the flexible choice. Refer students to the options from Handout: What to Do When We Disagree. Talk about the consequences of this choice and how the friends would feel. (Refer to Handout: Flexibility Skit Frameworks for a summary of choices and consequences.)
7. Repeat with Flexibility Skit 2 (bottom half of Handout: Flexibility Skits).

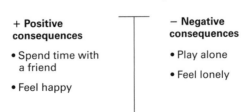

Choices and Consequences

+ Positive consequences
- Spend time with a friend
- Feel happy

– Negative consequences
- Play alone
- Feel lonely

Figure 9.4. Sample T chart.

ACTIVITY 2
Zinger

Materials

Not Included

- Die

Included

- Zinger Game Board
- Educator Guide: Zinger Game Rules (cut out game tokens before playing)
- Zinger Playing Cards (cut out before playing)

Instructions

Divide your students into groups of two to four students to play Zinger. Follow the directions on Educator Guide: Zinger Game Rules.

Flexibility Skits

LESSON 3 HANDOUT

TOPIC 9

Flexibility Skit 1

Who: _____ and _____

When: At recess after lunch

What: One student wants to swing, but the other student wants to play basketball.

Options	Consequences
The two students walk away from each other and go play independently.	→
The two students are flexible and decide to compromise. They decide to swing for half of recess time and play basketball for the other half.	→

Flexibility Skit 2

Who: _____ and _____

When: During class discussion

What: One student says that the Loch Ness monster is real, but another student believes that it is just a myth.

Options	Consequences
The student who disagrees says that the first student is crazy.	→
The student who disagrees listens to the first student explain his or her opinion. When that student is done, the student who disagrees explains why he or she believes differently.	→

What to Do When We Disagree

LESSON 3 HANDOUT

TOPIC 9

Look it up.

Agree to disagree.

Ask an adult.

Tell your friend that everyone can have his or her own opinion.

Do both things.

Let one person pick this time and the other person pick next time.

Find a different thing you both want to do.

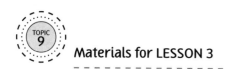

LESSON 3 EDUCATOR GUIDE

Flexibility Skit Frameworks

Flexibility Skit 1

Who: _____ and _____

When: At recess after lunch

What: One student wants to swing, but the other student wants to play basketball.

Options	Consequences
The two students walk away from each other and go play independently.	• Both students feel lonely because they had to play by themselves at recess. • Both students lost an opportunity to make and keep a new friend by sharing an experience.
The two students are flexible and decide to compromise. They decide to swing for half of recess time and play basketball for the other half.	• Both students are happy because they got to play what they wanted. • They also feel good because they made each other happy. • They were able to have fun at recess together, and each got to do the activity they wanted to.

Flexibility Skit 2

Who: _____ and _____

When: During class discussion

What: _Or_ one student says that the Loch Ness monster is real, but another student believes that it is just a myth.

Options	Consequences
The student who disagrees says the first student is crazy.	• The first student is really upset and feels hurt. The student had hoped to make friends with the other student, but now he or she sees that the other student doesn't know how to be a good friend. • Both students lost an opportunity to make and keep a new friend.
The student who disagrees listens to the first student explain his or her opinion. When that student is done, the student who disagrees explains why he or she believes differently.	• Both students then discuss what they like about each candidate _or_ arguments for and against the existence of the Loch Ness monster.
Write your own solution:	Write your own consequence:

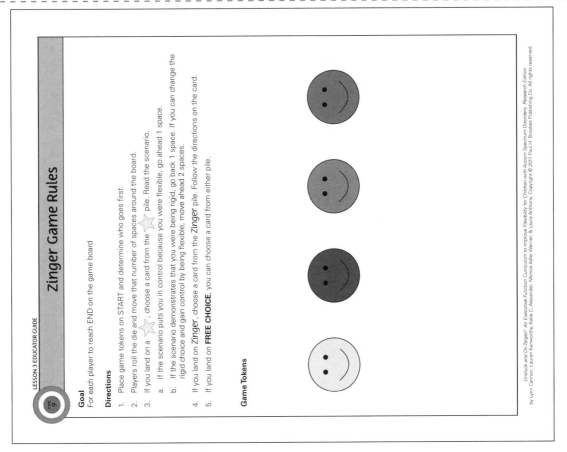

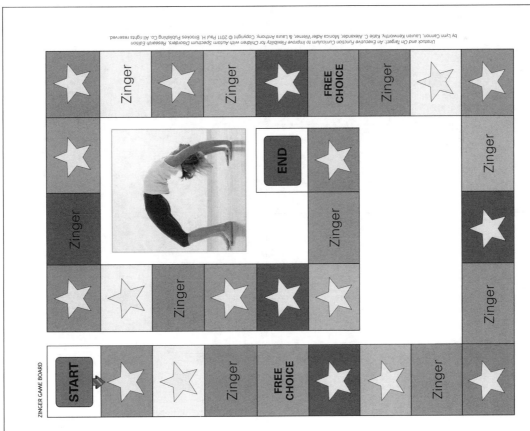

ZINGER PLAYING CARDS

The movie I wanted to see was sold out, so I chose to see another movie.

The board game my friend and I wanted to play was already being used, so we chose another one that we both liked.

I think the fastest car in the world is the Porsche. My friend thinks it is the Ferrari. We decided to look it up on the Internet.

I think *Mario Kart* is the best video game. My friend thinks *Dungeons and Dragons* is the best game. We decided to agree to disagree.

My friend and I played checkers and my friend won. He said, "Wow, I am an amazing checkers player!" Even though he was bragging, I decided to ignore it since I knew he was just excited.

I think we should go outside for recess. My friend wants to go to the gym. We decided to compromise and go to the gym for 10 minutes and outside for 10 minutes.

I think basketball is the best sport in the world. My friend thinks hockey is the best sport in the world. Instead of arguing, we decided to talk it through and name things that are great about both sports.

We only had 5 minutes to look at a book. I really wanted to look at the space book, but my friend wanted to look at the joke book. I decided to look at the joke book with my friend so w... at a boo...

My friend said she didn't like the color of my shirt. Instead of getting mad, I calmly told her she had hurt my feelings. She said she didn't mean to and apologized.

My friend was ... class. I decide... I know eve...

ZINGER PLAYING CARDS

ZINGER PLAYING CARDS

I wanted to see *Batman,* but the tickets were sold out. I refused to go to see any other movie.	I thought she was my best friend because we were exactly the same. Now I found out that she likes to swim, and I don't like swimming. I guess we can't be friends anymore.
I wanted to go outside and play soccer, but my friend wanted to play baseball. We spent the whole time arguing and never got to go outside.	If my friend doesn't choose to play hockey at recess, I just won't do anything at all!
I think the best pizza topping is pepperoni; my friend thinks the best topping is sausage. I think my friend is wrong, and I refuse to have lunch with him.	My friend told me she thinks cartoons are better than movies. I told her she is crazy!
I love to go sledding in the snow; my friend would rather have a snowball fight. I think we should just not play together anymore.	My friend said he was not feeling very well and wanted to rest instead of play with me at recess. I guess _____ friend.
I think the Loch Ness monster is real; my friend thinks it is a myth. I can't be friends with him if we don't agree.	My friend sai_____ with someboo_____ me tomorro_____

ZINGER PLAYING CARDS

ZINGER PLAYING CARDS

Create a PLAN A and a PLAN B for this goal:
I want to go to the movies.

Go ahead 2 spaces.

Create a PLAN A and a PLAN B for this goal:
I want to have fun at recess.

Go ahead 2 spaces

Give someone at the table a compliment.

Go ahead 1 space.

What do you do if PLAN A doesn't work?

Make a _____ .

Go ahead 1 space

Pretend you just won a game.
What is one positive thing you can say
to the person you are playing with?

Go ahead 1 space.

Jane wants to see *Shrek the Third,*
but it is sold out. She sits down and pouts.
What is the consequence of her decision?
What should she have done?

Go ahead 2 spaces.

Name one thing you have in
common with your friend.

Go ahead 1 space.

Billy wants to play with Joe at recess.
Joe has promised Sally that he will play
with her. Billy gets upset and sits at his
desk with his head down. What is the
consequence of his decision?
What sh

Go a

What is one thing that is different
between you and your friend?

Go ahead 1 space.

Jeremy
Jack says it is
Jack he is
What is the conse
What sh

Go a

ZINGER PLAYING CARDS

Zinger	Zinger
Zinger	Zinger
Zinger	Zinger
Zinger	Zinger
Zinger	Zinger

ZINGER PLAYING CARDS

Name one thing you can do
if you and your friend disagree.

Go ahead 1 space

Name one person you can talk to if you
are having a disagreement you can't resolve.

Go ahead 1 space.

Name three things you have in
common with someone at the table.

Go ahead 2 spaces.

Brendan wants to play video games,
but Kelly wants to play outside.
They decide to not do anything.
What is the consequence of their decision?
What could they have done?

Go ahead 2 spaces.

Name three things that are different
about you and someone at the table.

Go ahead 2 spaces.

True or false?

Everyone makes mistakes.

Go ahead 1 space.

Name one thing you like to do
with someone at the table.

Go ahead 1 space.

True or false?

Being flexible helps you keep being
friends even if someone makes a mistake.

Go

Name one thing you can do
if your friend is having a bad day.

Go ahead 1 space.

Name three reas

Go

ZINGER PLAYING CARDS

Zinger	Zinger
Zinger	Zinger
Zinger	Zinger
Zinger	Zinger
Zinger	Zinger

Extensions

Generalization

School Integration

- Distribute Educator Script: Friend Mistake Scenarios, Handout: Teacher Mistake Scenarios, Handout: My Similarities and Differences, and Handout: What to Do When We Disagree to all teaching staff.
- Start a bulletin board on reasons to be flexible (see Educator Guide: Bulletin Board Example).
- Highlight the similarities and differences students and teachers have with one another. Note how these contribute to making the classroom a wonderful, exciting place to be.

Home Integration

Topic 9 has no Home Extensions.

Flexible Futures

SPECIAL INSTRUCTIONS: The core goals of these lessons are to help students consolidate what they have learned about being flexible and learn how to generalize their new skills to future situations. These lessons are designed to be an enjoyable way to review the material in the curriculum. Make adaptations to facilitate your students' engagement with and enjoyment of the material.

Summary: The topic helps students review what they have learned in Topics 1–9 and plan generalization opportunities for their new skills.

Prerequisite skills: Vocabulary and concepts covered in Topics 1–9

Related skills: Ability to apply concepts to new situations (generalize)

OUTCOME—CRITERIA FOR MASTERY

1. In the context of a game, the student demonstrates the following:
    a. An understanding of the meaning of flexibility
    b. Familiarity with flexibility vocabulary and scripts
    c. An understanding of the value of flexibility with reference to a personal hero
    d. An understanding of internal feeling states and coping strategies
    e. An understanding of the definition of *goal*
    f. An ability to identify a Target Goal
2. The student identifies at least one plan to apply what he or she has learned to a future situation.

TOPIC BACKGROUND AND RATIONALE

Unstuck and On Target! presents many new concepts, definitions, scripts, and strategies to help students increase flexibility. Presentation of this material is designed to occur over the better part of a school year. As with any complex curriculum, review is important for the integration and mastery of the material. Students with ASD often have difficulty generalizing new knowledge to novel situations or contexts. To promote generalization, students must first demonstrate competency with the new skills. In the first lesson of this topic, students demonstrate their competency through games. In the second lesson, they plan generalization opportunities for the future.

Lesson 1 *Unstuck and On Target!* Review Game 1: Flexiac

 PURPOSE

Students review content material from the curriculum. There is one activity in this lesson.

Materials Required for All Activities

Not Included

All materials for this activity are included.

Included

- Flexiac Category Label Cards
- Point Cards (make 5 copies, 1 set per category)
- Educator Script: Flexiac Question and Answer Key

Generalization

School Integration

Continue to use flexibility language in the classroom.

Home Integration

There is no Home Extension for Lesson 1.

Modifications

Modify the game structure and presentation of questions as necessary for students' developmental level. Advanced students may want to create the questions for each other. Less advanced students may need a "hint" card they can use for help.

ACTIVITY 1

Unstuck and On Target! Review Game 1: Flexiac

Group Activity

~45 minutes

Materials

Not Included

All materials for this activity are included.

Included

- Flexiac Category Label Cards
- Point Cards (make 5 copies, 1 set per category)
- Educator Script: Flexiac Question and Answer Key

Instructions

Prior to having students play the game, go through the questions and answers to familiarize yourself with them and with the game structure.

1. Tell your students that today they will be playing a game called "Flexiac" to review all of the important information they have learned this year in the group.
2. You can divide your group into two smaller groups or have students play as one large group.
3. On a large table, arrange the cards into five columns with a Flexiac Category Label Card at the top of each column and Point Cards beneath each label card in ascending point values.
4. *Rules of the game:* Students will select a category. Within that category they will have five questions to choose from. The questions have a specific point value attached to them.
5. *Scoring:* You can choose a group point total goal (promotes cooperation and team work), or the team with the most points at the end wins (practices the skill of winning or losing the game).

POINT CARDS

10 points	20 points
30 points	40 points
50 points	

FLEXJAC CATEGORY LABEL CARDS

Flexible Body and Brain	Why Be Flexible?
Goal-Plan-Do-Check	Flexible Friends
How to Be Flexible	

LESSON 1 EDUCATOR SCRIPT

Flexiac Question and Answer Key

Category	Point value	Question	Answer
Flexible brain and body	10	A spaghetti noodle is ____ because it will break if it is bent.	Rigid
	20	A rubber band, string, and putty can all be described as ____.	Flexible
	30	You get to the swings, and all of the swings are taken. You decide you will go down the slide instead. You are being ____.	Flexible
	40	You are playing with your friend, and you both want to play different games. You decide you won't play anything. You are ____.	Stuck
	50	The brain and the body have this in common. They can both be ____.	Flexible
Why be flexible?	10	True or False: What you want is not always possible.	True
	20	If something doesn't go the way I want it, I have two choices. I can get stuck in the mud or be ____.	Flexible
	30	This is the person who decides if I will get stuck or be flexible.	ME!!!
	40	It always feels better to be flexible than to be ____.	Stuck
	50	I gain more privileges, more freedom, and more trust when I am ____.	Flexible
Goal-Plan-Do-Check	10	Something you want or need to do is a ____.	Goal
	20	Superman needed to save innocent people, Abraham Lincoln wanted to end slavery, and SpongeBob wanted to save King Neptune. These are all examples of the heroes' ____.	Goals
	30	What you do to achieve your goals is known as your ____.	Plan
	40	When Plan A doesn't work, you need Plan ___.	B
	50	When you stop and think, "Did my plan work?" you are doing this step of Goal-Plan-Do-Check.	Check

(page 1 of 2)

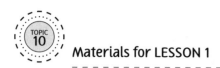
LESSON 1 EDUCATOR SCRIPT *(continued)*

Flexiac Question and Answer Key *(continued)*

Category	Point value	Question	Answer
Flexible friends	10	Play games, laugh, and share secrets are all things you can do with your ____.	Friends
	20	True or False: Everyone makes mistakes.	True
	30	True or False: A friendship has to end if you disagree or make a mistake.	False
	40	If you and your friend disagree, you have two choices about how to react. You can be flexible or you can be ____.	Rigid
	50	Agree to disagree, ask an adult, and tell your friend that everyone is entitled to his or her own opinion. These are things you can do when you ____.	Disagree
How to be flexible	10	A situation you can't get over quickly, can't ignore, or is very important is known as a ____ deal.	Big
	20	A situation you can ignore or is mildly annoying, or is a temporary problem is known as a ____ deal.	Little
	30	There are multiple ways to solve a problem. This means you have a ____ when you decide how to solve the problem.	Choice
	40	If there is only one way to do something, this means you do not have a ____ about how to do it.	Choice
	50	Being told in advance, stopping, taking a deep breath and remembering that you can be flexible, and asking questions so you can learn exactly what will change and what will stay the same. These are all things you can do when there is a ____ of plans.	Change

(page 2 of 2)

Lesson 2 *Unstuck and On Target!* Review Game 2: Four Corners

PURPOSE

Students review content material from the curriculum. There is one activity in this lesson.

Materials Required for All Activities

Not Included

- Paper to label four corners of the room A, B, C, D

Included

- Educator Script: Four Corners Question and Answer Key

Generalization

School Integration

Continue to use flexibility language in the classroom.

Home Integration

There is no Home Extension for Lesson 2.

Modifications

Modify the game structure and presentation of questions as necessary for students' developmental level.

Unstuck and On Target! Review Game 2: Four Corners

Full Group Activity

🕐 ~25 minutes

Materials

Not Included

- Paper to label four corners of the room A, B, C, D

Included

- Educator Script: Four Corners Question and Answer Key

Instructions

It is important to go through the game before introducing it to students and be prepared with the correct answers. You can have students demonstrate flexibility with their bodies—when they reach the corner they have to try and make their body look like the corresponding corner letter (i.e., in Corner A, you would make your body look like an *A*).

1. Label each of the corners of your room A, B, C, and D.

2. Tell your students today they will be playing a game called "Four Corners" to review all of the important information they have learned this year in the group.

3. *Rules of the game:* Students will work as a group to earn as many points as possible. An individual student will be asked a question and given four choices (Choice A, B, C, or D). The student will select an answer and move to that corner of the room.

4. If the student is unsure of the answer, he or she can pick a friend to discuss the answer with and go to the corner of the room together.

5. Each correct answer is awarded 10 points.

LESSON 2 EDUCATOR SCRIPT

Four Corners Questions and Answer Key

These people make mistakes.	A. Only teachers B. Only bad friends C. Everyone D. Parents	C. Everyone
You play games, you share secrets, and you sometimes disagree with ____.	A. Your friends B. Your pencil C. Your homework D. Your enemies	A. Your friends
If my Plan A doesn't work, I need ____.	A. To give up B. A Plan B C. To cry D. To quit	B. A Plan B
When I feel disappointed I should ____.	A. Scream B. Hit something C. Cry D. Take a break	D. Take a break
My face can feel hot, my stomach might hurt, and I might clench my teeth and fists when I feel ____.	A. Disappointed B. Tired C. Bored D. Happy	A. Disappointed
A hero is ____.	A. Silly and mean B. Rigid and cranky C. Angry and stuck D. Dedicated, flexible, and brave	D. Dedicated, flexible, brave
If you and your friend disagree, you have two choices about how you can react. You can be rigid or you can be ____.	A. Flexible B. Angry C. Stuck D. Sad	A. Flexible
Agree to disagree, ask an adult, and decide it is not a big deal are all things you can do if you ____.	A. Give up B. Don't care about your friend C. And your friend disagree D. Don't know the answer	C. And your friend disagree
A Target Goal is ____.	A. For playing in the ocean B. Silly C. The same for everyone D. Your most important goal	D. Your most important goal
Being flexible helps me be a good friend because ____.	A. People like to be around flexible people. B. Flexible people have more choices. C. When I am flexible my friends are happy. D. All of the above	D. All of the above

Lesson 3 Flexible Futures

 ## PURPOSE

This lesson engages each student in anticipating at least one way in which he or she will apply what has been learned throughout the curriculum. There is one activity in this lesson.

Materials Required for All Activities

Not Included

- Writing utensil
- Videocamera (if making videos)

Included

- Handout: Flexible Futures
- Handout: Graduation Certificate
- Home Extension 16 and Home Signoff

Generalization

School Integration

- Begin each student's day by helping him or her anticipate times during the day when flexibility may be useful. This should become a written GPDC. A student can do this with someone in the classroom or at an established safe address in the school. At the end of the day, review how the plan worked and what can be done differently in the future.
- The vocabulary introduced in this intervention should become an integral part of the educational team's verbal interaction with students across settings and curricula. Continue to check that the educational team applies the vocabulary.

Home Integration

- Upon completion of Lesson 3, send home a copy of Home Extension 16 and Home Signoff.
- If possible, send home a copy of the talk show video of each student to his or her parent(s). If this is not possible, send home a copy of the completed Handout: Flexible Futures.
- Send home a copy of Handout: Graduation Certificate.

Modifications

Use Handout: Flexible Futures as a format for a student interview without using the talk show medium.

ACTIVITY 1
Talk Show

👥 **Group Activity**

🕐 **~30 minutes**

Materials

Not Included

- Videocamera (if making videos)

Included

- Handout: Flexible Futures
- Handout: Graduation Certificate
- Home Extension 16 and Home Signoff

Instructions

1. Explain to students that they will be doing a talk show interview. If you plan to record the interviews on video, let the students know that.
2. Students can create their talk show script by completing Handout: Flexible Futures or by having a one-to-one conversation with you.
3. After the student's script is complete, he or she can pair with another student or with you to film the interview. Even if you do not plan to actually record, it would be helpful to have the students perform their interviews in front of one another.
4. Review Home Extension 16 with students.

LESSON 3 HANDOUT

Flexible Futures

Interviewer:	You've done an amazing job learning about staying unstuck and on target, and I hear that you're graduating today! You've learned so much, and our viewers would love to know more about how what you've learned will help you in the future. I'd like to ask you a couple of questions.
	You've learned the definition of *flexibility* and the definition of *stuck*. When is a time that you usually get stuck?
Me:	_____
	_____
	_____
Interviewer:	How will what you've learned help you in the future at school and at home?
Me:	_____
	_____
	_____
Interviewer:	You've done a terrific job practicing Plan A and Plan B. I would like to know at least one time when you plan to use it at school and at least one time when you plan to use it at home.
Me:	_____
	_____
	_____
	_____
	_____
	_____
Interviewer:	When is a time that you think you will use what you've learned about compromise?
Me:	_____
	_____
Interviewer:	What is the number one reason you think being flexible is good for you?
Me:	_____
	_____
	_____
Interviewer:	I understand that you're working on a Mission Possible. What are you working on now, and what is one thing you plan to work on next?
Me:	_____
	_____
	_____
	_____
	_____

(page 1 of 2)

TOPIC
10

Flexible Futures *(continued)*

Interviewer: When do you think Big Deal/Little Deal or Choice/No Choice will help you the most?

Me: _____

_____

_____

Interviewer: What is your top Target Goal?

Me: _____

_____

_____

Interviewer: How will being flexible help you be a better friend?

Me: _____

_____

_____

Interviewer: Which coping skills do you think you will use the most?

Me: _____

_____

_____

Interviewer: Thank you so much for spending time with us. I have one final question for you. What is one thing that you want our audience to know about being flexible?

Me: _____

_____

_____

Interviewer: Great! Congratulations on becoming unstuck and on target! (Presents certificate)

(page 2 of 2)

Home Extension 16

Summary: During this lesson, students have created an interview that helps them think about how they can use what they have learned about flexibility in the future. This is the final lesson of the flexibility curriculum, *Unstuck and On Target!*

There are several things you can do at home to help your child learn as fully as possible. The more experiences each child has outside the classroom, the better he or she is able to learn a concept and apply that learning.

1. You can use the same questions that you see on your child's talk show script to ask your child how he or she plans to use what has been learned about flexibility in the future.

2. Continue to use the flexibility vocabulary that you and your child have learned in your daily life.

3. Continue to use the flexibility strategies at home with your child.

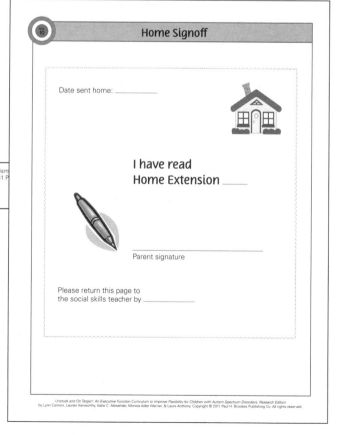

Home Signoff

Date sent home: _____

I have read
Home Extension _____

_____
Parent signature

Please return this page to
the social skills teacher by _____.

Extensions

Generalization

School Integration

- Continue to use flexibility language in the classroom.
- Develop a written GPDC with each student to help him or her anticipate times during the day when flexibility may be useful. At the end of the day, review how the plan worked and what can be done differently in the future.
- Continue to check that the educational team applies the vocabulary with students across settings and curricula.

Home Integration

- Upon completion of Lesson 3, send home a copy of Home Extension 16 and Home Signoff.
- Send home a copy of the video (if created) or the completed Handout: Flexible Futures.
- Send home a copy of Handout: Graduation Certificate

Materials for Home

- Home Extension 16 and Home Signoff
- A copy of the video (if created)
- Completed Handout: Flexible Futures
- Handout: Graduation Certificate

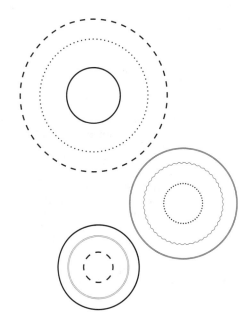

Index

Page numbers followed by *t* indicate tables.